Complete Series

APOSTOLIC APOSTLESHIP
The Age of

TRANSFORMING THE NATIONS
with miracle faith

On Behalf of
Connecting for Excellence
International Apostolic Network
CHURCHES AND MINISTRIES IN ASSOCIATION

By Dr. Alan Pateman

1. The Reality of a Warrior
2. Healing and Deliverance, A Present Reality
3. Control, A Powerful Force
4. His Life is in the Blood
5. Sexual Madness, In a Sexually Confused World (co-authored with Jennifer Pateman)
6. Apostles, Can the Church Survive Without Them?
7. Prayer, Ingredients for Successful Intercession, Part One
8. Prayer, Touching the Heart of God, Part Two
9. The Early Years, Anointed Generals Past and Present, Part One of Four
10. Revival Fires, Anointed Generals Past and Present, Part Two of Four
11. Why War, A Biblical Approach to the Armour of God and Spiritual Warfare
12. Forgiveness, the Key to Revival
13. His Faith, Positions us for Possession
14. Seduction & Control: Infiltrating Society and the Church
15. Kingdom Management for Anointed Prosperity
16. TONGUES, our Supernatural Prayer Language
17. Seven Pillars for Life and Kingdom Prosperity
18. WINNING by Mastering your Mind
19. Laying Foundations
20. Apostles and the Local Church
21. Preparations for Ministry
22. Developments and Provision
23. The Age of Apostolic Apostleship

24. Media, Spiritual Gateway (co-authored with Jennifer Pateman)
25. Israel, the Question of Ownership
26. Earnestly Contending for the State of Israel
27. The Temple, Antichrist and the New World Order
28. The Antichrist, Rapture and the Battle of Armageddon
29. Israel, the Church and the End Times
30. Introduction to all things APMI
31. Student's Handbook, Study Guide Volume 2
32. Empowered to Overcome
33. Equipped for Spiritual Warfare
34. Appropriations of African Territory
35. Understanding Coronavirus
36. China, Covid-19, World Domination
37. Watchers of the 4 Kings
38. Coronavirus – Communist and Marxist Uprising
39. The Global Coronavirus Pandemic (Complete Series)

BY DR. JENNIFER PATEMAN

1. Sexual Madness, In a Sexually Confused World (co-authored with Alan Pateman)
2. Millennial Myopia, From a Biblical Perspective
3. Media, Spiritual Gateway (co-authored with Alan Pateman)

AVAILABLE FROM APMI PUBLICATIONS, AMAZON.COM AND OTHER RETAIL OUTLETS

Complete Series

APOSTOLIC APOSTLESHIP
The Age of

TRANSFORMING THE NATIONS
with miracle faith

DR. ALAN PATEMAN

BOOK TITLE:
The Age of Apostolic Apostleship, Complete Series

WRITTEN BY Dr. ALAN PATEMAN
Paperback ISBN: 978-1-909132-65-8
Hardcover ISBN: 978-1-909132-93-1
eBook ISBN: 978-1-909132-66-5

Copyright 2017 Alan Pateman
Second Print/Update 2020

All rights reserved under International Copyright Law. Contents and/or cover may not be reproduced in whole or in part in any form without the express written consent of the Publisher.

Published By:
APMI Publications
In Partnership with Truth for the Journey Books
Email: publications@alanpateman.com
www.AlanPatemanMinistries.com

Acknowledgements:
Author/Design/Senior Editor/Publisher: Apostle Dr. Alan Pateman
Editing/Proofreading/Research: Dr. Jennifer Pateman
Computer Administration/Office Manager: Dr. Dorothea Struhlik
Cover Image Credit: www.PosterMyWall.com

Unless otherwise indicated, all scriptural quotations are from the HOLY BIBLE, NEW INTERNATIONAL VERSION ®. NIV ®. Copyright © 1973, 1978, 1984 by the International Bible Society. Used by permission of Zondervan Publishing House. All rights reserved.

*Where scriptures appear with special emphasis (**in bold,** italic or <u>underlined</u>) we have edited them ourselves in order to bring focused attention within the context of this subject being taught.*

Ministry Endorsements

Dearest Alan and Jenny, I wanted to thank you both for laying down your lives for others... In a world that is racing toward paganism, you have held the torch of the Lordship of our Christ high and with dignity... This requires sacrifice and a willingness to lose your life at any moment... I am humbled by your service...

Dr. Robb Thompson
Best-selling author, Pastor, Philanthropist, Mentor and Entrepreneur. Robb Thompson Ministries/Family Harvest Church
Chicago, USA

In founding LifeStyle International Christian University Doctor Alan Pateman has married the moving of the Holy Spirit and the authority of God's written word together. His many years and experience has caused him to be able to lead this university into the 21st century with a relevant edge.

I believe the students that participate in this university will have a healthy balance of the word and the Spirit and the maturity to fulfil their high calling. Remember preparation is never lost time.

Pastor Doctor Roberts Liardon
Best-selling author (over 7 millions copies sold)
Roberts Liardon Ministries/Embassy International Church
Orlando, USA

I have known Apostle Dr. Alan Pateman for almost two decades and I can confidently say that he is one of the Apostolic Generals of our time. With his gift and wisdom he has influenced and transformed many lives from all walks of life, regardless of their educational background and profession. In fact his ability in equipping ministry has impacted the nations of the globe.

I am always impressed any time Apostle Alan and I discuss Kingdom matters. He always inspires me because he doesn't consider the economical challenges in Italy as a hindrance but rather as an opportunity to spread the gospel; he is a man of faith and lives by faith.

Apostle Doctor Benjamin Ayim Asare
Author and Pastor of Followers of Christ Intl. Church
Novara, Italy

Doctor Alan Pateman, whom I know for many years now, is very well rooted in the Word of God and at the same time he is an inspirational and motivational teacher. He is widely recognized as a prolific author, profound knower of the Word and a strong Apostle of God.

He has all my appreciation and I strongly recommend his university to all those who want to combine a solid preparation with a strong impact of the Holy Spirit in their lives

Pastor Pietro Evangelista
Publisher of Evangelista Media/
Centro Cristiano "Il Buon Samaritano"
Pescara, Italy

My Prayer

My prayer for all of you, who read this book, is that God blesses you and that He will enlarge your territory. Taken from the following scripture is this wonderful prayer, which I recommend you confess and pray over your Church, Ministry & Family etc. Cry out as Jabez did and see God grant your request!

"Oh, that you would bless me and enlarge my territory! Let your hand be with me, and keep me from harm so that I will be free from pain." And God granted his request.
(1 Chronicles 4:10)

Dedication

I dedicate and submit this book "The Age of Apostolic Apostleship" to God the Author and Perfecter of all things and pray that the anointing of His Holy Spirit will rest upon all those who read this book.

A special big thanks to my wonderful wife Jenny. She is a true intercessor and Woman of God; she is truly bone of my bone and flesh of my flesh. For her practical help in guidance, typing and editing skills.

A ministry like this cannot exist without the practical support and the many prayers of those prayer warriors, which we call our partners.

Partners!
Thank you for your love and support.

Personal Invitation

Dear Friend, Greetings in the Name of Jesus, He is building His Apostolic Church, restoring righteousness and *spiritual government,* which no gate of hell can prevail! *Amen.*

Please receive this book as a personal invitation to become part of the "Connecting for Excellence Apostolic Network."

Within these pages I have the privilege of sharing with you and introducing to you the work of this ministry and **the vision** behind it. I hope you find it an exciting discovery! And become a part or member of this network of association, *(or affiliation)* or just support, then don't delay we would love to hear from you.

You may also ask yourself the question, Do I have the training needed? My prayer is that *"LifeStyle International Christian University"* is the answer to those questions.

He's looking for History Makers.

In His Presence

Apostle Doctor Alan Pateman
(Overseer)

Acknowledgements

Most of the credit for this book, "The Age of Apostolic Apostleship" must go to all those I've been mentored by directly and those I've had the privilege to study their ministries and material over many years.

It is impossible to grow into maturity without the knowledge and wisdom that comes from the impartation of others, through their dedication and relationship with God. Therefore you will find some sections from other writers; I hereby acknowledge their insight and challenging motivation and contribution.

Many thanks are not enough to express my appreciation to people like Ian Andrews, apostolic director of the International Association of Healing Ministries and the founder of Citadel Ministries; the late Reverend Dr. Bob

Gordon whom I learnt so much from in my early years, who laid many solid foundations within my life; Dr. Roberts Liardon who has inspired me over the years to fulfil the apostolic call on my life; for Reinhard Bonnke, in seeing how an international organisation of great multitude is run.

Also Kenneth and Gloria Copeland who are both true witnesses of stature, unmovable faith and presentation; Dr. Robb Thompson who is an exceptionally skilled relational and leadership strategist. Dr. Bill Hamon for his leadership in bringing much needed truth, a father of the apostolic and prophetic movement.

This list is endless, some I have known personally and others I have learned and watched from afar. These are true mentors. How we need fathers in the faith.

Personal Encouragement

I cannot express my gratitude enough to all those who have encouraged me to establish that which you will find in this book, "The Age of the Apostolic Apostleship."

But this is not something that one wakes up to one morning and decides to begin or develop. It was not my intention to develop a network out of some response, because of a lack of associations or denominational structures, *remember there is only One Body.*

It is not because someone encouraged me to put down on paper my thoughts of how and what a network is or consists of. As you will see in my introduction, there are many wonderful and well-established organizations that I would only be too pleased to submit under and help to develop.

But God over the years, to my surprise, has led me in a direction to *help develop others in their quest to fulfil the dream* that God has placed within their heart. This began to materialize in the late 1980's, although at the time, I did not know that the word apostle existed. We were always encouraged by the pastoral gift, with the occasional glimpse of perhaps that evading evangelist.

At the beginning of the 1990's God began to speak to me prophetically through men of God, like Doctor Roberts Liardon with words of direction and encouragement, that God was raising me up in the apostolic ministry. This was apparent as time went on for I found that different ministries were coming to me for prayer, impartation, anointing and ordination.

This developed into the establishing of "Friends in Ministry" in relationship with Pastor Andy Wall, then at the advice and direction of Doctor Robb Thompson into **"Connecting for Excellence"** International Apostolic Network (2000), a multi-facetted missions organization as I have travelled widely throughout Europe, Africa, Asia and America.

Serving more than 500 ministers that I have to-date ordained in over fifty nations along with ministries, churches and schools in association or affiliation from around the globe.

I pray as you read this book that you will find that the Holy Spirit will impart to you the vision of Apostolic Networking, and then together we can work for the glory of the Almighty God.

Apostle Alan Pateman, Ph.D., D.Min., D.D.

Table of Contents

Foreword..25

Preface...27

Introduction...29

Part One **LAYING FOUNDATIONS**

Chapter 1 Passing the Baton between Generations............39

Chapter 2 Signs of the Times................................49

Chapter 3 The Transition into the 21st Century.............59

Chapter 4 A Network of Relationships.......................65

Chapter 5 The Kingdom Reign of God.........................71

Chapter 6 The Church Age Begins............................85

Chapter 7 Replacement Theology.............................93

Chapter 8	Laying Foundation	99
Chapter 9	The Objective of an Apostle	105
Chapter 10	Types of Apostles	111
Chapter 11	Marks of an Apostle	119
Chapter 12	Apostles Today?	129
Chapter 13	The Apostolic Ministry Functions Today	133

Part Two   APOSTLES AND THE LOCAL CHURCH

Chapter 14	Relationship between the Apostolic and the Local Church	147
Chapter 15	Establishing Leadership	157
Chapter 16	Discernment of Gifting	161
Chapter 17	Spiritual Gifts vs. Governing Authority	167
Chapter 18	Authority - Who has it?	173
Chapter 19	Who Ordains Who?	185
Chapter 20	The Office of an Elder	197
Chapter 21	Church Government	205
Chapter 22	Elders are Territorial	211
Chapter 23	Women in Ministry	217
Chapter 24	Mandate for Fellowship with God's Spirit	221

Part Three   PREPARATIONS FOR MINISTRY

Chapter 25	Apostolic Pitfalls	235
Chapter 26	Promoting the Lord or Self?	245
Chapter 27	Your Destiny is Developed in Adullam	251

Chapter 28	The Strength of the Anointing	257
Chapter 29	Humanism vs. The Spirit of God	263
Chapter 30	Divination and the Python Spirit	269
Chapter 31	A Work of Sovereign Grace	275
Chapter 32	Staying Accountable	281
Chapter 33	Honouring your Apostle	289
Chapter 34	God in Three-Perfect Deity	297
Chapter 35	Baptism of the Holy Spirit	307
Chapter 36	New Days – New Ways	317
Part Four	**DEVELOPMENTS AND PROVISION**	
Chapter 37	Interest and Concerns	331
Chapter 38	Apostolic Association Network	337
Chapter 39	Preventing Ministry Burnout	343
Chapter 40	Team Ministry	347
Chapter 41	Thoughtful Questions	353
Chapter 42	Financial Economy	359
Chapter 43	Ministry Ordination	365
Chapter 44	What is Ordination?	369
Chapter 45	Covenant Partnership	373
Chapter 46	Responsive Thoughts	377
Chapter 47	Theological Education	381
Chapter 48	The Apostolic Doctrines, Articles of Belief	385

Foreword

Over the years increasing numbers of men and women have been ordained and received impartation and anointing through this apostolic network.

To help them with their quest, God put a resolution in my heart that now is the time to put together teaching that would not only help to prepare but would also help identify the seasons along the road to achieving maturity. Very often we think that God calls, we obey, He anoints and then we wonder why we're not in some dynamic, overflowing and internationally *recognized-by-all* ministry!

We need to understand that there is a process in God, not only of achieving maturity but also reaching that recognized place of success.

I believe through this book "The Age of Apostolic Apostleship," you will begin to understand and discover the many patterns regarding your failures or successes. Plus the reasons for those frustrated, unbelievably lonely periods when you begin to wonder whether you were ever really called at all.

You will discover that this is part of the road that one must tread to reach that fullness of maturity, which others will then recognize as being of God.

Preface

The characteristics of the apostolic will be at the forefront of what God is doing within and through the church at this time. To reveal the heart of God in stirring up and drawing forth the dynamic potential that has been deposited in each born-again believer.

In so doing, exposing the darkness that has for so long gripped the church to become silent, inactive and powerless, therefore our cities, nations and the world remain gripped in the hands of Satan.

At first the apostolic will be strongly resisted but the Spirit of God will bring conviction, the presence of God will be felt everywhere, the atmosphere will be divinely changed as the word of God is preached. Only God's Spirit can reveal the true condition of our hearts.

It is important for all of us to have that (for some rare) intimate communion with God where we can say, like Evan Roberts of the Welsh revival of 1904, "Bend me! Bend me! Bend us!" Evan prayed so fervently that perspiration poured down his face and tears streamed quickly saying, "I am coming, coming Lord to Thee!"

The apostolic is not a popular style but essential, one that mirrors the lives of many who have dared to live the life of Christ in their day. Those who have taken the inspiration and motivation solely from the fundamental simplicity of the word of God and backed by the power and might of the Holy Spirit.

God is challenging everything that can be challenged. This is the time for the restoration of the apostolic *(Ephesians 4:11)*, the prophetic, the time for the church to rise up and take possession of the land.

The apostolic is in full swing, the best is yet to come, now is the time to take the cities. To take the land with a shout! This has to be the most exciting and privileged time to live in. To be able to see with the eyes of the Spirit, both all that has past and that which is to come. The church, the bride of Christ, will leave this planet in triumph, not in defeat.

Introduction

Over the years I have been hosting leadership gatherings around the world, something I am very grateful and honoured to do. However, in my travels I have been consistently challenged by the lack of understanding that prevails.

Firstly the lack of understanding of what it means to be a leader and what qualifications are necessary. Secondly the lack of insight people seem to have of leadership from a New Testament point of view and the subsequent "out-working" of church structure, as seen in scripture.

It's disconcerting because as a result of this ignorance we tend to get caught up in the extremes that exist which provide no real way forward at all. So within these chapters, I want to discuss *"what's next?"* And what it means to be a leader. What qualifies us and who appoints us?

Titles are also misused, certainly within the apostolic movement today. Therefore we will also discover what it means to be self exalted as a bishop! As many currently perceive that the title of bishop exceeds that of the apostle. We must clear up this confusion within the body of Christ.

However let it be understood from the very onset of this subject that it is not, nor will it ever be, my intention to use this material to violate, manipulate or control others, which is often wrongly perceived about the apostolic ministry.

Shedding Some Light

Instead my heart towards this vast subject is to help bring much needed clarity, as there is so much out there that helps bring much confusion-to-the-table. My intention in teaching about the apostolic is only to shed some light on all-things-apostolic as they should be according to the New Testament.

None of us should ever manipulate or control the work and move of the Holy Spirit or the lives of any individual committed to networking apostolically - in any capacity.

Dr. Bill Hamon in his book titled, **"Apostles, Prophets and the Coming Moves of God,"** on page 49 says, "Although 'structure' is good and necessary we must never lose sight of the fact that we are ONE BODY. When structure stands in the way or when we worship or idolize our structures rather than Jesus Christ who is the HEAD of ONE BODY, then we have moved away from the Holy Spirit and truth.

Unity recognizes that there is ONE BODY. Disunity segregates and divides. We do not become members of a club or organization – we are members of the APOSTOLIC BODY of CHRIST (Ephesians 2:19-22).

We must not present ourselves in a said 'Association' or 'Network' in such a way to imply that those who do not believe and worship the same way as ourselves are out of order with God or are in some kind of error. This is not the prerogative of some kind of Pope Initiative, whether it is the Catholic, Charismatic, Pentecostal, Evangelical, Kingdom, Faith, Prophetic or the Apostolic kind.

We all need to appreciate that each person and fellowship has a responsibility to follow their own revelations, convictions and practices, but not to impose them upon the corporate body of Christ. Such presumptuous declarations, teachings and actions cause divisions in the body of Christ. Every erroneous Christian group has established certain doctrines and practices that are unique to them. This then makes them an exclusive, 'elected' group that sees itself as superior to all others" (Hamon 49).

Exclusivism Leads to Cults

He also says, "exclusivism leads to cults" and that, "the manifestations of this attitude are seen in the extreme groups that arose during the time of the Holiness and Pentecostal Movements: Mormonism, Christian Scientists and Jehovah Witnesses. But sad to say, there are also some of the extreme right that are still counted as 'mainline' Christian denominations who believe that they are the only true people of God.

They base this conviction on a certain baptism formula, way of worship, church order or some other unique doctrine or practice.

No one man or group has it all. The New Testament scriptures emphatically and repeatedly declare that Christ has only ONE church here on planet earth. No denominational, fellowship, network, association or restoration camp makes up the entirety of the Church.

Every born again, blood washed, sanctified child of God is a member of Christ's Church. They may be Charismatic Catholics, Evangelicals, Pentecostals, Prophetic people or Present-Truth Apostolic people. We are only parts of the whole and members in particular of the corporate body of Christ.

Life is found in the Cluster

All truth and life are found in the whole, not just in one particular part or member. We need each other and will never come to maturity and fullness of truth without each other. The New Wine is in the cluster – not just in one individual grape (Isaiah 65:8)" (Hamon 49).

This however does not detract from the responsibility of any church or network from fulfilling the commission given by the Lord Jesus Christ to "go and make disciples… teaching them…" (Matthew 28:16-20)

According to the grace of God which was given to me, as a wise master builder I have laid the foundation, and another builds on it. But let each one take heed how he

Introduction

builds on it. For no other foundation can anyone lay than that which is laid, which is Jesus Christ.
(1 Corinthians 3:10, 11 NKJV)

"The great need of the day is growth, balance and maturity in sonship."

This is the time of new beginnings especially as we have entered the New Millennium. Perhaps some might say, "Now is the count down for the Lord's return..." But the fact remains there is much work to be done. We need stable, trained and Spirit led harvesters that are willing to go out into the harvest field.

The Call of God is to fulfil the Purpose of God

The call of God is not to be a good Christian only, is not to be successful in family life as an end in itself, is not to be successful in business pursuits, except it be the will of God. The call of God is to fulfil the purpose of God: "We are called according to His purpose." The purpose of God is made known to us through the knowledge of the mystery according to Ephesians 3:1-11.

We are called to be part of an apostolic church, to be joined together "in one accord," and "of one heart and one soul" as the body of believers in Acts 1-4.

In these days the Lord is raising up apostolic companies, led by apostles with all the five fold ministries in place, to fully function as a body.

Each part of the body is "Joined and knit together by what every joint supplies, according to the effective working by which every part does its share, causing growth of the body for the edifying of itself in love" (Ephesians 4:16 NKJV).

Apostolic Vanguard

Apostolic companies are the vanguard that God is raising up in these days to demonstrate to His people the victory He has given us over the devil. As apostolic companies begin to function in the fullness of our Messiah's authority in the earth, then a multitude of believers will flock to embrace the apostolic and the church will finally come to her destination, to rule and reign with Jesus our Messiah in Zion.

Paul Galligan from Revival Ministries Australia says, "The Pentecostal revival that began in the early twentieth century and has continued since was the restoration of the infilling or baptism of the Holy Spirit. It was not the restoration of the fullness of the Spirit of sonship. The Spirit of sonship is being restored today!

It is time for maturity, not time for Pentecost. Finally Pentecost is one of the foundations but sonship is the means by which the mature church reaches the destination, which is the glory of Christ revealed in His saints in the earth" (http://www.revivalministries.org.au).

Fulfilling your Mandate to the Community

We as Christians are called to more than just sub-culture; that calling and vocation are not limited to the narrow religious confinement of the Church, but to fulfil Christ's

Introduction

mandate to reclaim all that has been lost. Christians must influence their communities.

C. Peter Wagner says, "The strongest word that the Spirit is currently speaking to the churches relates to God's desire for His people to take dominion over every area of our society! The best template for designing the strategies to accomplish this is known as the seven mountains or the seven molders of culture."

"We need to affect the entire world and prepare the way of the Lord before His return. According to Scripture, Jesus will sit at God's right hand until all of His enemies are put under his feet." (Psalm 110:1)

"Those who are sons of God and led of the Holy Spirit will "accomplish this as God's end-time emissaries confront the seven nations of the – Hittites, Girgashites, Amorites, Canaanites, Perizzites, Hivites, and Jebusites (Deuteronomy 7:11).

These nations correspond to seven 'Mountains' of global society – Media, Government, Education, Economy, Religion, Celebration/Arts, and Family" (Johnny Enlow).

The Church then must equip its people for such a commission!

Part One

LAYING FOUNDATIONS

CHAPTER 1

Passing the Baton between Generations

Let's look in detail at recent church history in order to view how the apostolic "baton" was successfully passed from one generation to the next. Knowing that through the perseverance and obedience of others - history as we know it was altered forever! In particular we are going to look at how things progressed from the "Azusa Street Revival" onwards and how certain individual's affected their own era, while still affecting our lives today.

> *One generation will praise your deeds to the next. Each generation will talk about your mighty acts.*
> *(Psalms 145:4 GW)*

To begin with and in addition to the ministers who received their Pentecostal experience at Azusa Street, thousands - millions of others were indirectly influenced by the revival in Los Angeles. Among them was Thomas Ball Barratt of Norway, a Methodist pastor who became known as the Pentecostal Apostle to Northern and Western Europe.

After being baptized in the Holy Spirit and receiving tongues in New York City in 1906, Barratt returned to Oslo where, in December 1906, he conducted the first Pentecostal services in Europe. From Norway, Barratt travelled to Sweden, England, France and Germany where he sparked other national Pentecostal movements. Under Barratt, such leaders a Lewi Pethrus in Sweden, Jonathan Paul in Germany and Alexander Bobby in England were brought into the movement.

The Chicago Influence

From Chicago, through the influence of William Durham, the movement spread quickly to Italy and South America. Two Italian immigrants from Chicago, Luigi Francescon and Giacomo Lombardy founded thriving Italian Pentecostal movements after 1908 in the United States, Brazil, Argentina and Italy.

In South Bend, Indiana - near Chicago - two Swedish Baptist immigrants, Daniel Berg and Gunnar Vingren, received the Pentecostal experience. Believing they were called prophetically to Brazil, they embarked on a missionary trip in 1910 that resulted in the formation of the Brazilian Assemblies of God.

The Brazilian Assemblies developed into the largest national Pentecostal movement in the world and had some 25 million members by 1990. Also hailing from Chicago was Willis C. Hoover, the Methodist missionary to Chile who in 1909 led a Pentecostal revival in the Chilean Methodist Episcopal Church.

After being excommunicated from the Methodist Episcopal Church, Hoover and 37 of his followers organized the Pentecostal Methodist Church, which has some 1.5 million adherents in Chile.

African Pentecostalism

African Pentecostalism owes its origins to the work of John Graham Lake (1870-1935), who began his ministry as a Methodist preacher but who later prospered in business as an insurance executive. In 1898 his wife was miraculously healed of tuberculosis under the ministry of Alexander Dowie, founder of the religious community called Zion City near Chicago. In 1907, Lake was baptized in the Holy Spirit and spoke in tongues.

Zion City also produced almost 500 preachers who entered the ranks of the Pentecostal movement. After his Pentecostal experience, Lake abandoned the insurance business to answer a long-standing call to minister in South Africa. In April 1908, he led a large missionary party to Johannesburg where he began to spread the Pentecostal message throughout the nation.

Lake succeeded in founding two large and influential Pentecostal churches in South Africa. The white branch took the name Apostolic Faith Mission in 1910, borrowing from the name of the famous mission on Azusa Street. David du Plessis, known to the world as "Mr Pentecost," came from this church.

The black branch eventually developed into the Zion Christian Church, which had six million members by 1993. Soon after Lake returned to the United States, the movement reached the Slavic world through the ministry of a Russian-born Baptist pastor Ivan Voronacv, who received the Pentecostal experience in New York City in 1919.

Through prophecies, he was led to take his family with him to Odessa, Ukraine in 1922. There he established the first Pentecostal church in the Soviet Union. Voronacv was arrested, imprisoned and martyred in a communist prison in 1943. The churches he founded survived extreme persecution and have become today a major religious force in Russia and the former Soviet Union.

Japan and Korea

Pentecostalism reached Korea through the ministry of Mary Rumsey, an American missionary who had been baptized in the Holy Spirit at Azusa Street in 1907. At that time, Rumsey believed that she was called to Japan and Korea.

It was not until 1928, however, that she landed in Korea. Before World War II, she had planted eight Pentecostal churches there before being forced out of the country by the Japanese. In 1952, those eight churches were turned over to the AG, whose missionaries immediately opened a bible school in Seoul.

One of the first students to enrol was a young convert by the name of Paul Yonggi Cho. After he graduated from bible college, Cho pioneered a Korean church that became the Yoido Full Gospel Church. By the time it had over 700,000 members it was heralded the largest single Christian congregation in the world.

As for the Neo-Pentecostals, Charismatics & Third Wavers - the first wave of the Pentecostal pioneer missionaries produced what has become known as the Classical Pentecostal Movement, with more than 14,000 Pentecostal denominations throughout the world.

This phase was followed by organized Pentecostal denominational mission efforts that produced fast growing missions and indigenous churches. The final phase was the penetration of Pentecostalism into the mainline Protestant and Catholic churches as *"charismatic renewal"* movements with the aim of renewing the historic churches.

New Waves

It is worth noting that these newer *"waves"* also originated primarily in the United States. They included the Protestant Neo-Pentecostal movement, which began in 1960 in Van Nuys, California, under the ministry of Dennis Bennett, Rector of St Marks Episcopal *(Anglican)* Church. Within a decade, this movement had spread to all the 150 major Protestant families of the world, reaching a total of 55 million people by 1990.

The Catholic Charismatic Renewal movement had its beginnings in Pittsburgh in 1967 among students and faculty at DuQuesne University. After spreading rapidly among students at Notre Dame and the University of Michigan, the movement spread worldwide.

In the subsequent years since its inception, the Catholic movement not only has gained the approval of the church but also has touched over 90 million Catholics in 120 countries. The newest category that was added to these was called the *"Third Wave"* of the Holy Spirit.

It originated at Fuller Theological Seminary in 1981 under the classroom ministry of John Wimber, founder of the Association of Vineyard Churches. This "wave" comprised mainline evangelicals who experienced sign and wonders but who disdained labels such as Pentecostal or Charismatic. The Vineyard was the most visible movement of this category. By 1990, the Third Wavers were credited with some 33 million members worldwide.

Evangelists & Healers

Throughout the previous century, Pentecostals produced many evangelists who were known for their mass healing crusades.

These included Maria Woodworth-Etter, Aimee Semple McPherson *(Founder of the International Church of the Foursquare Gospel in 1927)*, Oral Roberts, Kathryn Kuhlman, Reinhard Bonnke, Benny Hinn and Peter Youngren. Beginning in the 1950's with Oral Roberts, the "televangelist" genre appeared bringing healing, tongues, prophecies and other spiritual gifts into living rooms across the nation.

Some of the most successful ones included Pat Robertson's Christian Broadcasting Network and Paul Crouch's Trinity Broadcasting Network. Notable evangelists Jimmy Swaggart and Jim Bakker fell in the televangelist scandals of the 1980's.

Most religious and secular press carried news of the renewal. This was paralleled by the publication of millions of books and tapes sold in conferences and crusades internationally. New periodicals spawned by the movement included Dan Malachuk's *Logos* magazine and Stephen Strang's *Charisma and Ministries Today* magazines.

In the late 1970's a newer movement of *"faith"* teachers drew national attention. These included Kenneth Hagin Sr., Kenneth Copeland and Fred Price. In this 1990's millions of people tuned in to the teachings of Copeland and Price, while others enrol in Hagin's Rhema bible college in Broken Arrow, Oklahoma, and a host of other Spirit-filled bible schools.

Massive Crusades

Overseas, the crusades of the German Pentecostal evangelist Reinhard Bonnke regularly drew crowds of up to 500,000 in cities throughout Africa; *(then later on up to one million in one crusade; truly phenomenal!)* the same is true of Rev. Peter Youngren's crusades in India.

Major educational institutions arose during the 20th century as well. Healing evangelist Oral Roberts founded a university under his name in Tulsa, Oklahoma, in 1965, and Pat Robertson founded Regent University in Virginia Beach, Virginia, in 1978. In addition, liberal arts colleges and bible colleges were planted worldwide.

In a sense, the charismatic movement in the United States reached a peak in 1977 when 50,000 people from all denominations gathered in Arrowhead Stadium in Kansas City, Missouri, for the General Charismatic Conference led by Kevin Ranaghan. Planners for this conference were confronted by the major controversy of the era, which involved the *"shepherding"* teachings of four charismatic leaders from Fort Lauderdale, Florida: Derek Prince, Bob Mumford, Charles Simpson and Don Basham. This movement fell apart after the four separated in 1986.

Exotic Manifestations

In the 1990's, Pentecostals and Charismatics were reinvigorated by new waves of revival that featured such Pentecostal spiritual manifestations such as *"holy laughter," "falling under the Spirit,"* and other "exotic" manifestations.

Leading in this new wave was the South African Pentecostal evangelist Rodney Howard Browne. Beginning in 1993, manifestations appeared at the Toronto Airport Vineyard church led by Pastor John Arnott. Although Arnott's church was disfellowshiped by John Wimber and the Vineyard movement, the force of the revival has continued throughout the decade.

Another wave came in 1995 when a notable revival began at Brownsville Assembly of God in Pensacola, Florida. Led by Pastor John Kilpatrick and Evangelist Steve Hill, the Brownsville meetings have attracted more than two million visitors, and recorded almost 200,000 conversions.

Those resulting *"times of refreshing"* revealed at the end of the Pentecostal century that the movement was far from over and poised itself when entering the new millennium with undiminished power. Only time can reveal the true impact on the world that the Pentecostal movement had throughout the 20th century.

Finally - from the likes of Rev. Charles F. Parham, William J. Seymour, John Wesley, Thomas B. Barratt, John G. Lake, Alexander Dowie, Maria Woodworth-Etter, Aimee Semple McPherson, Oral Roberts, Kathryn Kuhlman, Reinhard Bonnke, Benny Hinn and Peter Youngren, Kenneth Hagin Sr., Kenneth Copeland and Fred Price, John Wimber, Pat Robertson, John Kilpatrick, Steve Hill to the infamous Rodney Howard Browne (the list is endless); everyone of these above mentioned gifts to the body of Christ had a responsibility to "catch" the baton held out to them.

Had they dropped their baton, then life, as we know it today, just wouldn't be the same! These men and women of God, epitomize what it is to RUN WITH THE FAITH OF THE SON OF GOD.

CHAPTER 2

Signs of the Times

Take your everyday, ordinary life... and place it before God as an offering... ***Don't become so well-adjusted to your culture that you fit into it without even thinking*** (Romans 12:1 MSG).

The question that the last hundred years leaves us is this: **"What next?"** The only answer that can be given is that we must surrender to the move of the Holy Spirit and the authority of God's word! Only this marriage of God's Spirit and God's word will move us forwards in this generation.

Let me insert something here that came out during a conversation between Dr. Robb Thompson and Oral Roberts, which I happen to agree with very much indeed. In Oral's living room one day they began discussing how the Lord produced such great believers in the past. To which Brother Oral made the following comments:

THE AGE OF APOSTOLIC APOSTLESHIP

"IN THE LAST CENTURY – WE NEVER HEARD ABOUT THE WORD COMMITMENT. THE WORD WE CONSISTENTLY USED WAS SURRENDER."

I also would like to suggest that SURRENDER is a key word for any of us wanting to move on with the Holy Spirit today. We must learn once again what it means to be fully surrendered to the Lord.

In Psalms 37:7 it says "Surrender yourself to the LORD, and wait patiently for him. Do not be preoccupied..." (GW) However the Authorized Version uses the word "rest" in place of "surrender" here - which basically means to "stop yourself, to hold your peace and to quieten yourself!"[1]

To continue and to answer the question: "what next?" I will simply suggest that this has already begun taking place by what is known as **"The Apostolic and Prophetic Movement."**

Apostolic Ministries Formed

To qualify this point of view, let me add something that Roberts Liardon and I spoke about recently; he said, "The most successful students and ministers now come from schools that are birthed by Apostolic Ministries.

In the times of the reformation, seminaries were the place where great ministers were formed, but over time many of them have become places where God's word and the present day workings of the Holy Spirit are discredited. It seems that God has moved the place where He trains and launches His ministries and this increasingly is within the apostolic streams."

Church Historians

In addition to this, it's true to say that Church historians do recognize that the restoration of truth has been and is being restored to the church. You might say this began as far back as 1517.

We can recognize these individual movements according to a particular century and decade. But to summarize, **it is important to identify that the Church age could not be brought to a place of full maturity until the fivefold ministry gifts were restored,** that every one as a church member could be prepared to be part of a ministry team (i.e. a vehicle to reach society as seen in Ephesians 4:11–16).

These major truths have been restored:

- **Salvation by grace through faith** *(Ephesians 2:8-9)* was the beginning *(1500)*, which we now call *"The Protestant Movement."*

- In the 1600's *"The Evangelistic Movement"* began with water baptism and the separation of Church and State.

- In the 1700's *"The Holiness Movement"* came into being with sanctification, the Church being set apart from the world.

- In the 1800's *"The Faith Healing Movement"* with divine healing for the physical body and the recognition that healing was provided for in the atonement.

- In the 1900's *"The Pentecostal Movement"* exploded on the scene at a small bible school in Topeka, Kansas with former Methodist pastor Charles Fox Parham, with the Holy Spirit baptism, the evidence of speaking in tongues, and the gifts of the Spirit, the forerunners being Evan Roberts of the Welsh Revival *(1904)* and also William J. Seymour *(from 1906 onwards)* of the famous Azusa Street Revival USA.

- Then in the 1950's the *"Latter Rain Movement"* began with the prophetic presbytery, singing praises and melodious worship.

- Now from this time forth, *The Five Fold Apostolic Ministries* have been placed back in the Church, with recognition. *The Evangelist Ministry* and mass evangelism was reactivated.

- Then in 1960, *The Pastoral Gift* was restored to being the sovereign head of the local church, with renewal of all restored truth to all movement churches; this was known as *"The Charismatic Movement."*

- Then in 1970, *"The Faith Movement"* began with faith confessions, prosperity and victorious attitudes for life; with *The Teaching Ministry* re-established as a major *"five fold ministry."*

- In the 1980's we saw *"The Prophetic Movement"* begin with the prophet ministry restored and the company of the prophets brought forth. We also saw through this prophetic movement, a release of certain characteristics and revelations, such as the activation of warfare praise and prophetic intercession and much teaching on the Joshua generation, which challenged us to cross over into the Promised Land.

- Then in the 1990's *"The Apostolic Movement"* began with the **Apostle's ministry** being restored to bring divine order, structure and finality the restoration of the five fold ministries. Along with this gift, there have been fresh appearances of the miraculous, signs and wonders, unity amongst leaders and a great harvest of souls.

These are not competitive, controlling authorities, **but servant-hood** governments **that have come to serve the people of God and help them fulfil their course and purpose.** They will teach spiritual principles and not just mechanics of the word. They will understand that there are different mechanics for different things in different parts of the world.

However, the spiritual principles remain the same. These churches will train the people to use their unction and to follow the leading of the Holy Spirit to reap a bountiful harvest of souls, wherever they go in the earth.

- In 1975, Bill Bright, founder of Campus Crusade and Loren Cunningham, founder of Youth With a Mission (YWAM), developed a God-given, world-changing strategy, **"The Seven Mountains of Societal Influence."** Their mandate: Bring Godly change to a nation by reaching its seven spheres, or mountains, of societal influence.

They concluded that in order to truly transform any nation with the Gospel of Jesus Christ, these seven facets of society must be reached: Religion, Family, Education, Government, Media, Arts & Entertainment and Business.

Connecting for Excellence International Apostolic Network's primary goal is to be a catalyst, through prayer and righteous activism, which will bring change to these areas of societal influence.

The Seven Mountain Mandate

The following seven principles were taken from Generals International, a prayer based organisation founded by Mike and Cindy Jacobs in 1985, that exists for the purpose of changing lives and transforming nations.

1. Religion:

"Every society has some type of belief in a superior being or beings. In the east, religions tend to be polytheistic (many gods) or outright idolatrous (such as Hinduism and Buddhism). Although these religions are thousands of years old, they nonetheless continue to thrive today. In the west, Christianity and Catholicism are predominant, but postmodern views are increasingly being accepted and the concept of God is being rejected. This is especially true in Europe.

The Christian Church is described in the Greek language as the ecclesia. Literally translated, the word ecclesia means 'governing body.' Although we don't condone theocracies, this translation suggests that the Church should have great influence in all other spheres that make up a society. With a plethora of categorized religions around the world, it's the Church's responsibility to reach the lost with the love and Gospel of Jesus Christ, and expand the Kingdom in ministerial efforts, both nationally and internationally.

2. Family:

In any functional society, the family is the 'building block' of the community. Throughout the Bible, you will find familial examples that portray how we ought to live our lives today. God desires that men, women, and children within a family be united as one in His love. After all, He is the ultimate Father (Romans 8:14-17).

The families of the United States have been under constant and prolonged attack. Today, the assailants are fatherlessness, divorce (50% rate in secular and Christian marriages), abuse, homosexual marriage, pornography, and other negative influences have brought great dysfunction to American life.

God is calling fathers and mothers (both spiritual and biological) to bring order to the chaos that the enemy has unleashed against families in America. He also wants to bring healing to marriages and relationships within families in order to maintain a moral foundation for children in the future to stand upon.

3. Education:

At one time the education system of America unapologetically incorporated the Bible, prayer to the God of the Bible, and biblical values in every aspect of school life. Not coincidentally, this system produced a people that produced the most powerful and prosperous nation the earth has ever seen.

Now, the children of our nation are inundated with liberal ideologies, atheistic teaching and postmodern principles in our public schools and in most universities (including many Christian institutions). Put simply; they are being indoctrinated with often false, biased and anti-biblical information.

A re-introduction of biblical truth and Bible-centric values is the key to renewal and restoration in America's failing educational system.

4. Government:

Proverbs 14:34 states that, 'righteousness exalts a nation, but sin is a reproach to any people.' Many times, as exemplified in the Old Testament, a nation's moral standards are dependent on those exhibited by its leaders (or predominant political party). While each individual is responsible for his or her own sins; the fact remains that people are greatly influenced by those moral (or lack thereof) that popular leaders adopt.

The progressive liberal agenda, empowered by well-known men and women in the arts and entertainment industries, have made significant gains in the political arena over the past few decades. In fact, many liberal groups, such as the ACLU, seek to remove anything related to God or Christianity from the governmental and educational systems because of a misapplied interpretation of the phrase, 'separation of church and state.' We must see a shift in this arena in order to preserve the Christian heritage that America was founded upon. The goal is to put in place righteous political leaders that will positively affect all aspects of government.

5. Media:

The media mountain includes news sources such as radio, TV news stations, newspapers, Internet news and opinion (blog) sites and etc. The media has the potential to sway popular opinion on current issues based upon its reporting, which is not always truthful or accurate. In the 2008 elections, the liberal 'elite' media played a vital role, especially in the Presidential race. Their generally supportive and positive reporting greatly influenced the outcome.

There has been a rise in Christian news services, which is needed. However, to bring transformation to the mountain of media, Christians who are gifted for and called into this type of work must be willing to report righteously and truthfully in the secular marketplace.

6. Arts & Entertainment:

In this mountain we find some of the most influential forces shaping our society. Music, filmmaking, television, social media, and the performing arts drive the cultural tastes, values and standards of a nation's citizens, particularly its youth.

With a heavy reliance on the strong appeal of sex, drugs and alcohol, the arts and entertainment industries wield significant influence. The body of Christ needs powerful, righteous men and women who are not afraid to take their God-given talent into the arts and entertainment arenas. People ready to further His purposes, while impacting those who are lost in darkness and would not otherwise be interested in any kind of Christian message in traditional forms.

7. Business:

The ability to literally create wealth through ingenuity, enterprise, creativity and effort and is a God-given gift and a universal impulse. The markets and economic systems that emerge whenever people are free to pursue buying and selling become the lifeblood of a nation. This includes anything from farms to small businesses to large corporations.

Of course this realm is prone to corruption through idolatry, greed and covetousness. In response, the Church must embrace its responsibility to train up those who are called into the marketplace to manage businesses and provide leadership with integrity and honesty. We believe it is the Lord's will to make his people prosperous and that He desires for His Church to use its wealth to finance the work of Kingdom expansion. Simply put: Prosperity with a purpose" (https://www.generals.org).

Chapter 3

The Transition into the 21st Century

Throughout church history there have been certain pioneers who have helped mark their generation for the Lord; leaving a legacy for others to follow. Commendable - but not many of those same pioneers were able to "transition" from one move of God to the next. The transition can be crucial and just as important as the pioneering efforts to begin with.

> *I'm going to send you food from heaven like rain. Each day the people should go out and gather **only what they need for that day**. In this way I will test them to see whether or not they will follow my instructions...*
> *(Exodus 16:4-5 GW)*

It is not my intention here to try and cover church history in this one short chapter, but I do however encourage you to go look for yourself and see what notable figures you can find of recent and not-so-recent within church history, who **"moved-on" when the Spirit of God began to blow a new wind of divine direction,** and made the transition into the new move of God. You will find those who made the transition and those who got lost because somehow the past had become their logos!

Cucumber Mentality

It is wonderful to be used of God, in any generation, but we must not get stuck. So that when God wants to do a new thing, we are not stubbornly attached to what He did in the past. Not many have been able to move on throughout church history, and notoriously prefer to stay with the familiar.

Consider the Israelites who were thinking of something as small-minded as **"onions and garlic"** when they were in the wilderness! Especially after experiencing all the adventure and enormity of God's deliverance, with the years of torment and suffering still fresh in their minds. Nonetheless they soon began to pine for the familiar.

Listen to their murmuring and contempt:

> *If only we had meat to eat! Remember all the free fish we ate in Egypt and the cucumbers, watermelons, leeks, onions, and garlic we had? But now we've lost our appetite! Everywhere we look there's nothing but manna!*
> *(Numbers 11:4-6 GW)*

Sadly this is a common human weakness; that we begin to crave the very thing that we were set free of! We become so familiar with the bondage that had us captive for so long, that we actually prefer it; a re-occurrence for us all especially if we stay in the wilderness.

It is true to say that not many people are able to experience God in their generation, *(pioneer, be in the forefront)* and then move on with Him and keep the impact on the next generation alive! Instead they get stuck in the last move... and don't know how to stay with what God is doing today.

We can call this the now move or wave of God *(which is relevant to any current generation...)* Most folks can only relate to their own experiences - so when something new happens - they can't flow with it. They miss it... lots of folks - even well intentioned folks miss God. *(It's easy to be "sincere" but "sincerely-wrong" at the same time!)*

Pioneers that made it!

By way of a short example I want to make mention of a few names that we are all so familiar with, those of recent church history; **pioneers such as Lester Sumrall, Morris Cerullo and Oral Roberts...** of course the list could go on.

Dr. Sumrall for instance **had the likes of Howard Carter and Smith Wigglesworth as his mentors and received some of their "anointing" for his generation.** He was ordained way back in 1932 and was considered the father of Christian Television because he helped secure the first license for 24-hour Christian television, amongst many other achievements.

But with all of his accolades Lester was one of those men *(of his calibre)* who did not get stuck in yesteryear... he moved on... and was one of the few who was able to do so. Right up until the end, he kept current with his finger on the pulse of what God was doing and saying in the now *(remember Hebrews 11:1 calls it "now-faith!")*

No Retirement for the Genuine

There is no retirement for genuine men and woman of God! They walk with God like Enoch did and then they are not..! They are too "black n white" to enjoy the "grey!" *(see Genesis 5:24)*

Lester Sumrall kept hearing God, keeping relevant to the day that he was in rather than aligning himself with the experiences of the past *(regardless of how successful they might have been)* he kept himself aligned to God. In fact the more successful a move may have been, can prevent folks from moving on to the next wave... somehow they imagine that God could only be successful in their generation - no matter how long ago that was - and don't ever move on because of that premise.

To qualify this, let me say that there is always a balance to everything. We are not talking about being politically correct or relevant in that context but in regards to what God is doing and saying today.

Dr. Sumrall was a good example for us to follow; not to get stuck in yesterday... but **stay hooked up with what God is saying and doing today.** If that means moving on from what we have known all our lives... moving away from the familiar - then yes... we must move on and not miss God. We must not get stuck in a generational or denominational rut!

If we refuse to move on with God, then what might have been successful in the past has now become a deception especially if it prevents us from hearing and moving on with God today.

Reading books and studying history can be of great value and is great in its place. BUT... if we are so caught up in the past, that we fail to hear God for today, then we have been caught in deception. **It takes a very brave man or woman - to move on with God. Especially if they helped pioneer the old!**

Yesterday and Today

Of course when we talk about what God is saying today this does not in any way change **His "Logos-word"** *(written)*... this always remains the same *"yesterday, today and forever."* However His *"Rhema-word"* - that which **He "speaks" today** - is fresh and is NOW manna. It never contradicts His written word. But it is for today. Otherwise we would all still be wearing sackcloth and ashes!!!

Let's make sure that we move with the tide, God's tide. Not with the popular opinion or political correctness of our day; but with God. **What is He saying right now? What is on His heart for our world right now?** If we know more about previous centuries and what God said to them, than we do today, then we have missed God for today.

Let's not make that same mistake that so many others have made and <u>move on</u> with God into the 21st century.

Nothing is holding us back. **We must make the "transition" into the apostolic,** which is only possible when we hear God's voice.

> *I am the good shepherd, and know my sheep, and am known of mine... they shall hear my voice...*
> *(John 10:14-16 KJV)*

❖

CHAPTER 4

A Network of Relationships

The Holy Spirit directs us to focus on building "spiritual relationships" so that a strong NETwork can be produced, relationships willing to work together for the purposes of the kingdom of God.

> *So then, as Christians, do you have any encouragement? Do you have any comfort from love? Do you have any spiritual relationships?* **Do you have any sympathy and compassion?** *Then fill me with joy by having the same attitude and the same love, living in harmony, and keeping one purpose in mind.*
> (Philippians 2:1-2 GW)

Such a network of relationships is *apostolic* in nature and is what the Holy Spirit continues to develop for this end time move of God. These relationships look for apostolic support and encouragement from other apostolic men and women of God in order to move forwards boldly and powerfully in the Holy Spirit; released to fulfil their destinies for the glory of God.

Networking People

A network literally means: a linking of people with a common interest or area of concern. Therefore as time develops, we will see a new emphasis on the development of such networks, working together across the board denominationally and via association. Networking does not imply that all groups should come under one "Pope" type figure, a specific apostolic movement, or "his holiness archbishop."

> *Again, **<u>the kingdom of heaven is like unto a NET</u>**, that was cast into the sea, and gathered of every kind: which, when it was full, they drew to shore, and sat down, and gathered the good into vessels, but cast the bad away.*
> *(Matthew 13:47-48 KJV)*

Instead, kingdom networking simply involves associations and groups working together, just like large "fishing nets." This can be explained like so: each member of a network represents a single **KNOT** that helps tie the overall net together.

In addition, those with the grace, vision and wisdom enough, that is needed to network together with other networks - will eventually make up the greater fishing net that God will use to draw in the vast end time harvest of souls. A net that will both be large enough and strong enough to catch and to hold such multitudes!

Dr. Bill Hamon says of such networks, "This gives the Holy Spirit the opportunity to bring a greater unity and corporate vision within the body of Christ." This will enable all available resources to be harnessed to work together towards assisting the body of Christ to initiate and sustain an effective thrust towards souls. "The common meeting ground is to have the corporate vision of reaping the great end time harvest and proclaiming Jesus Christ as Lord over all the earth."[2]

Nets to Equip

In the Amplified version of the above scripture (Matthew 13:47-48), it aptly uses the word DRAGNET: **"Again, the kingdom of heaven is like a <u>dragnet</u> which was cast into the sea and gathered in fish of every sort."** The Message Bible calls it a "fishnet" and the Authorized simply uses the word "net" as above.

The Greek word used for "net" does refer to fishing nets but also to PACKSADDLES, which in the East were simply bags made of *netted-rope*. However perhaps even more interesting is the Greek root meaning for the word "net" used in the Authorized, which means TO EQUIP![3] *(See also Matthew 4:19; 9:35; 13:49; John 21:1-ff; James 3:13; 4:1-8; 1 Peter 5:5-10).*

Therefore a strong and effective network largely depends upon the people involved *(especially pastors and leaders)* to be totally committed - in every aspect of their lives - to the Lord Jesus Christ. Cheerfully willing to pool their talents and abilities for the "over-all" without begrudging the personal cost.

Such relationships of association through networking are not meant to threaten or contradict denominational loyalties or even cause division; instead they are meant to assist, help bring strength, secure unity and a much greater clarity; especially in enhancing better skills in sharing the word of God.

One specific aim of a network is to help establish ministry centres of excellence and influence. Such can be called: *"Spiritually Governmental Hubs,"* that enhance God's kingdom and provide a significant "platform" *(for all the ministry gifts)* to speak into cities and nations with maximum effectiveness.

Such spiritual hubs help to develop ministries; enhancing and bringing them into positions of leadership that will influence every area of society. Utilizing skills individually and corporately to impact local regions as spheres of influence, for the *kingdom of God* and the glory of Jesus Christ.

Knots of Divine Appointments

Lastly let's take a look at the significance of knots, we could say that divine appointments are like "knots" in a net. They are **strong-connections** that can take the strain of apostolic relationships! In other words each relationship can be seen as a knot in the overall net. And any net is only as strong as its individual "knots" and "connections!"

A Network of Relationships

Any fisherman will affirm that it's the knots that bring stability to the net and empower the net. Equally true for the kingdom of God, all of its knots *(divine connections and relationships)* strengthen its net. When such relationships *(knots)* are strong and in place they always breed more of the following: security, prosperity, encouraged abilities, healing, unity, trust and harmony.

> *Behold, how good and how pleasant it is for brethren to* **dwell together in unity!** *It is like the precious ointment upon the head, that ran down upon the beard, even Aaron's beard... for there the LORD commanded the blessing...*
> *(Psalm 133:1-3 KJV)*

FACT: fishermen spend a great portion of their time mending and cleaning their nets; perhaps more time than actually fishing! Likewise we too must spend larger portions of our time securing sound relationships that help develop the net - the kingdom! Only then will we be more effective.

FACT: fishing nets can catch vast amounts of fish, with a high percentage of what's caught being thrown directly back into the sea, *(wrong type or size!)* It's a stark reality that many "undesirables" will be caught in the kingdom's net, that will also be thrown back! **Even God is looking for a certain type of fish - that can be *gutted* correctly!**

Cleaned and Gutted

In other words, those ready to "give" themselves to the kingdom are kept and all else are thrown back. Those who are kept in the net (kingdom) are then "CLEANED" and "GUTTED!"

The emphasis in all of this is the "kingdom of God," as Matthew 13:47 clearly stated; **"the kingdom of heaven is like a net..."** which was a direct teaching about the kingdom and not just a meagre net! In fact, including this particular parable about the NET, Jesus told **seven short parables** in total, about the kingdom of God.

- The Hidden Treasure - Matthew 13:44
- The Pearl of Great Price - Matthew 13:45-46
- The Yeast - Matthew 13:33-35, Luke 13:18-19
- The Mustard Seed - Matthew 13:31-32, Mark 4:30-34, Luke 13:18-19
- The Household Treasures - Matthew 13:52
- The Sprouting Seed - Mark 4:26-29
- **The Dragnet - Matthew 13:47-50**

So based on our knowledge of nets it's been easy to ascertain the basic characteristics of the kingdom; the restoration of the net equals the healing of relationships. Knots equal the need to submit one to another in effective cooperation and finally anyone who remains in the net *(kingdom)* will be cleansed and gutted!

Conclusion:

The kingdom of God is only as strong as its relationships *(knots!)* Making DIVINE NETWORKING a *major* part of kingdom activity. Therefore we must always be ready to work together, safe guarding strong and effective *connections* - with purity of heart - and a willingness to be steered by the larger plan and kingdom business of the Holy Spirit.

CHAPTER 5

The Kingdom Reign of God

We have been looking at "knots" and how the New Testament referred to the kingdom of God as being like a "net." We looked briefly at the vital role of "knots" in a net and how they bring stability and strength. We talked about how each knot represented "divine relationships" or "contacts" within God's kingdom by using this powerful statement, "divine connections produce strong relationships that in turn develop and enhance God's kingdom."

> *Thy Kingdom come, Thy will be done, on earth as it is in heaven.*
>
> *(Matthew 6:10 KJV)*

So in keeping with this emphasis on the kingdom, let's move on to talk more about what the kingdom really is all about. To begin with, when the bible refers to the "kingdom of God," it is actually referring to the "reign" (authority) of God more than the "realm" over which He rules or over which His authority resides.

In other words, it is more about His authority than anything else! However in our modern day vernacular this has gotten a little lost, either in translation or in cultural references and we tend to assume that "kingdom" refers to a "place" or "territory" more than to "authority."

Clearly this makes it vital for us to correct our focus a little so that the true context is not lost and where we can properly adhere to the true meaning of kingdom as seen in scripture. That kingdom is essentially more to do with reigning, ruling and exercising authority than it is about the realm where that authority functions.

Predominant Meaning

I would say this is a far more dynamic concept. Much less passive! And it is within the New Testament that the predominant meaning of "kingdom" was God's-reign or rule; with any other meaning seldom used.

For instance if we were to say, "the gospel of the kingdom of God," this would best be understood as *"THE GOOD NEWS OF THE REIGN OF GOD."* The gospel is the good news and the kingdom is His reign. Hence the good news of His reign! We must consider this and make it personal; His kingdom is His rule, His authority and His government, therefore when we receive the kingdom of God, we receive, accept His government and rule over our lives and hearts.

To solidify this concept, we can remember what Jesus said, that we must *"receive the kingdom of God like little children" (Mark 10:15)*. In other words, **we must receive the government of God over our lives in childlike trust,** because He has our best interests at heart. **Besides when He "governs" our lives, nothing else can!**

Consider this a little further. Every time we have prayed the "Lord's Prayer," we have actually petitioned God to reign over us, ("...thy kingdom come..." Matthew 6:10 KJV) The correct context being that "His will" must be obeyed on earth (by men) just as it is obeyed in heaven! Because when He is obeyed by men, and His will is done in this present life, then the kingdom of God has already come!

Obedience Enhances His Reign

It is already here! It is upon us! And obedience is always the key to truly dwelling in the kingdom of God. If we truly live in the kingdom of God NOW, by allowing Him to govern over us, this in turn must mean that we see the things of His kingdom coming to pass, not occasionally but regularly and routinely. We know that what is normal to the kingdom of God is not normal to this world (healings and miracles) but must be common-place to us!

When the bible was written, the hearers of the gospel possessed this early understanding of *"kingdom,"* and had a better grasp of its meaning than we do today. When they heard that the kingdom of God was at hand, they understood that it meant God's authority was being restored to the earth and that to enter the kingdom of heaven meant entering

God's reign and experiencing the benefits of this in our immediate lives.

Or perhaps today we would say in "real-time" which simply means "right-now!" Religion always keeps God "out-there" somewhere, but He and the rule of His kingdom is "right-here" and "right-now!"

Many preachers have told us that entering the "kingdom of heaven" means going to heaven when we die. While this is true, it leaves us with very little understanding of the purposes of God and His intentions for His Church. **Failure to preach and understand the "kingdom" of God is the reason that few Christians live the life of "OVER COMERS" today.**

Kingdom of God becomes a Present Reality

It is when the kingdom of God becomes a "present reality" and not just a "future hope," that mankind is able to enjoy the blessings of God's rule and reign in their individual lives. Where they enter the more abundant and victorious life that is promised in scripture, yet sadly is only enjoyed by a minority of Christians today.

Those who enjoy true kingdom benefits today are not some elite group who live opulent lifestyles, but rather those who have genuine *"...righteousness and peace and joy in the Holy Spirit,"* as mentioned in Romans 14:17. This IS the kingdom of God!

This is not to say that there is no future realm when Christ returns, but it opens to us the marvellous possibility that He will return to a world where His reign is already well established. Not to the fractured and feeble Church we have become, that is divided and has lost its grasp on what the true biblical concept of the kingdom really is.

When the kingdom of God is proclaimed to the Church and by the Church we will have returned to the original biblical truth of the matter. Even more importantly, we will be obeying the instruction of our King Jesus, **to proclaim the supernatural gospel of the kingdom of God, hastening the day of His return** *(see books by Dr. Myles Munroe – "Kingdom Principles" and "Rediscovering the Kingdom" – www.destinyimage.com).*

The kingdom of God is the only thing that Jesus ever called the "gospel." Few people understand this fact. And the fact remains that if we fail to proclaim the "gospel of the kingdom," we are not actually obeying His instruction to preach the "Good News of God's Reign and Authority!"

The government of God is the best news that anyone can ever hear, because it is God's only solution to all of man's ills. When we accept this "King Jesus" as the ultimate "ruler" of *every* aspect of our lives, then and only then can we truly experience kingdom living as it should be.

Ambassadors of His Kingdom

As ambassadors of His kingdom our role on this earth is to administer His kingdom justice here, His rule, reign and righteousness. This is the role of every single believer, to reign spiritually and administer His spiritual justice in order to put into affect His kingdom right here and right now.

To administer in the dictionary means to manage the affairs of, formerly give out, and to apply. This explains our role quite well in contemporary terms, because we have to minister into our everyday circumstances simply by applying God's spiritual truth and spiritual laws.

We do this without denying or breaching natural laws, in order to do things from a kingdom perspective! BUT **the laws of God's kingdom obviously supersede all others and we can apply these truths into the spiritual realm and let it take effect there.** Remember that everything originates in the spiritual realm first anyway (Genesis 1:1-2) and has its eventual effect here on the earth.

Take for instance such scriptures as Matthew 6:10 for example, where it says, "...as it is in heaven" and in Matthew 18:18 especially in the Amplified version where it talks about binding and losing on earth, just as it already is in heaven. **We are enforcers who enforce the things of God** but in the spirit realm FIRST. Because **that's where the struggle is, it is a spiritual battle and not one of flesh and blood (Ephesians 6:12).**

There are places of course where preaching is illegal and believers are forced underground but traditionally this has not hindered the gospel, on the contrary that's often when it runs the fastest, spreads hardest and supersedes all obstacles. But this is another discussion altogether!

What we are talking about here is applying God's spiritual truth into the atmosphere, letting it supersede all else; yet without breaching natural or political laws, to

the best of our ability! Remember just being righteous in an unrighteous world is spiritual warfare in itself. We don't have to open our mouths to create conflict, just being here – spiritually speaking - is conflict in itself! Remember we are light and light always disperses darkness.

Even our worship is warfare, because it creates an atmosphere that is "contrary" to the atmosphere of this world. Therefore even before we open our mouths, we are not welcome! Anything we engage in is spiritual warfare! Our very presence on earth creates a contradiction and a conflict. Essentially we represent a real and present "resistance" to evil – particularly when yielded to the Holy Spirit.

More Than Numbers

Dr. Paul Y. Cho in his book, **"More Than Numbers"** writes: "Since the beginning of recorded human experience, men have always tried to fathom an ideal society. Plato, the well-known Greek philosopher, that dreamed of an ideal society based upon an ethical political framework and social philosophies, that were too idealistic ever to be executed to his desired perfection.

The Old Testament prophets spoke of a future age when men would live together without armaments of war. Isaiah spoke of spears being turned into pruning hooks, and nations not lifting up swords against each other. In fact, the peace of the world would be so dramatically different that he used the images of a wolf lying down with a lamb, leopards with kids, and calves with young lions to signify the radical change in world affairs, which would come in the future.

The message, which Jesus preached, was one of repentance because the beginning of a new era was at hand. *'Repent, for the kingdom of heaven is at hand' (Matthew 4:17 KJV).* His teachings, illustrations, and parables were all primarily dealing with the kingdom of God. In fact the prayer he taught the disciples to pray was, *'Thy kingdom come, thy will be done on earth as it is in heaven' (Matthew 6:10 KJV).*

To the very end, Jesus continually emphasised the kingdom to his disciples. Although it is obvious to all who study the gospels that Jesus' main emphasis was on the kingdom of God *(Matthew called it the kingdom of heaven because he wrote primarily for the Jews),* I find little agreement on what the kingdom of God is and what the message of the gospel of the kingdom should be.

Synonymous to the Church

Augustine perceived the kingdom of God to be synonymous with the church. The Reformed movement had a large part in redefining the meaning of the kingdom of God. Calvin basically agreed with Augustine. He differed on what aspect of the church represented the kingdom of God. His feelings were that the true church, which was within the obvious church, was the earthly manifestations of the kingdom of God.

The task of the church would be made possible by the use of a special power called the gospel of the kingdom of God. This gospel of the kingdom of God would so affect the lives of first men and then nations that there would be a mighty transformation of social, political, and economic reality.

The Kingdom Reign of God

The church was likened to leaven which would slowly so permeate the dough of the earth that at a point in history the earth would proclaim Jesus Christ as Lord and King. At this point the Lord Jesus Christ would return to earth to accept the kingdom prepared for him by his heavenly Father.

There has been another school of theology, which does not try to explain the kingdom of God in terms of the future but tries to understand the kingdom of God in its present social context. **Harvey Cox** is just one of many modern theologians who view the kingdom of God as a social order brought about by the church.

The problems of inequality, prejudice, as well as the rest of our social concerns are to be addressed and dealt with by a church, which is conscious of its mission. Biblical terms are redefined to make them more relevant of today's problems. Many of our liberal church leaders are motivated by what they see is the lack of concern within the more conservative evangelical church leaders."

Basic Flaw of Theology

Cho continues, "Although my view of the kingdom of God will be given, I believe that there is a basic flaw in just a theological view of the kingdom of God. Although I believe in reason, I don't believe in reason's infallibility. There is a greater foundation than reason in establishing what the kingdom of God really is. That foundation is the simple and yet profound word of God. Let us look at some basic biblical principles, which will help us understand what the kingdom of God is.

The kingdom of God is not only for the future, but also for the present. *'For the kingdom of God is not meat and drink; but righteousness, and peace, and joy in the Holy Ghost'* (Romans 14:17 KJV). Paul reveals to us that the kingdom of God transcends the natural existence of man and causes him to experience in the here and now, the fruit of the Holy Spirit. That if you associate with the Holy Spirit you will become like the person you are associating with.

The natural result of association with the Holy Spirit will be a way of life, which is more concerned with the quality God bestows to life rather than the essential aspects to life, eating and drinking.

Changing Sides

Paul also reveals that the kingdom of God is something that we have entered into as a result of our being regenerated by the Holy Spirit. *'[God] hath delivered us from the power of darkness, and hath translated us into the kingdom of his dear Son'* (Colossians 1:13 KJV). The word, *'translated,'* used in our English text, in the Greek is *metestasen,* which literally means to change sides.

As I study this verse, I see a picture of a football game. Each team is on the opposite end of the field. On one side is the team, which represents the kingdom of darkness. On the other side is the team, which represents the kingdom of God. During the game, one of the main players of the darkness team takes off his shirt and number, goes to the opposing bench and puts on the kingdom of God shirt. Then he goes on the field to play against the darkness boys. He simply switches sides. This is what happened to us. We were transformed from one kingdom to the other, the kingdom of our Lord.

The kingdom of God is also described in its future prospect for eternal blessedness:

Wherefore the rather, brethren, give diligence to make your calling and election sure: for if ye do these things, ye shall never fall: For so an entrance shall be ministered unto you abundantly in the everlasting kingdom of our Lord and Saviour Jesus Christ.
(2 Peter 1:10-11 KJV)

In Matthew Jesus spoke of the future when he said, *'Many will come from the east and west and sit at the table with Abraham, Isaac and Jacob in the kingdom of heaven' (8:11).* Yet in Matthew 13, our Lord tells parables which give further clarification to what he meant by the kingdom of heaven. He says that once the kingdom is purged, the righteous would shine like the sun.

Jesus is the representation of what it is like to be in the kingdom. **'The kingdom of God is not coming with signs to be observed; nor will they say, 'Lo, here it is!' or 'There!' for behold, the kingdom of God is in the midst of you'** *(Luke 17:20-21 RSV).*

This verse can be applied to the fact that the kingdom of God was there in their midst. The *'you'* here is the plural, which in English is hard to understand. Jesus was there in there midst. The Pharisees were not to look for a glorious manifestation in the future, but the kingdom was before them and they were too blind to observe that God was working without a lot of fanfare.

The Kingdom Paradox

The kingdom's paradox has to be viewed on the basis of a balanced understanding. Jesus told Pilate in John 18, *'My kingdom is not of this world.'* Yet he also said in Luke 13 that the kingdom of God would start out rather unobservable, like a mustard seed. Yet, this seed, almost unnoticed, would grow up and affect the entire world.

Rather than seeing opposing views in scripture as contradictory, I consider them as a balance. **Therefore, the kingdom of God is *future*, but it is *present*. It is not of this world, but it affects this world. It can be entered into at the present time, but there is a future fulfilment. You can't see it with the natural eye, but the kingdom of God is everywhere Christ is.**

As we analyse the kingdom further we realise that the word kingdom can be understood in different ways.

Both the word *baileia*, the Greek word translated kingdom; and the Hebrew word *malkuth* signify the rank and authority exercised by a king. Our present thinking deals with the people who are under the king's authority or the actual territory over which kingly authority is exercised. So the nature of the authority may be closer to the understanding of the biblical concept of kingdom than the actual subjects of the authority.

Psalm 145:13 expresses in poetic terms something of this idea, *'Thy kingdom is an everlasting kingdom, and thy dominion endureth throughout all generations.'* In classical

Hebrew poetry, the two verses of the poem are to express the same idea in differing ways. Therefore the poet's concept of the kingdom was that it was God's actual dominion.

Kingdom Legitimacy

Herod the Great was not a popular king of Israel. Although he rebuilt the temple to majestic grandeur and built a great many fine public buildings in Jerusalem, he had no real kingdom. There was no genuine basis for his authority apart from Roman might. He had gone to Rome and had been given the kingship over Israel without a legitimate basis for having this kind of authority.

He was not born to it. A recognised prophet did not anoint him. He was not a descendant of Judah. He had no legitimacy. Although he lived in a palace, wore a crown and was called King Herod, his kingdom was bought and not earned. In Great Britain there are estates that can be bought which will carry a title with them. So if you have enough money, you may buy a title. Yet, this is not the same as being given a title by the queen, or being born into a noble family. Money might buy you a title, but that title is not legitimate.

As we analyse this thinking further, it causes us to understand the prayer, which Jesus told us to pray: *'Thy kingdom come. Thy will be done in earth, as it is in heaven.'* More than asking God to take over the world in a cataclysmic event, there seems to be the desire in the heart of the Lord for the authority of God to be as obvious to the earth as it is obvious in heaven.

Conclusion:

Therefore I believe that the kingdom of God is the nature of His reign or His authority. It is genuine, it is indisputable, and it is eternal. The reign of God is present, but it will also be in the future. God has always been in charge! He is the Creator of the earth and for that matter the entire universe. He is all-powerful.

However, in this human arena called earth, God has allowed Himself to be limited. Satan was given a realm of authority; he is the god of this present age. He has authority over this world's systems. His seat of authority is in the immediate atmosphere surrounding the world.

God has provided an escape from the territory over which Satan has authority. He provided Jesus Christ, the last Adam."[4]

CHAPTER 6

The Church Age Begins

Bob Walker in 1952 prophesied, that the Assemblies of God and other Pentecostals had planted the seeds of a mighty "Charismatic" revival. He stated that soon the revival would break out in all denominations. **It has come to pass.** We are now seeing the end-time outpouring of the Spirit.

Satan is raging. We are at war. But the prophet said, *"that when the enemy comes in like a flood the Spirit of God will raise up a standard against him."* One of the greatest dangers facing the Evangelicals, Pentecostals and Charismatics is a rejection of our biblical heritage and radical changes of our views on the end-times. The non-Kingdomists and Dominionists are examples of this. New and extreme winds of doctrine seem to blow around us with gale force. Nevertheless many stand firm and proclaim God's truth for these last days. Indeed, we are *"set for the defence of the gospel."*

Earnestly contend for the Faith

After Jesus' death and resurrection came the Day of Pentecost, the Holy Spirit was poured out and the church was born.

The church grew, thousands of Jews believed that Jesus of Nazareth was the Messiah, and that His death and resurrection was exactly what the prophets had foretold. Many went out as Jesus had commanded them *(Matthew 28:19)*, "Go into all the nations." The result was that even Gentiles were professing Jesus Christ as their Lord. Questions arose among Jewish believers about whether the Gentile believers were required to keep the Mosaic Law or not?

Tensions grew between Jewish and Gentile Christians led early to each side, having to define in great discussion their relationship regarding both the Law and circumcision. The Gentile believers should simply abstain from certain kinds of food, such as blood and from fornication *(Acts 15)*.

For the Jews both the Abrahamic and the Mosaic covenants had the same validity, and it was unthinkable to interpret history with its promises in an allegorical or spiritual manner.

Neither Jesus nor the apostles denied the historical testimony of the Old Testament but they gave its texts an added perspective. Paul described the Non-Jewish believers as branches, taken from a wild fruitless olive tree *(the heathen nations)*, and grafted into cultivated, fruitful olive tree with a nourishing sap filled root *(Israel)*.

> *If some of the branches have been broken off and you though a wild olive shoot have been grafted in among the others and now share in the nourishing sap from the olive root, do not boast over those branches. If you do, consider this: you do not support the root, but the root supports you.*
>
> *(Romans 11:17-18)*

Despite Paul's explicit warning to the Gentile churches not to boast against the *"Fathers"* and the *"root,"* i.e. the Jewish people, it was not long before the official church developed the theology that God had completely rejected *"old Israel"* and replaced it with the *"church."* All the promises in the Old Testament were taken to mean the "church" in the capacity of *"the new Israel."*

Greek Gnosticism secured a foothold in the church, by means of various rites, as did Babylonian mystery cults. Struggles for power by certain bishops also had an effect, as well as local superstitions. Then in the fourth century the Roman Caesar Constantine, declared that the struggle against Christianity was lost. So he proclaimed religious freedom throughout the Roman Empire and Christianity was declared the official religion.

The Religious World Opposes Revival

The Church became an institution for authoritarian politics, this in turn developed into the Roman Catholic and Greek Orthodox religions we know today. Religion, supremacy, legends, superstitions and human traditions gained power, but Christianity gradually disappeared. Mariology and veneration of saints came increasingly to the forefront within society. This seemingly brought a twofold development that led an assault against bible-based revival movements and against Jews.

After Christianity was accepted by the State, it became distorted. Doctrines on grace, faith, repentance and salvation were perverted. Repentance from the heart and the new birth were no longer emphasised. People believed that God's grace was obtained through the sacrament — infant baptism, communion, confirmation, confession, marriage, priesthood, ordination, and finally, extreme unction.

It was said you could only become a Christian by doing all these things! The most sacred was infant baptism. It was taught that an infant was born again through water baptism, as God's Spirit was imparted through the water. Then as the child grew and participated in the various sacraments within the church system, then the child was a Christian.

Biblical Revelation

Assurance of salvation was lost, the result, an enormous doctrine of works, which combined various occult elements. The forming of *"holy orders"* and *"holy places"* with *"holy objects,"* *"saints."* All these were nothing more than man's contrived attempts to reach God and obtain His approval.

Many superstitions began to flourish together with the worship of saints, fetishes, fables, myths and unbiblical traditions. Biblical revelation was lost and withheld from ordinary people who were lost in a maze of condemnatory fabrications and superstitious beliefs. Holy lifestyles and reverence for God were lost and replaced by liturgy, pilgrimages, flagellation, monks and holy orders. Candles and crucifixes became holy objects. Icons became an occult medium through which it was said, life and grace were imparted from heaven. As the papacy developed so too did the worship of saints *(ancestor worship)*, and Mariology. Latin became a holy language and the liturgy was read with Latin prayers like occult incantation.

Religion had now taken over, New Testament Christianity had lost its power, extinguished by demonic imitation, the life had gone.

Replacement Theology

Unbiblical features became part of the norm as the church moved away from its Jewish and biblical roots. As Christianity was proclaimed the official religion of the Roman Empire, becoming legal requirement, replacement theology became increasingly prevalent.

A false charge has echoed from this time, with lasting accusation, the Jews are still being charged with the same violent attacks. This accusation is the most serious because it has theological root. ***Did the Jews murder Jesus?***

Augustine *(354 to 430AD)* systematically developed, "*Kingdom Now Theology.*" He did this with reference to the theology of the kingdom of God, applying this to the Jewish thinking about themselves as God's kingdom. Augustine developed the thought that their dispersion *(the Jews)* was a sign to Christians who when they saw what had befallen the Jewish people who had rejected and murdered Jesus, their own Messiah. This then would be a warning concerning what would happen to anyone falling away from the church — the *"Mother"* of all believers.

He also argues that the church's interpretations of the Old Testament injunctions are shadows. He maintains that these shadows become realities in the new life Christ gives! Declaring that the Old Testament is a prophecy concerning Christ, and therefore Christians now possess all the promises contained therein. The application is that the *"church"* is in itself an institution, and the *"Heavenly State"* to be — set up on earth.

Fugitive Status and Vagabonds

Furthermore all Jews were condemned to fugitive status, vagabonds wondering the earth as punishment for putting to death Christ. This fever had now spread the excitement of a fight and being in good stead for it was a new phenomenon. The theologians and so-called church fathers who were to be examples, Christ like, were also involved and quick to embrace anti-Semitism.

Because of the anti-Semitic view many people shut the Jews out, unless of course they became Christians like everyone else. Some treated this as a new fad, meaning that everyone else was *"doing it,"* like the latest fashion. The question was and is: **Did the Jews murder Jesus? Was it justifiably, biblical?**

Let's find out.

First: the Roman authorities sentenced Him to death and the Roman soldiers carried out the execution. According to history both Romans and Jews were involved, so to be consistent all Romans and Italians and Jews ought to be persecuted.

Second: theologically speaking Jesus was to be the Lamb who would be sacrificed for the sins of all mankind. Sinners then killed Him! Jesus repeatedly told His disciples that He had to go to Jerusalem to suffer and die there. Much earlier John the Baptist had prophesied over Him saying, "Look the Lamb of God who takes away the sin of the world" *(John 1:29)*. When Peter tried to defend Jesus' life with a sword in Gethsemane, Jesus declared:

> *Do you think I cannot call on my Father, and he will at once put at my disposal more than twelve legions of angels? But how then would Scriptures be fulfilled that say it must happen in this way?*
>
> (Matthew 26:53-54)

Jesus also said:

> *The reason my Father loves me is that I lay down my life — only to take it up again. No one takes it from me, but I lay it down of my own accord. I have authority to lay it down and authority to pick it up again. This command I received from my father.*
>
> (John 10:17-18)

Third: is there any room for hatred towards the Jews? The bible says in 1 Corinthians 13:5 that Love... keeps no record of wrongs. Persecution, personal hatred, revenge has no place in a believer's heart. The Jews are not eternally damned; God loves them as He does the entire world. **The Jewish people will always be in God's plan.**

> *When you pass through the waters, I will be with you; and when you pass through the rivers, they will not sweep over you. When you walk through the fire, you will not be burned; the flames will not set you ablaze.*
>
> *(Isaiah 43:2)*

> *Since you are precious and honoured in my sight, and because I love you, I will give men in exchange for you, and people in exchange for your life. Do not be afraid, for I am with you; I will bring your children from the east and gather them from the west.*
>
> *(Isaiah 43:4-5)*

> *I ask then, did God reject his people? By no means! I am an Israelite myself, a descendant of Abraham, from the tribe of Benjamin. God did not reject his people, whom he fore knew. Don't you know what the Scripture says in the passage about Elijah — how he appealed against Israel?*
>
> *(Romans 11:1-2)*

I believe the question is answered,
No one took the life of Jesus!
"He gave it."

CHAPTER 7

Replacement Theology

We know that Replacement Theology is prevalent in all Christian groups to some degree, but to one man's experience it became too much to bear — Martin Luther *(1483-1546)*. Luther protested about Replacement Theology by nailing a 95-page thesis to the church door at Castle Church, Wittenberg, on 31st October 1517.

The veil was lifted when he received a revelation on Romans 1:16-17, like a flashing light.

> *I am not ashamed of the gospel, because it is the power of God for the salvation of everyone who believes: first to the Jew, then to the Gentile.*
>
> *For in the gospel, righteousness from God is revealed, a righteousness that is by faith from first to last.*

He realised that righteousness; peace, justification and mercy were not earned through man's efforts or religious deeds. God imparts them through Christ's sacrifice on the cross. Everything he has done for us on the cross, He works in us when we received Christ Jesus. *"For we maintain that a man is justified by faith apart from observing the Law"* (Romans 3:28).

Up to this point in his life he was a Roman Catholic, a monk, with all its teachings on works, superstitions, human traditions and church politics. Doctrines on grace, faith, repentance and salvation were perverted. Repentance from the heart and New birth was no longer emphasised. People believed that God's grace was obtained through the sacraments — infant baptism, communion, confirmation, confession, and priesthood.

Luther a monk, then priest, and later Professor of Theology, was hoping to find peace with God through all his good works, but the opposite was true. He religiously fasted and prayed to Mary and the saints. He wore horsehair shirts, made regular confessions and pilgrimages, and bought indulgences hoping to find peace with God. But it was seemingly futile.

During this period Luther visited Rome, Christianity's religious capital. He staunchly prayed, fasted and gave alms. He even walked on his knees praying on Sancta Scala. He did everything in his power to please God, yet he remained empty inside.

When he gradually became aware that the whole religious system to which he belonged was absolute, he intended to reform it. He began to realise that the church had totally perverted the gospel. Legalistic works had replaced the gospel of grace; faith had been substituted by superstition and religious actions. Human legends, traditions and the Canon Law had replaced the bible. Instead of the outworking of the word and the Spirit through ministerial gifts, there were Popes, Cardinals, Bishops and Priests whose word took precedence over the bible.

Selling indulgences was particularly loathsome to Luther. The church taught that monks and priests could be paid to pray for the souls of the dead. The Pope at the time, proclaimed a special indulgence called *"Peter's penny"* which was used to build St. Peter's in Rome.

This money, recovered through this indulgence, was supposedly to save your relative years of suffering in purgatory.

The Reformation is Born

The reformation is born! The grip of Catholicism over Europe was giving way to this restoration of teaching. And Luther was excommunicated and out-lowed by the Catholic church.

Luther who God had used and was diligent in his cause also fell into *"Replacement Theology."* Like the Catholic theologians, Luther had interpreted all the promises of salvation in the Old Testament as fulfilled in Christ. The belief is salvation, which the Old Testament saints held, is what is known as *"anticipated belief in Christ."* In other words, the Christian Church is also anticipated in the Old Testament. This is true and in accordance with the witness of the New Testament but if one by reasons thinks that the role of the Jews in God's plan of salvation is concluded, then one is *"walking in darkness and does not know where one is going."*

Postulations of the anti-Jewish kind by Luther once fuelled the Catholic church in its persecution of the Jews, can be summed up as follows:

- God's judgmental wrath abides upon unbelievers and He alone can annul it. God Himself has appointed the Jews to judgement as punishment for what they did to his Son Jesus.
- Jews cannot repent of their own free will. There is no way in which they can be brought into the church; they are stiff-necked unbelievers and incurable despite all efforts to help them.
- Their continual blasphemy of Christ and God proves their religions to be still alive but hostile toward God.
- This appointed suffering abides likewise upon other enemies of Christ and God. The Israelites rejection of Christ is constantly being repeated within Christianity, and the Jews personify the belief, which is perpetually breaking out within the church.[5]

Bitter controversy was the result of three connected writings produced by Luther in 1542-1543.

He wrote, "A man who doesn't know the devil may well wonder why the Jews above all others, are so hostile towards

Christians. Moreover, they are so without cause, for we show them all goodness. They live here among us and have the use of our land, streets and lanes while our leaders are still sitting back, snoring open-mouthed, allowing them to lift from their purses and coffers, and to steal and rob them as they fancy. How? By allowing their own subjects and themselves to be fleeced and impoverished by the usury of the Jews, and so, with their own money, they make themselves beggars."

Luther in giving proposals to Evangelical leaders of the day said, "*They dishonour God and worship the devil when they, in their blasphemous fables, make Christ out to be a witch-doctor."* And all the atrocities which had been ascribed to the Jews such as poisoning water, child-stealing, blood-guiltiness were probably true. He suggested that the Jewish houses should be demolished and the occupants removed to temporary huts built by gypsies. There right to safe-conduct should be abolished prohibition of usury, slave labour for able-bodied Jews and Jewesses and the burning of all synagogues and Jewish schools.

Thankfully there was some sanity among those Evangelical leaders, one cannot help thinking where the Love of Christ was, where Luther was concerned!

The Jews account Luther as one of history's worst anti-Semites. They consider him as one who laid the foundation for the extermination of the Jews during the Second World War.

Through the preaching of the clergy, the church was not only compliant with, but in many cases supportive of, anti-

Jewish tendencies in the Third Reich. One of Hitler's leading men, Streichner defended the extermination of the Jews at the Nuremberg trials by quoting from Martin Luther's writings!

In conjunction with the celebration of Luther's 500th anniversary, the Lutheran World Council issued the following statement:

"We Lutherans can neither accept nor overlook the vehement verbal assaults made by the Reformer upon the Jews... Luther's sinful anti-Jewish statements and his fierce attack upon the Jewish people must be acknowledged with deep sorrow. All possibility of similar aggression, both now and in the future, must be removed from our churches."

Chapter 8

Laying Foundation

Many years ago I was ordained a "bishop" and this is just one of the *titles* that I have gained over the years but I have certainly not chased titles, rather they have chased me! However through the process of my own personal journey I have discovered the importance of such titles, simply because God gave specific gifts to the church and we *must* be able to recognise, *who is who.*

> *Built on the foundation of the apostles and prophets, with Christ Jesus Himself as the chief cornerstone. In Him the whole building is joined together and rises to become a holy temple in the Lord. And in Him you too are being built together to become a dwelling in which God lives by his Spirit.*
>
> *(Ephesians 2:20-22)*

God is not the author of confusion; He knows exactly who he has anointed to serve the purposes, what *gifts* He bestowed on each and exactly how they should operate *(not excluding how others should address or recognise them!)*

Even though many *extremes* exist out there, this is still not reason enough to *totally* dismiss or be in denial about God's gifts for the local church. When we behave like this it is either out of fear or just plain unbelief! In fact many have chosen to *discourage* the use of such titles, based exclusively on their own perceptions and then taught such *perceptions (perceived truths)* to the rest of the body. But this is not based upon the word of God, as scripture itself is very clear concerning the correct use of titles.

Avoiding Error

This means that the very people who attempt to avoid error concerning titles, end up embracing it and then propagating it! All because it feels more *acceptable!* This type of *"replacement theology"* occurs when people literally *"replace"* truth for what allows them to stay within the confines of their own religious comfort zones!

Of course all of us cannot go further than what we have been taught or that which has been revealed to us personally by the Holy Spirit. For example, in the Faith Movement everybody is considered a "pastor!" But in the Evangelical Movement there is a greater emphasis on "eldership" and having a "set" minister.

So generally speaking, there is wide recognition for the pastoral gift, the evangelistic gift and the teacher, but when it comes to the apostle and prophet, they are commonly denied or ignored! People tend to forget that Jesus was indeed our apostle and high priest; with many more titles besides, but not least our *apostle!*

> *Therefore, holy brothers, who share in the heavenly calling, fix your thoughts on **Jesus, the apostle and high priest** whom we confess.*
>
> *(Hebrews 3:1)*

I can share from personal experience, that when I travel throughout Europe, it's easier to use the word *apostle* than *bishop!* Yet when I travel throughout the African churches, there is a much greater emphasis on the "bishops," who are held in great esteem, while all others are perceived as being beneath such *hierarchy.*

Diocese Episcopate

I would suggest that this is a little backward! Yet I'm not saying we should now throw-the-baby-out-with-the-bath-water and get rid of all the bishops. Not at all! Though correct and balanced teaching *must* be brought back into the church, especially where leadership positions and titles are concerned. Now if the anointing flows *down* and not up, this means that church leaders must get this accurate or the rest of the body will be confused.

There is nothing in this system, which corresponds exactly to the modern diocese episcopate; bishops, when they are mentioned *(Philippians 1:1)* are from a board of local congregational officers and the position occupied by

Timothy and Titus is that of Paul's personal lieutenants in his missionary work. It seems most likely that he was then specially designated with the title of bishop; but even when the monarchical bishop appears in the letters of Ignatius, he is still the pastor of a single congregation.

The word **episkopos** occurs five times in the NT: once of Christ *(1 Peter 2:25)* and in four places of "bishops" or **"overseers" in local churches** *(Acts 20:28; Philippians 1:1; 1 Timothy 3:2, Titus 1:7)*. The verb **episkopeo** occurs in Hebrews 12:15 *("watching")* and *(in some NT MSS)* 1 Peter 5:2 *("exercising the oversight")*.

A bishop then has "oversight of," he is an "overseer." 1 Peter 5:2 says, "Feed the flock of God which is among you, taking the oversight thereof" *(KJV)*. The Greek word for "oversight" is **episkopeo** - to oversee, to beware, to look diligently, take the oversight. Extra words given: direction *(about the times)*, have charge of, take aim at *(spy)*, regard, consider, take heed, look at *(on)*, mark.[6]

Take for instance when I was on a ministry trip to Africa, I was asked to be involved in a *presbytery*, during a particular ordination service. Some of those individuals to be ordained that day, I might add, were accomplished men in their own right, one in particular was acting chaplain to a very high-ranking government official within his own country and was held in high regard himself.

However during the process of this extremely ceremonial meeting, they proceeded to make such a fanfare of these prospective bishops, to the point that it was almost ridiculous! The last person they ordained that day was a woman evangelist, whom they ordained as an apostle and whom they gave very little prominence to at all. **They clearly misunderstood the *governing role* and *office* of an apostle, versus the general *overseeing role and office* of a bishop,** *(I had the unpleasant job of trying to straighten out their theology before I left).*

However we cannot allow *confusion* to reign unchallenged, in the body of Christ, especially concerning such important matters as these. This fuels my passion even more, to help *restore* some clarity back into the church, about the true position, nature and role of the apostle; in regards to the other five-fold-ministry gifts, as well as putting the record straight about "bishops" who were originally and basically commissioned as "overseers" for the local-church!

Apostolic and the Prophetic

Only by turning to scripture can we reveal the true *position-that-goes-with-the-title* and show up whether or not certain "replacement doctrine" has crept into the church. Again, once error is embraced, it readily circulates throughout the rest of the body like a virus that must be stopped and corrected!

It's important for us to realise that we are currently in the move of the apostolic and the prophetic - so let's define the gift of *apostle* in particular and whether such a gift truly exists today! **Please at this point - don't decide that titles do not matter, they do have their place, even today!**

Consider Paul in whose writings he often declared himself, "Paul an apostle." Why? Because Paul knew exactly who he was and what he was commissioned to do. This should be true of the rest of us, because there is clear foundation and structure to the body of Christ, which Jesus Himself put into place.

CHAPTER 9

The Objective of an Apostle

By the grace God has given me, I laid a foundation as an expert builder, and someone else is building on it. But each one should be careful how he builds... *(1 Corinthians 3:10) Strong's architekton (ar-khee-tek'-tone); from 746 and 5045; a chief constructor, i.e. architect, KJV -* **masterbuilder**.[7]

Let's look at the following 5 objectives:
The First Objective of an Apostle:

He is more than just an architect; He is like a "superintendent" of the building process. *Strong's tekton (tek'-tone); from the base of 5098: an artificer (as producer of fabrics), i.e. (specifically) a* **craftsman** *in wood: KJV - carpenter.*[8]

This apostolic function is the necessary basis for every local church, which forms part of the household of God.

"Consequently, you are no longer foreigners and aliens, but fellow citizens with God's people and members of God's household, **built on the foundations of the apostles and prophets,** with Christ Jesus Himself as the chief cornerstone" *(Ephesians 2:19-20).*

Secondly He Lays a Foundation of Life in Christ:

By the grace God has given me, I laid a foundation as an expert builder, and someone else is building on it. But each one should be careful how he builds. For no one can lay any foundation other than the one already laid, which is Jesus Christ.

(1 Corinthians 3:10)

This is done very importantly via the word of truth but also by fatherly relationship. In other words, it's not just achieved by endless impersonal teachings; "For though ye have one thousand instructors in Christ, yet have ye not many <u>fathers</u>: for in Christ Jesus I have begotten you through the gospel" *(1 Corinthians 4:15 KJV).*

Note: speakers only have *hearers,* where fathers have children! A father-in-the-faith is not a remote and austere figure that separates himself from the people but is *real* and *approachable,* just as a father with his son.

However even though an apostle takes on that fatherly role, another major emphasis must be established here, that an **apostle is a BUILD-ER** and not just a **BLESS-ER!** For example he is not easily given to emotions and shallow-short-term-solutions, *(which are often miss-represented as "blessing!")*

No! He is in it for the *long-term* and is willing to go the extra mile with people, in order to *build* something substantial into their lives. In other words, an apostle is never committed to the popular **"hit-n-run"** or **"quick-fix"** solutions, but sticks with the process until he sees real fruit appear in people's lives! **"My dear children, for whom I am again in the pains of childbirth *until* Christ is formed in you..."** *(Galatians 4:19)*

Third, He Lays a Foundation of Obedience towards Christ:

He stresses clearly from the beginning the Lordship of Jesus Christ for whom he is pledged to make disciples. He aims to bring about the "obedience of faith" and looks for that obedience to be complete.

> *Through him and for his name's sake, we received grace and apostleship to call people from among all the Gentiles to the obedience that comes from faith.*
>
> *(Romans 1:5)*

One definite fact is that it's hard to get away with *anything*, when an apostle is around! His aim is to help each individual in the church to build his house upon the only sure foundation of obedience - the commandments of Jesus.

> *Then Jesus came to them and said, "All authority in heaven and on earth has been given to me. Therefore go and make disciples of all nations, baptizing them in the name of the Father and of the Son and of the Holy Spirit, and teaching them to obey everything **I have commanded** you. And surely I am with you always, to the very end of the age."*
>
> *(Matthew 28:18-20)*

> *Therefore everyone who hears these words of mine and puts them into practice is like a wise man who **built his house** on the rock...*
>
> *(Matthew 7:24)*

Fourthly, He Lays a Foundation of Doctrine:

Before the church can go on to maturity, the foundational doctrine must have been clearly laid. **This is the responsibility of the APOSTLE not the bishop.** To build and to work, making sure that every member of the church is clear on repentance and faith, baptism in water and the Holy Spirit; on eternal judgment and the resurrection from the dead.

> *Therefore let us leave the elementary teachings about Christ and go on to **maturity**, not laying again the foundation of repentance from acts that lead to death, and of faith in God, instructions about baptisms, the laying on of hands, the resurrection of the dead, and eternal judgment. And God permitting, we will do so.*
>
> *(Hebrews 6:1-3)*

He will establish them on the same sure foundation of their death and resurrection with Christ.

> *So then, just as you received Christ Jesus as Lord, continue to live in Him, rooted and **built up in Him**, strengthened in faith as you were taught, and overflowing with thankfulness.*
>
> *(Colossians 2:6-7)*

He confirms in them the dynamic of what it means to be united with Christ *(Romans 6:1ff)*. He contends with every error and distortion that would detract from the fullness of Jesus and diminish the believer's fullest experience of Him.

> *See to it that no-one takes you captive through hollow and deceptive philosophy, <u>which depends on human tradition and the basic principles of this world</u> rather than on Christ. For in Christ all the fullness of the Deity lives in bodily form, and you have been given fullness in Christ, who is the Head over every power and authority.*
> *(Colossians 2:8-10)*

Legalism, asceticism, mysticism and pseudo-spirituality are all refuted and corrected. The word of God is for the apostle, the *only* existing basis for building.

Five, The "master-builder" is responsible for the whole construction and supervises the entire work:

He is especially concerned for the fitting-out of the building for its intended use. A house must be finished so that the occupants can take up residence.

An apostolic leader is equally concerned for the house of God. He sees that the parts of the building are fitted and equipped to serve their function. All this is so that the church may once more be a dwelling place fit for God and his Holy Spirit *(Ephesians 2:20)*.

❖

CHAPTER 10

Types of Apostles

In this particular chapter we are going to clearly differentiate between the two *major* types of apostles *(as there are others, such as regional or international apostles and so forth)*. However to begin with the word apostle means: "to-send-forth;" someone with a commission to fulfil; representing the same authority that sent them.

> *Paul, an apostle -* **sent** *not from men nor by man, but by Jesus Christ and God the Father, who raised him from the dead...*
>
> *(Galatians 1:1)*

We see this in the following scriptures; "Jesus said to them, 'If God were your Father, you would love me, for I came from God and now am here. I have not come on my own; but He sent me...'" *(John 8:42)* "Because of this, God in his wisdom said, 'I will send them prophets and apostles, some of whom they will kill and others they will persecute'" *(Luke 11:49).* "Again Jesus said, 'Peace be with you! As the Father has sent me, I am sending you'" *(John 20:21).*

Therefore an "apostle" is not someone who is sent by men or appointed by men, but by God. Again we go straight to scripture in order to see this, "Paul, an apostle - sent not from men nor by man, but by Jesus Christ and God the Father, who raised him from the dead..." *(Galatians 1:1)* "Paul called to be an apostle of Christ Jesus by the will of God..." *(1 Corinthians 1:1)* "He who receives you receives me, and he who receives me receives the one who sent me..." *(Matthew 10:40 - see also Acts 14:14; 15:23; Romans 16:7; 2 Corinthians 8:23; 1 Thessalonians 1:1)*

Increasing Apostolic Revelation

Now before I go any further, let me add to this by taking an excerpt from one of Ulf Ekman's books called, **"The Apostolic Ministry."**

"Apostles and prophets lay the foundation for the church: This century has seen increasing revelation on the ministry gifts. We have begun to understand what a pastor is, how an evangelist functions and what a teacher does. However, there are two special gifts that we need to understand so that God can develop strong local churches in the Last Days.

There is a fierce struggle concerning these gifts going on right now across the earth. The devil hates strong churches. He tries to crush them, tear them down and render them passive and ineffective. If he can remove the gifts that develop strong local churches, then he'll be satisfied. Apostles and prophets are the gifts that do this more than any other.

The apostle and the prophet are like spearheads, and the church is built on the foundation they lay (Ephesians 2:20). If they are not allowed to lay a proper foundation, then the church will lose direction, strength, anointing and spiritual insight. You can have good meetings, interesting conferences and fantastic campaigns without these gifts. But when the preachers leave and the crowds disappear, where is the strength that's needed for the local church? If you look closely, you'll see that the church is small, exhausted, confused and unsure of its direction.

The apostle and the prophet, especially the apostle, channel strength to the churches that helps them grow on a daily basis. **Churches are not built on conferences, campaigns and seminars. They are built by the steady labour of ordinary people, who are constantly developing and maturing.** Maturity, in a biblical sense, refers to increased vigour and stability, which makes us stronger. The apostle's ministry is vital and the bible gives us many examples of this."[9]

Balanced Concept

Therefore it is important that we have a balanced concept of what an apostle is and what an apostle is really sent to do. Otherwise *(and just as I have witnessed around the world)*, this authentic and much needed role of the apostle is "misunderstood" and is desperately "lacking" within the church.

Often it is misconstrued as something intolerable, domineering and threatening. However in reality it couldn't be further from the truth and totally robs the church of a vital element that will help it to grow strong and STAY strong! So instead of complaining about all the weaknesses in the church we must allow the apostles to take back their rightful position in the body of Christ. Only then can we witness the kind of power, strength, authority and single-mindedness of the early church that we all crave to see.

I agree with Apostle Doctor Christian Harfouche; he says, "We believe in the pure unchanged, first century doctrine of Jesus Christ, as delivered by Jesus to His Body the Church by His servants, the Apostles, affirmed by the fathers and doctors, and agreed upon by the whole Church."

He go's on to say,

> *"If there is anything that the world needs today, it is to see the Church living and walking in the power of the first-century faith."*

The devil fears this kind of strength and will do anything to uphold the myth that apostles *(and prophets)* are obsolete and no longer necessary. The devil IS a liar! Oh how we need the apostolic ministry today and how little will be achieved without it.

Spiritual Puff Pastry

However in order for the church to be of significance once again, we need the apostolic ministry to do what it was sent *forth* to do. To bring: stability, maturity and growth.

None of us want to create works that have no substance. Puff pastry looks substantial on the outside but once you break through its veneer and crust there is no substance underneath! It looks impressive and glazed sitting up top but has little *(if any)* foundation. Spiritual puff pastry is a far cry from what God has planned for His church and for that which Christ died.

Resurrection Apostles

Now let's differentiate between the following types of apostles: **the resurrection and ascension apostles.** The original twelve *(minus Judas)* make up the first group, as they were directly commissioned by Jesus and received the inbreathing of resurrection life directly from Him, *(as the first fruits of His new creation).*

From Jesus they received proof of His being alive and the principles of His kingdom first hand. And once reinforced by Matthias *(Acts 1:12f)* they received the promised Holy Spirit at Pentecost. They are also known as the **APOSTLES OF THE LAMB.** "The wall of the city had twelve foundations, and on them were the names of the twelve apostles of the Lamb" *(Revelations 21:14).*

Furthermore Paul must be included in this particular group of apostles for the reason we see here, **"...and last of all he appeared to me also, as one abnormally born"** *(1 Corinthians 15:8).* And it is the testimony of this exclusive group of men that forms the definitive standard of teaching and doctrine for us. For example, we believe Jesus through *their* word, in the context of what Jesus spoke here in John

17:20, "My prayer is not for them alone, I pray also for those who will believe in me through their message..."

Strictly speaking *(concerning "resurrection apostles")* their only true successor is the New Testament itself; which preserves the record of their inspired testimony.

> *I have much more to say to you, more than you can now bear. But when he, the Spirit of truth, comes; he will guide you into all truth. He will not speak on His own; he will speak only what he hears, and he will tell you what is yet to come. He will bring glory to me by taking from what is mine and making it known to you...*
> *(John 16:12-14)*

All subsequent apostolic ministries *("ascension apostles")* must *submit to* and *accurately reflect* their testimony. It can be said like this; the words of the "resurrection apostles" are still primary and still scripture; but however, any other apostolic word is only *derivative (non-scripture)*.

Unfortunately this is just where some of our modern-day apostles *(recent-past and present)* have made their errors. Some of them have wrongly imagined that this status of being an "apostle" gave their own words the same footing and weight as scripture itself! Clearly mistaken they have misunderstood their proper boundaries.

No Additional Revelation

To be clear about this, no one today is receiving any "additional revelation" that can add or take away from the original foundation of the gospel. We already have the revelation of the New Testament. Paul said, **"But though we, or an angel from heaven, preach any other gospel unto you than that, which we have preached unto you, let him be accursed"** *(Galatians 1:8 KJV)*. Paul warned that we are to take heed how we build upon the foundation that has already been laid *(1 Corinthians 3:10)*. Quite simply we can't add to it or take *anything* away from it.

Ascension Apostles

As mentioned already above, there exists a clear distinction between these two sets of apostles, those of the resurrection *(apostles of the Lamb)* and those of the ascension. In addition to this fact and to further explain this, it can be said that Paul was very much a "pivot" in that he was not only the last of the resurrection apostles *(who actually saw the risen Lord Jesus Christ)* but was also the first of a new series of apostles, called the **ascension apostles.**

To appreciate another *(ascension)* apostle, I turn again to the writings of Ulf Ekman and insert a paragraph from his book: **"The Apostolic Ministry - Can the Church Live Without It?"**

"The Apostolic Ministry has long-term effects: we must be set free from the idea of a religious 'St Paul' as portrayed in marble statues, icons and ancient historical images. We must see him in the unique role he had. It was Paul who received the revelation of Jesus' resurrection and wrote one-third of the New Testament. He remains the most important example of a Christian today after Jesus - our primary example.

Paul is an example in two areas: first he shows us how a Christian should live... lives of consistency. Second, he exemplifies the ministry of an apostle. He demonstrates the function of an apostle and the results that follow... Every ministry gift operates within the restrictions of time. The ministry of John the Baptist was effective for only a short period of time, yet his influence was great. Paul not only affected his era, but his influence has remained from generation to generation up to our present day.

An examination of the apostolic ministry will show that its influence continues even after the apostle has died. History speaks of men who weren't called apostles but were in fact just that. Wycliffe was definitely an apostle, as his degree of influence demonstrates. Huss, Luther, Calvin, Knox and Wesley were also apostles. How do we know? From their preaching, their message, their ministry and the enduring legacy they left behind. These are some of the signs of the apostle."[10]

Yes! The apostle is certainly in it for *long haul* and not even his natural death can limit his influence. That's exciting! But there is much more to an apostle than this, we have only discussed some of the signs of an apostle - there is more.

In closing this particular chapter let me summarize by clearly saying, that not all apostles were like Paul. Some had lesser and some greater anointing, including different gifting. But the fact remains; there are two distinct categories of apostles: those of the resurrection and those of the ascension. Today apostles are still *commissioned* and *sent-forth,* and still possess great influence. Even today we can refer to them as **ascension apostles.**

Chapter 11

Marks of an Apostle

In our last chapter we defined the difference between resurrection and ascension apostles. We looked at the basic meaning of the word apostle as being "sent-forth" by God. In this chapter we proceed by discussing the major *functions* and *characteristics* of an apostle.

> *The things that mark an apostle - signs, wonders and miracles - were done among you with great perseverance.*
> *(2 Corinthians 12:12)*

There are clear elements that dominate the calling and gifting of an apostle; which causes all apostles to act in similar ways. In other words, they can be very different in personality and background, but their gifting will have similar functions and boundaries.

Firstly and arguably the most important is that apostles are very good at *working-together,* whereas other gifts are more prone to being *competitive!* Although a true apostle will not build on the foundation of another *(usurp),* he will always allow other apostles to work together *with* him, in the spirit of relationship and collaboration.

In fact I would say that this is one of the *quickest* ways of detecting whether someone is an authentic apostle or not! **True apostles will work together.** Those who compete and clamber over others to "get-ahead," are ruthless like businessmen, *not* apostles.

Apostles do NOT Compete

Instead they have a unique understanding about foundations and just how *counter-productive* it can be to build upon the foundation that another has laid, and to usurp the authority of another. He will not waste his time. He would rather work in *conjunction with* or go somewhere else and lay down a whole new foundation!

Another feature or characteristic of the apostle is that of a PIONEER. They go first. When scripture said, "**...first apostles**" in 1 Corinthians 12:28, this was *not* just a sentiment of hierarchy but literally meant that apostles would *go-first, in front and pioneer!*

They break-open new ground and are not at all shy of ploughing where it has never been ploughed before. Nor do they shy away from *hard work*. **In fact you have never known real hard work until you have been around a true apostle** *(ask those who know!)* Their work ethic is second to none and they have *durability* and *spiritual backbone* that others even half their age can lack!

Their ability to endure hardship is another trait of the apostle. They are not fragile or delicate in their approach; they can be tough at times, yet remain loving and fatherly. They will observe and watch maturely, while others race and chase opportunities. They possess unequalled wisdom with a *panoramic scope* of view that keeps track on the pulse of where everything's up to, in the overall development of things!

This is unique to the apostle, whose spiritual scope and sight is much more *far reaching* than the other gifts of the body. Even though the prophet is considered the "seer," it is the role of the apostle to over-see the wider production and development of God's kingdom. This is why the prophet and apostle need each other and must work closely together - including the other gifts.

Apostles can have different gift mixtures, such as an apostle who is a pastor or an apostle who is a teacher and so forth. Still, regardless of gifting, we see during many different instances throughout scripture, how the apostles would work *together*.

One example for this is found in Acts 2:42 where it says; **"They devoted themselves to the _apostles_' teaching... to the breaking of bread and to prayer."** Notice how the plural was used - **"apostle-s"** - showing that more than one apostle was involved in teaching those people.

No Fame-Game

Authentic apostles do not get caught up with the fame-game. In fact they are not driven by the need for fame, rather their need for **accomplishment!** Apostles are productive wherever they are, just as Paul was never found *stifled* by circumstance. Even when left to languish in prison for a season or under house arrest, Paul wrote some of his best works during those specific periods. **Nothing deterred him from his mission and nothing could chain down his revelation.** In fact hardship helped propel it!

In addition to all of this, apostles are not generally nervous about money - the abundance or lack of it! Scripture shows that Paul was very robust, knowing how to abase or abound. Whatever the situation *(or season)* called for, he was willing. And not just for the sake of proving how robust he could be, but for the furtherance of the gospel and advancement of the cause.

The Life of Preparation

So apostles are ready for just about anything and regular variations of season do not shake them, they just live prepared. All of which is another characteristic of an apostle. Apart from being extremely hard working and focused, they have a deep appreciation for "PREPARATION." They are always preparing, which is why they are always prepared. THEY LIVE PREPARED!

An apostle who does not feel *prepared* is generally not a happy apostle. This is when he can get a little gruff! It is also why you will never find an apostle sitting around doing nothing *(even in his sleep he is building or preparing **something!**)*

Sturdy is equal to "nerdy" in the world's eyes, but for an apostle **spiritual-backbone** is everything. One of their greatest satisfactions is derived from seeing "spiritual-maturity" outworked in the people. To help people *realize* and *release* the gifting that is within them.

In short, an apostle will always stir up the saints for ACTION and bring an explosion of life and activity wherever they are. *(Whether it's a good or bad reaction that's stirred, there's **always** a re-action around an apostle).*

So being lazy is a luxury around an apostle! No one gets away with it! They are hard wired to motivate people and therefore no one feels comfortable doing *nothing* around them! *(They can make even a hardened and self-confessed workaholic feel lazy!)*

However, it's all taken in their stride, by the inspiration of the Holy Spirit and each apostle possesses a specific *time-frame* to work in. They are uniquely aware of "time" and hate to waste it, working tirelessly to achieve the goals set before them.

*(Note: seasoned apostles don't tire with age because they have grown in wisdom and therefore also in their ability to **delegate** - most apostles could put an army to work, quite easily!)*

Spiritual Carelessness

Nothing displeases them more than to see rampant apostasy amongst God's people and spiritual carelessness or sloppiness. Therefore it's also good to point out that the apostle is not heavily prone to taking spiritual short cuts. No architect would do it. The safety of their overall structure would be compromised and the apostle sees things much the same way!

Another characteristic is ORDER; the apostle has an affinity with all-things-order. They generally bring order into chaos and restoration where there is brokenness. They are the ones trusted with God's blue print, as they are God's builders. Likewise, just as Nehemiah discovered he must remove the rubbish-heap before he could proceed building the walls of Jerusalem, an apostle will equally deal with the chaos that tries to hinder God's plan *(Nehemiah 1-3)*.

In fact no other gift can maintain the level of order that an apostle can effectuate *(put into force or operation)*. By his powers of delegation and skills of origination, he deals with any chaos *(naturally or spiritually speaking)* within his given sphere of influence and looks to permanently remove any obstacles that threaten to hinder or delay the successful completion of God's design.

Eight points to remember:

- **Plurality - apostles work as part of a team** *(1 Thessalonians 1:1; 2:6)*. Let's look a little deeper at the apostle's ability to work alone but also as part of a team. He is not easily threatened and likes to work with others. In fact over "twenty men," at one time or another, were associated with Paul in his apostolic travels. **True apostles are not charismatic lone-**

rangers who lack and even despise the checks and balances of plurality. This is one reason that they like to bring on younger men in their calling in God, such as Paul did with Timothy.

- **Gifts and anointing** *(1 Thessalonians 1:5a)*. They have spiritual "power" not just ecclesiastical "status." **They enjoy the charisma of the Holy Spirit rather than their ordination papers** or may not even be officially ordained by a denomination.

God is rising up a new breed of apostolic ministers who will readily admit that they are embryonic and earnestly desire and covet the wonders and miracles that are one of the signs of a true apostle. **"The things that mark an apostle - signs, wonders and miracles - were done among you with great perseverance"** *(2 Corinthians 12:12)*.

- **Has a proven character** *(1 Thessalonians 1:5b)*. We see in scripture that the apostles were men of integrity with mastery over wrong motives. For example they were not out to deceive, flatter or make money from those they ministered to *(1 Thessalonians 2:2-6)*, men worthy of imitating.

- **Is a man of patience and gentleness** *(1 Thessalonians 2:6-7)*. Because he is a man of faith he can afford to wait. Because he is a man of love he does not have to throw his weight about. **Building with living bricks takes time and trouble.** Taking another look at the sign of a true apostle, *(2 Corinthians 12:12)* we find the word **perseverance** *(patience KJV)*.

This reveals that true apostles are not mere remote office managers presiding over some new charismatic empire, which they lay claim to "covering." True apostles are prepared to spend time with individuals and not *just* leaders at that *(unless one is called to leaders specifically)*. They are *"on-site"* superintendents of the work.

- **A bearer of God's word** *(1 Thessalonians 2: 13).* "And for this purpose I was appointed a herald and an apostle - I am telling the truth, I am not lying - and a teacher of the true faith to the Gentiles" *(1 Timothy 2:7)*. No man can ultimately be recognised as an apostle, who does not have a proven ministry as a preacher and a teacher of the word of God, for it is that which is the root of his authority, the source of his life and the dynamic of his ministry, he is a preacher and teacher of the word *before* he is an apostle.

- **He stands or falls by the church** *(1 Thessalonians 1:6-7)*. Like Peter, he should have been a fellow-elder in a local body. There, he can be tested and checked as he learns like everybody else, what it is to submit to one another in the fear of the Lord. As a local elder, he knows the responsibility of rule and pastoral care, which leaders in the church have, and then as an apostle, will be able to speak into other churches with greater sensitivity.

To the elders among you, I appeal as a fellow-elder, a witness to Christ's sufferings and one who also will share in the glory to be revealed: Be shepherds of God's flock that is under your care, **serving** *as overseers - not because you*

must, but because you are willing, as God wants you to be; not greedy for money, but eager to serve...
(1 Peter 5:1-2)

- **One who is "sent-out" by the church to which he belongs,** an apostle carries credibility with him. Those who receive him can expect that he will have worked out *(learnt)* at home whatever he is laying on them as counsel; in this way Paul and Barnabas were "released" by the church at Antioch *(Acts 13:1-3)*.

Being sent out by the church of which they were a part - they are eager to return to give their support and report.

From Attalia they sailed back to Antioch, where they had been committed to the grace of God for the work they had now completed. On arriving there, they gathered the church together and reported all that God had done through them and how he had opened the door of faith to the Gentiles.
(Acts 14:26-27)

- **Finally and most importantly true apostles appreciate being "accountable."** This gives them a sense of security, saves them from the wrong kind of independence and reminds them they exist to serve the body and not themselves. They desire the best for the church *(1 Thessalonians 2:19)*.

CHAPTER 12

Apostles Today?

Much of what is in this current book, "The Age of Apostolic Apostleship," has been taken from my articles called, "Truth for the Journey." Many across the Internet enjoy these articles; likewise we enjoy the tremendous feedback and positive responses they provoke!

In particular, an apostle who lives in Spain called, "Emilio Sevilla" dropped me a line to encourage but also to elaborate a little deeper on the meaning of the word apostle.

I quote him: "The word apostle means *'sent-to-establish'* because the word is made up of two words which are, *APO-STELLO* - *APO* means to be sent forth and *STELLO* means to establish… this is why apostles should not rest until they have established the kingdom in their given area…" End quote.

To see this in its various forms, we simply go to the Strong's Greek Concordance. To do so we take the precise place in scripture where Paul emphatically introduces himself as an "apostle" in his letter to the Corinthians, "Paul, called **to be** an apostle of Jesus Christ through the will of God..." *(1 Corinthians 1:1 KJV)* or as the Young's Literal Translation puts it, "Paul, a called *apostle* of Jesus Christ..."

The Greek word that was used here is the compound word apostolos *(ap-os'-tol-os)* specifically meaning a delegate; specially, an ambassador of the gospel; officially a commissioner of Christ *("apostle") (with miraculous powers):* - apostle, messenger, **he that is sent.**[11] However there are actually numerous compound words that help make up or have influence upon the meaning of this word apostle - which we have all become familiar with.

An Indispensable Ministry

For sure, the more we see what apostles do, the more we realize how indispensable their ministry is. The Acts of the Apostles is a book with no ending, as it records that which Jesus began to do and teach; He continues to do and say through His apostles, apostolic men or women who have the ability to father the church, its pastors and people. They are blessings from God, so much needed for today.

Yet there are still those who ask, **"are there apostles for today?"** Of course the answer has to be an unequivocal "Yes!" But let us qualify this answer because there are many who would answer, "No." To those who still question the validity of apostleship for today I would say that if there are prophets, evangelists, pastors and teachers then there must be apostles too.

Why? Because Jesus Himself gave and commissioned **all five** of these gifts to His bride and as long as this institution that we call church remains upon the earth - until Christ returns for it - then these five gifts will remain in full!

As stated before, apostles willingly work together just as the twelve did in the beginning, to lay the foundation for the very first church in Jerusalem. However were they really "unique" as some like to suggest, in an attempt to imply that apostles had their rightful place in the beginning, but are *obsolete* for today.

"Unique?" Yes, in the context that only they walked with Christ from the time of His baptism by John the Baptist, until He rose from the dead. They were also eyewitnesses of all that Jesus said and did. Some of them even recorded what they experienced *(testimony)*, which became part of the New Testament that we have and love today. In addition they not only received divine revelation, but also communicated that revelation *once and for all*. Yet even with this fact in place, the bible *never* stipulated that these were the first and final *(only)* apostles for the church.

Outside of the Original Twelve!

The most prominent apostles of all were Peter and Paul and arguably that the most important was Paul - who was not even among the original twelve, yet neither was Barnabas who we also found being called an apostle in scripture *(see Acts 14:14-15)*. This is the point. Scripture clearly states that they were both apostles. Furthermore, we find in Galatians 1:19 that James the brother of Jesus was also considered an "apostle."

In addition to this we find Paul writing about the apostolic ministry of Silvanus and Timothy *(who incidentally were also not part of the original twelve)* in his letter to the Philippians and there exists many more examples of this in scripture. So it appears there were indeed many more apostles that the bible identifies - outside of the original twelve!

They even lived and functioned during the same lifetime as the original twelve but were not included into that band. This identifies that the apostolic ministry was in circulation and was not limited to a certain number.

So the purpose of the apostles for the early church was clear. They helped lay the foundations and continued to establish and build upon what Christ had said and done. With this in mind then, let us ask the following question regarding today's church:

- Is the building finished?
- Is the bride ready?
- Is the church full-grown and are the saints completely equipped?
- Has the church attained its ordained maturity and unity?

I dare say this: only when the answer to these few questions is a **"YES,"** can we dispense with the apostolic ministry.

CHAPTER 13

The Apostolic Ministry Functions Today

So we are slowly establishing the fact, using scripture to qualify, that the apostolic ministry was indeed something that Christ ordained Himself and is still in function today.

For the same God who worked through Peter as the apostle to the Jews also worked through me as the apostle to the Gentiles.
(Galatians 2:8 NLT)

Now in order for such apostolic ministry to function correctly and be at it's best *(as God intended and not as man-made hierarchy prefers it)*, we must be "in-charge-of-our-egos" especially where clerical *titles* are concerned! Even though Christ Himself gave such gifts their titles, we must not think of ourselves more highly than we aught *(Romans 12:3)*.

A Government of Liberty

Rick Joyner says, "Church government under the original apostles was so unique, free, and effective that it defied definition. It was such a radical departure from anything the world had ever seen that it was impossible for the world to understand using any authority structure that was known. Like the other great principles of the faith, when there is an attempt to overly define it, the essence of what it is intended to be is often lost.

The first-century church government was not dependent on just one form, but on the anointing of the leaders who held the positions. Because of this, it had to be defined by the ones leading more than the system itself.

The apostles did not have a constitution, which decreed that they could dictate policy. Their authority came from something much higher—they had been with Jesus, and they were anointed by Him. Therefore, the only ones who could recognize their authority had to know the Lord and know the anointing.

The exercise of authority in the first-century church was both hierarchical and democratic. The main function of the apostles was to lay a solid foundation of doctrine and to establish a church government, which promoted liberty, not conformity. They accomplished this for a time. The freedom this allowed enabled the hearts of men to be converted by the power of truth and the conviction of the Holy Spirit - they were not converted by coercion.

From the beginning, this was intended to be the mode of operation for the spiritual authority exercised in the church. There was room for discipline and correction, but the ultimate penalty that the authorities of the church could exercise was the removal of the offender from fellowship until there was repentance.

The adherence of the apostles to this course of leadership was in such contrast to anything that had been known before, and certainly to the culture of the times, that it constituted the most extraordinary leadership ever exercised by any government at any time. As the church drifted from the genius of this extraordinary style of leadership, oppression grew, and the power of truth was replaced with a terrible, barbaric force intended to compel men to bend their knees to the dictates of church leaders without first bending their hearts to the truth."[12]

First a Servant

Consider that in addition to holding-office, the apostle is also a ministry-gift to the body; nevertheless he is first a **SERVANT,** as are all the other gifts/offices that Christ ordained.

> It is the apostles who are assigned to take what the Spirit is saying to the churches and implement it by developing a strategy for moving forward.
> **Peter Wagner**

It is undeniable that Satan will try and destroy the anointed "structure" that God is restoring through His apostolic ministries. Satan knows full well that a house in division against itself *(against its own ordained structure)* will collapse. He capitalizes on this by triggering some of the "infighting" that exists between the different "gifts" in the body, *(making them totally counter-productive)*.

Individual gifts are deceived very effectively when simply steered down wrong paths *(that are not ordained for them)*. Let's be honest, a little "steering" here and there, is all it takes to make even the most "sincere" amongst us, totally ineffective! In other words our adversary might not be able to influence our love for Christ or dampen our zeal but he certainly can and does influence our egos, time and time again!

All apostolic ministries must never forget that they have been called to serve the church and not their own egos! Whenever power is involved, this can prove challenging *(1 Peter 5:5-8)*.

It's important to look at the apostle in relation to the other apostolic gifts. By way of a simple illustration, take the hand and imagine each of the fingers to represent one of the five fold ministry gifts that Christ gave to His body.

- **The index finger:** represents the prophet - the one who points the way and says just like Isaiah "This is the way; walk in it..." *(30:21)* Therefore he gives direction, tells of the spiritual condition of the church and exposes its sin!

- **The middle finger:** represents the evangelist. His ministry is more widespread than others. He reaches further. He is stifled if left in the confines of the church. He loves to be out in the field. He needs to be let loose to do his job, supported and equipped by the church that sends him out - to go beyond its confines and be effective.

- **The ring finger:** represents the pastor's ministry. He is totally committed to his flock - loving as a shepherd would - caring, encouraging and meeting the individual needs of his sheep.

- **The little finger:** represents the teacher's ministry - the finger small enough to clear away the wax in the ears so that folks can hear well and understand better!

- **Lastly the thumb:** represents the apostle. It is sturdier than the other fingers and can touch all of the others with ease! This implies that an apostle can function in all of the other ministry gifts - when necessary. He brings stability and flexibility, which is essential for the body to grow with strength and maturity.

However and perhaps most importantly is the fact that without a thumb it is impossible to "grasp" anything. **In fact only when the other fingers cooperate with the thumb - can the job get done!**

It's elementary then, that just as the fingers of one hand must work together, so too must apostolic ministries cooperate and collaborate together so that they can be of benefit to the body that they are called to.

Apostolic Gifts flowing Together

In his book, "Apostles, Prophets and the Coming Moves of God" Dr. Bill Hamon brings out the following:

"**Fivefold Ministries:** these are the fivefold ascension gift ministries as revealed in Ephesians 4:11 - apostle, prophet, evangelist, pastor and teacher. They are not gifts of the Holy Spirit per se, but an extension of Christ's headship ministry to the church. Their primary ministry and function are to teach, train, activate and mature the saints for the work of their ministries *(Ephesians 4:12-13)*.

Apostle: one of the fivefold ministries of Ephesians 4:11. The apostle is a foundation-laying ministry *(Ephesians 2:20)* that we see in the New Testament establishing new churches *(Paul's missionary journeys)*, correcting error by establishing proper order and structure *(first epistle to the Corinthians)*, and acting as an oversight ministry that fathers other ministries *(1 Corinthians 4:15; 2 Corinthians 11:28)*.

The New Testament apostle has a revelatory anointing *(Ephesians 3:5)*. Some major characteristics are **great patience** and manifestations of **signs, wonders and miracles.** We will know more and see greater manifestations concerning the apostle during the peak of the apostolic movement.

Prophet: he is a man of God whom Christ has given the ascension gift of a 'prophet' *(Ephesians 4:11; 1 Corinthians 12:28; 14:29; Acts 11:27; 13:1)*. A prophet is one of the fivefold ascension gift ministers who are an extension of Christ's ministry to the church. He is an anointed minister who has the gifted ability to perceive and to speak the specific mind of Christ to individuals, churches, businesses and nations.

Greek: 'prophetes' *(prof-ay-tace)* a foreteller, an inspired speaker *(Strong's Concordance, Vine's Concordance)*. A proclaimer of a divine message, denoted among the Greeks as an interpreter of the oracles of gods.

In the Septuagint it is the translation of the word 'roeh' - a seer - indicating that the prophet was one who had immediate intercourse with God *(1 Samuel 9:9)*. It also translates the word 'nabhi,' meaning either, *'one in whom the message from God springs forth, or one to whom anything is secretly communicated' (Amos 3:7; Ephesians 3:5).*

Prophetess: Greek 'prophetis' - the feminine of phrophet *(Gk. Prophetes)*. A woman of God whom the Holy Spirit has given the divine prophetic ability to perceive and speak the mind of Christ on specific matters to particular people. Strong's - a *'female foreteller or an inspired woman.'* She is a specially called woman who functions like the New Testament prophet to minister to the body of Christ with inspired speaking and prophetic utterance *(Acts 2:17; 21:9; Luke 2:36; Isaiah 8:3; 2 Chronicles 34:22; Jude 4; Exodus 15:20).*

Prophetess is the proper title for a woman with this ascension gift and calling. **Prophet** is the proper title for a man with this ascension gift and calling.

Evangelist: the traditional view of the evangelist is a bearer of the *'Good News,'* proclaiming the gospel to the unbelieving world; exemplified by modern-day evangelists who preach the message of salvation in crusades and the like. However, Philip, the New Testament evangelist mentioned in Acts 21:8, demonstrated a strong supernatural dimension to the evangelistic ministry.

Philip preached the gospel to the lost *(Acts 8:5)*, moved in miracles *(8:6)*, delivered people from demons *(8:7)*, received instructions from an angel *(8:26)*, had revelation knowledge *(8:29)*, and was supernaturally translated from Gaza to Asotus *(8:26, 40)*. We are looking forward to the restoration of this type of prophetic evangelist to the body of Christ.

Pastor: Greek 'poiment' - a shepherd, one who tends, herds or flocks *(not merely one who feeds them)*, is used metaphorically of Christian pastors. Episkopeo *(overseer, bishop)* is an overseer, and Pesbuteros *(elder)* is another term for the same person as bishop or overseer. They normally give the title to the senior minister of the local church, regardless of his fivefold calling. It is a shepherding ministry to feed and care for the flock.

Responsibilities that appear connected with the pastoral ministry include oversight and care of the saints, providing spiritual food for their growth and development, leadership and guidance, and counsel. Prophetic pastors not only do the things normally associated with pastoring, but also move in supernatural graces and gifts of God *(prophesying, word of knowledge, healing)* and have the vision and willingness to develop the saints in their gifts and callings.

Teacher: an instructor of truth. *'All scripture is given by inspiration of God, and is profitable for doctrine, for reproof, for correction, for instruction in righteousness' (2 Timothy 3:16 KJV).*

A New Testament apostolic-prophetic teacher is one who not only teaches the letter of the word, but also ministers with divine life and Holy Spirit anointing *(2 Corinthians 3:6)*. He exhibits keen spiritual discernment and divine insight into the word of God and its personal application to believers.

Apostolic-Prophetic Lifestyle: these are the people who live their lives according to the logos and rhema word of God. The *logos* is their general standard for living and the rhema gives direction in specific areas of their lives. The fruit of the Holy Spirit is their characteristic motivation, and the gifts of the Spirit are their manifestation to meet the needs of mankind.

They are allowing their lives to become a prophetic expression of Galatians 2:20 *(KJV)*; *'I am crucified with Christ; nevertheless I live; yet not I, but Christ liveth in me: and the life which I now live in the flesh I live by the faith of the Son of God, who loved me, and gave Himself for me.'*[13]

The apostolic is in full swing. The best is yet to come. Much is being restored back to the church and we will see the power of the early church. The days of "Ananias and Sapphira" will return - where the fear of God will reign again and those outside the church walls will respect her position of authority on the earth.

There is power and authority when the apostolic ministry is allowed to function and flow by the Spirit of God, just as they were supposed to. I look forward with great expectation and anticipation to the complete restoration of all such things.

Notes

1. Strong, James. S.T.D., L.L.D. 1890. Strong's Exhaustive Concordance; Dictionaries of the Hebrew and Greek Words. e-Sword ® version 7.6.1 Copyright © 2000-2005. All Rights Reserved. Registered trade mark of Rick Meyers. Equipping Ministries Foundation. USA www.e-sword.net. #H1826

2. Hamon, Bill. Apostles, Prophets and the Coming Moves of God. Copyright © 1997. Published by Destiny Image Publishers, Inc. Printed in USA. p.14

3. Strong's Exhaustive Concordance. #G4522

4. Cho, Paul Y. More Than Numbers. Copyright © 1984. Published by Word Publishing. Printed in UK. p.77-81

5. Maurer, Wilhelm. Kirche und Synagoge. ed. by Karl-Heinrich Rengstorf and Siegfried von Kortzfleisch. Copyright © 1968. Published by Ernst Klett Verlag. Printed in Germany. p.56

6. Strong's Exhaustive Concordance. #G1983

7. Strong's Exhaustive Concordance. #G753

8. Strong's Exhaustive Concordance. #G5045

9. Ekman, Ulf. The Apostolic Ministry. Copyright © 1995. Published by Word of Life Publications. Printed in Sweden. p.20-21

10. The Apostolic Ministry. p.23

11. Strong's Exhaustive Concordance. #G00652

12. Joyner, Rick. Shadows of Things to Come. Copyright © 2001. Published by Thomas Nelson, Inc. Printed in USA. p.92-93

13. Hamon, Bill. Apostles, Prophets and the Coming Moves of God. Copyright © 1997. Published by Destiny Image Publishers, Inc. Printed in USA. p.279-281, 289

Bible Translations:

- Unless otherwise indicated, all scriptural quotations are from the HOLY BIBLE, NEW INTERNATIONAL VERSION ®. NIV ®. Copyright © 1973, 1978, 1984 by the International Bible Society. Used by permission of Zondervan Publishing House. All rights reserved.

- Scripture references marked GW are taken from GOD'S WORD®, © 1995 God's Word to the Nations. Used by permission of Baker Publishing Group.

- Scripture references marked KJV are taken from the King James Version of the bible.

- Scripture references marked MSG are taken from The Message. Copyright © 1993, 1994, 1995, 1996, 2000, 2001, 2002. Used by permission of NavPress Publishing Group.

- Scripture references marked NKJV are taken from the New King James Version. Copyright © 1982 by Thomas Nelson, 1982 by Thomas Nelson, Inc. Used by permission. All rights reserved.

- Scripture references marked NLT are taken from the Holy Bible, New Living Translation, copyright © 1996, 2004, 2007 by Tyndale House Foundation. Used by permission of Tyndale House Publishers, Inc., Carol Stream, Illinois 60188. All rights reserved.

- Scripture references marked RSV are taken from the Revised Standard Version of the Bible, copyright 1952 [2nd edition, 1971] by the Division of Christian Education of the National Council of the Churches of Christ in the United States of America. Used by permission. All rights reserved.

Part Two

EARNESTLY CONTENDING FOR THE STATE OF ISRAEL

Chapter 14

Relationship between the Apostolic and the Local Church

Let's look at the relationship that should exist between the apostle and the local church - how they should relate. We will look at how the authoritative structure within the church works. Also we will look at gifts - for example is an apostle a position of **"office" or "gift?"** This we can answer straight away.

First the Apostle

First the apostle was given as a gift, as seen in Ephesians 4:11ff; 1 Corinthians 12:28. God has appointed ministry gifts in the church and this guarantees that they *(the church)* will function properly.

Ulf Ekman explains it like this: "When the bible says that God has appointed 'first apostles,' it does not mean that He has placed them up on a pedestal. Instead, it means that the apostle has been placed *at the very front.*

The idea of a vertical triangle with some sort of pope seated at the top should be discarded. Imagine instead a horizontal triangle that looks like a plow. God has positioned the apostle at the tip of this plow. The apostle can be likened to a *general practitioner.* He has the ability to operate in all of the ministry offices."[1]

"Apostle and prophet teams then set pastors and pastoral elders over the churches to guard, feed and lead the flock of believers like a shepherd *(Acts 15:32; 16:4,18,25; 2 Corinthians 1:19; 2 Thessalonians 1:1; Acts 20:28).*"[2]

In other words the apostle has a governing office and can function in any of the gifts. Therefore the apostle has an **office to govern,** along with ministry gifts and the authority to establish.

Sent or Stayed

Not all apostles travel, some are senior pastors of apostolic churches; apostle James is an example, he was considered an apostle in scripture, he did not actually leave the church in Jerusalem. Seemingly, he never ministered outside of Jerusalem. But apostle Paul travelled continually during his thirty-plus years of ministry.

His longest stay at any local church was two years in Ephesus. So this begs the question; **"can an apostle be a**

'sent-one' and be a 'stayed-one' at the same time?" Yes! So long as he is *establishing, building* and *fulfilling* a mandate that he has ultimately been sent by God to fulfil.

However this depends largely on his "gifting" too and not just his "office." Now his *office* is one thing, and his *gifting* helps him to carry out the mandate upon his *office*. For example, an apostle whose main gifting is to be a pastor is able to *build* right where he is. He is able to have an international mind-set *(not parochial in his vision)* and possess the spiritual capacity to travel and be "sent" but also has the capacity to "stay."

Now in addition to this, it must be stated that all the gifts are EQUAL - they just have different tasks to do. Likewise all the "offices" are *equal;* they just operate with different gifting. For example a local elder who has a governing-office to "oversee," is one who has been given dominion in a certain area.

The Great Connector

However when it comes to the local church in relation to the apostle - it has to be said that being part of one body - includes being **"connected"** with the rest of the body. And a great part of what the apostle does is through "connections." **He is a great connector.** The Holy Spirit uses the apostolic ministry more than any other to do His great global networking!

Now having said all this - any position of authority or given office of governing authority *(whether apostle, elder/ bishop)* is not dictatorial but submissive - particularly the apostle who is able to "recognise" what God has already established and continues to establish.

It is also crucial to observe here that once the local elders have been set in and their role established - it is THEY who have the authority over the local church and *not* the apostle. Now of course he still has authority to bring correction like a shepherd-father-figure would - but he does not stay around to carry this out. His role is to oversee.

To view this in scripture we go to the verses quoted below in order to highlight or showcase this point perfectly - when Paul was troubled to write with much concern to warn the church in Corinth of his pending rebuke!

> *I'm afraid that I may come and find you different from what I want you to be, and that you may find me different from what you want me to be...*
>
> *I already warned you when I was with you the second time, and even though I'm not there now, I'm warning you again. When I visit you again, I won't spare you. That goes for all those who formerly led sinful lives as well as for all the others. Since you want proof that Christ is speaking through me, that's what you'll get. Christ isn't weak in dealing with you. Instead, he makes his power felt among you. He was weak when he was crucified, but by God's power he lives.*
> (2 Corinthians 12:20; 13:3-4 GW)

Obviously the apostle has a continuing position of responsibility when it comes to the local church but he is not there to stay and to run the local church or implement the local vision! This again is the role of the set leading elders.

Let us move on now to the next step and take a look at how apostolic teams in particular should function and work together. Before we do this let me point out ever so briefly how important structure is. The spine or backbone is our natural structure. None of us can live without it! And spiritually speaking the same is true also. Even Satan's kingdom has structure to it.

We see this show-cased in the sixth chapter of the book of Ephesians and verse 12 where it says; "This is not a wrestling match against a human opponent. We are wrestling with rulers, authorities, the powers who govern this world of darkness, and spiritual forces that control evil in the heavenly world" *(GW)*. It is very distinct here that there are varying levels in the kingdom of darkness, levels of authority or hierarchy to execute its mandates.

Kingdom has Structure

This represents none other than a governing "structure," yet perhaps in reverse from that of the kingdom of God. And by saying, **in reverse** I don't suggest for a moment that this means *equal-to* God's kingdom, by no means! Yet Satan once knew just how the kingdom of God functioned and was internally structured… therefore he most certainly would have modelled his best attempts at organizing his hordes of darkness - upon what he saw working with pristine order and condition within the kingdom of God!

Structure is valued by those who understand how it works and by structure I don't mean that we get all wrapped up in knots because we have adopted some form of legalism. Nevertheless "structure-less-ness" is far from freedom - but more like anarchy and chaos and who can have success in the midst of confusion?

Anyhow take business for example; they could never thrive without structure. Organizations would collapse the world over without structure and so would every great building of antiquity that we know! From the tower of London and Big Ben to the Eiffel tower - still known as the tallest structure in Paris! Nothing of significance can remain standing without some form of structure holding it up!

So **we must not be "structure-shy" especially within the church** where we tend to feel obliged to run a "free-for-all" and expect it to work! **It must not be said by our enemies that the body of Christ has no backbone or that we are spineless!** But nor let us try and create our own image of structure based upon what we think church should be like... No! Rather we should submit ourselves to what God has already laid out in scripture to work irrespective and notwithstanding our misguided reservations towards... the apostolic ministry!

Void of Spiritual Backbone!

Instead we should shout, "Welcome back!" For the church as we know it - has indeed been feeble and without strength - yes even much of it has been guilty of being spineless and void of spiritual backbone! But now is the time to embrace true spiritual structure as Christ deemed fit to bestow upon the church and to recognize once again the importance of this "apostolic ministry" within His body. Who are we to resist? We must work-with and not against true spiritual structure.

It is true to say that it has never been enough for the spiritually immature - "floppy-n-floaty" *(freshly filled with new wine Christians)* to get this great and awesome job done! Nor has it ever been enough just for the "stuffy-n-religious-bookworm-types" to give their official nod to everything! What we need is the precious working of God's Holy Spirit, the power of His Word and the coming together of His mighty body worldwide - "a-great-working-together" - to get this great and divine commission complete!

So as we continue then, from our brief look at the supposed "hierarchy" of Satan's kingdom - let's us now look at the "structure-of-authority" as it should exist within God's kingdom - according to scripture *(in other words apostolic teams working together)* - as follows:

1). Main forces of human leadership:

A] Apostolic teams and presbyteries *(elders)*

1. Both usually PLURAL
2. A shepherd is a pastor
   a) Shepherd *(singular)* always refers to Jesus *(Acts 20:17)*
   b) Elders *(plural)* are overseers *(or bishops)* or shepherds *(see also 1 Peter 5:1-2)*
3. As shepherds *(elders)* are united, so will their flocks be

B] Elder's responsibility is to govern - conservation (1 Timothy 5:17; Titus 1:5)
- a) In the OT the elder's place was at the gate
- b) Their function: judgement, counsel and government
- c) The NT concurs with this

C] Apostolic team's function is extensive (Romans 15:20-21)
- a) Reach the unreached
- b) They did not operate alone

D] Governing body in an area is sovereign
- a) Same applies to a family, mother and father are sovereign

    Independence and sovereignty are not the same
- b) Sovereign: accountable to God
- c) Independent: out from under God's authority possibly?

E] Apostolic teams

Mobile

Top authority of church extension

Presbyteries

Local/resident

Govern locally conservation

- a) Balance is 50% emphasis on either side in NT church

b) The current balance is 98% conservation and 2% extension

F] There is *no place for independence* in Christianity

2). Interdependence:

A] Apostles appoint elders *(Acts 14:21-23)*

a) After elders become installed, a group of believers becomes a church

B] Apostles sent out by elders *(Acts 13:1-4)*

a) They became apostles after being prayed for and sent out *(Acts 14:14)*

b) They were selected by the Holy Spirit from the most experienced and fruitful

c) Then new leadership emerges from the less experienced

C] Reproductive cycle *(Acts 16:1; 1 Thessalonians 2:6)*

a) Apostle means: one sent forth

b) It all starts with God the Father

3). Jesus set the pattern:

A] The first Apostle *(Hebrew 3:1)*

a) Women have a place *(Luke 8:1-3)*

B] The Early Church was mobile

C] Apostolic attestation

a) It takes the supernatural to make Gentiles obedient *(Romans 15:18-19)*

b) *(2 Corinthians 12:12)*

D] Marks of the apostle
  a) Perseverance, character, not giving up
  b) Signs, wonders and mighty deeds

E] The issue is NOT apostle succession, but apostolic ministry *(1 Corinthians 4:20)*

CHAPTER 15

Establishing Leadership

It is my desire in this chapter to help people understand whether they are *called or appointed* by God, to whatever position or realm He has decided. We are not looking here to discover the depths of how a ministry operates in its function, but simply how to be prepared in the positioning of ourselves within the body of Christ. Only then will those in authority be able to recognize that which God has imparted within us; which in turn *releases* us into our destiny.

The democratic society we live in is far removed from the definition of a kingdom, where a king rules because he inherited the throne! Democracy differs in that her leaders are elected and not inherited. A system where leadership roles are open to the talented and asserted, but as for the kingdom of God, it operates on an entirely different premise.

...I warn everyone among you not to estimate and think of himself more highly than he ought [not to have an exaggerated opinion of his own importance], but to rate his ability with sober judgment, each according to the degree of faith apportioned by God to him.
(Romans 12:3 AMP)

Jesus Himself appointed offices of service, found in Ephesians 4:11, only Jesus Himself through the Holy Spirit gives this authority to men. **When we assume authority rather than receive authority we are on dangerous ground.** Self-exaltation is the promotion of self-purposes rather than seeking first the kingdom of God. Consider those who have been called but not yet appointed, who then commission themselves and who end up serving themselves; our commission can only come from the Lord.

Chosen from among Men

Spiritual leaders are **"...chosen from among men"** and are "...**appointed** to act on behalf of men in things relating to God." Furthermore, **"one does not appropriate for himself the honour... but he is called by God..."** Just as Jesus, "...did not exalt Himself...but was **appointed**..." *(Hebrews 5:1, 4, 5 AMP)*

Appointment comes from God alone, even Jesus did not assume His place, but was appointed by the Father. We may be called, but we also require appointment. Consider Paul who in Romans 1:1 in the NIV states that he was both *"called"* and *"separated."*

The call comes first then the appointment! You may have been called before the earth began or while you were still in the womb but that was not when you stepped into your **"office!"** You step into your call *[salvation]* before you ever step into your office.

Testing of Years

Note: Paul went through years of testing once he submitted himself to the leaders at Antioch. *"They must first be tested; and then... let them serve..." (1 Timothy 3:10)*

Separated actually means chosen, Jesus said *"Many are called, but few are chosen..." (Matthew 22:14)* **Meaning that not many make it through those *testing* periods**, but the few who make it are those who have been successfully *separated* unto the Lord! All ministries must go through a period of testing and preparation *(this preparation varies from gift to gift)* before we go through or move through into our assigned assignment, our appointed time!

There are *offices* and *positions of service,* mentioned in the bible, *(1 Corinthians 12:28)* **"And God has appointed** these in the church: first apostles, second prophets, third teachers, after that ... helps..." *(NKJV)* Paul during those first years in Antioch did not occupy a five fold office *(Ephesians 4:11)* **in fact he served in the ministry of helps, then was promoted to the office of a teacher (2 *Timothy* 1:11; Acts 13:1).**

John Bevere says in his book **"Thus Saith the Lord,"** "Not only would Paul be tested in the realm of helps but in the office of teacher as well. When Paul was promoted from teacher to apostle we again see how God chooses and separates those that He wants to fill certain offices or positions."[3]

In Acts 13:1-2 we can see how Paul is listed along with other teachers in Antioch and how the Holy Spirit wanted them to be separated unto Him. The appointed time had finally come, the one who had been called to be an apostle all those years earlier on the road to Damascus in Acts 9:15 had finally, after many years of testing and loyal service, now been separated unto God to be an apostle.

First he was *called* then he served in *helps,* later in the *office of a teacher* and then lastly in that of an *apostle.* Why? Because Paul was faithful to promote the Lord and not himself *(1 Corinthians 4:2).*

Note: God used the established leadership whom Paul had faithfully served...

Then, having fasted and prayed, and laid hands on them, **THEY SENT THEM** *away. So, being sent out by the Holy Spirit, they went...*

(Acts 13:3-4 NKJV)

God did not use anyone Paul was not already in submission to; instead he used an established authority that had already been set up in Antioch. **God will not undermine the leadership in the body of Christ in order to raise someone up into a position of leadership. Why, because your character is far more important than your *gifting.***

CHAPTER 16

Discernment of Gifting

Let us continue and move on and look at the concept of **"gift discernment."** Exactly what has God graced our lives with? Just like Paul, we must be able to "recognise" who we are in Christ and what we have been called to "do," without this, it is inevitable that we will both be "unfruitful" and "ineffective" *(regardless of any good intentions!)*

Therefore we must discover what God's plan for our individual lives really is and more importantly what His plan is to benefit other people's lives through ours. Gifting is "always" for others and not for self! So along with the gift we must also recognise who is going to "benefit" and what exactly is He looking to "influence" with His kingdom. God always has a strategy plan!

Before I formed you in the womb I knew you, before you were born **I set you apart; I appointed you** *as a prophet to the nations.*

(Jeremiah 1:5)

Evidently it becomes a major necessity for us to have clarity on this issue. We must begin by accepting the fact that "divine distinction" does exist and that we must work together with it not against it. Quite simply, there are many folks today who are failing to see this "divine distinction" not only in their own lives but also in the lives of others.

As a result many are "struggling" and "straining" themselves to be something that God has not called them to be. We often succumb to the peer pressure of becoming what others perceive for us rather than what God has "appointed" for us.

Today it would be true to say that there exists so much confusion between **"body gifting"** and **"ministry calling,"** something that has caused pain, heartache and much "disillusionment."

To help clear this up let's look at four major factors that need to be considered when it comes to ministry gifting.

The Sense of Call

Today I believe that we often mix up "desire" with "call." Of course, the scripture tells us to desire the best gifts *(see 1 Corinthians 12:31)*. However desire can never override call. First and foremost any desires must line up with the will of God for our lives.

Discernment of Gifting

The Desire for the Work

The call always comes first from God's point of view as we see here in Jeremiah 1:5; "Before you were formed in the womb I called you" *(appointed, sanctified, set apart, separated, consecrated and dedicated)*. However this was news to Jeremiah. Who was less than ecstatic about the proposal. Rather he went into an immediate verbal inventory of all the excuses and reasons why the opposite was in fact true. Not unlike the rest of us do!

Inadequacy often rears its ugly head in the face of stepping up to the call. Nevertheless in the midst of trauma we can discover the "desire" to serve the Lord.

With all this in mind we need to distinguish what desire in this context actually means. It goes beyond just a human sense of looking to enjoy something. Rather in this context it is more of an "inner yearning," a "knowing" that we must face this call or we are going to die! *(It can feel this intense; like your whole life depends on it, even before you really understand why).*

And while it might be possible to enjoy serving God, desire from the inner man is something quite different; that inward yearning we spoke of, goes much deeper; according to the Strong's it is akin to "jealousy" or being "zealous."[4]

Exercise the Gift

A man's ministry makes room for itself. A genuine call from God will manifest itself - if it is exercised properly. God does not appoint us to a position of "spiritual inertia" *(inactivity, lethargy, disinterest, inaction or unwillingness).* Rather He appoints and anoints for ACTION *(faith without works is dead!)* So there is a built-in dynamic to this "call" of God that we all face and it only finds *expression* through continual practice and not "theory!"

Fruitfulness, a Sign of Ministry

So many people lay claim to ministries in advance of "fruitfulness" and "appointment," when in fact fruitfulness is the real sign of ministry. **"Do not neglect your gift**, which was given you through a prophetic message when the body of elders laid their hands on you" *(1 Timothy 4:14)*; "...**fan into flame the gift** of God," *(2 Timothy 1:6)*; "Each one should **use whatever gift** he has received to serve others, faithfully administering God's grace in its various forms" *(1 Peter 4:10)*.

There is a distinction in kind, between a talent, which we were born with and a gift imparted by the Holy Spirit. It is noticeable in Paul's ministry that he was not averse to using his natural talents in his service for the Lord. For example he was obviously intellectually gifted but also practically so and at times used his natural abilities to support his own ministry *(see Acts 18:3 for tent making)*.

But it is also important to see how Paul laid such talents aside when it came to operating in revelation *(see 1 Corinthians 2:1-3)*. God uses both in the leader but in fact, it is dedication of all that we have and are, which removes the clear distinction between natural talent and divine gift in the leader.

Discernment of Gifting

Every Called Person has a Handicap

The great heroes of the bible had handicaps even those with mighty signs and wonders; they were mere humans with many limitations and flaws. Moses committed murder and had a terrible speech impediment. Miriam fuelled a conspiracy against Moses during the wilderness journey of the Israelites. David committed adultery and murder. A harmless little old lady intimidated Elijah. And when the chips were down, Peter denied even knowing Jesus! Saul of Tarsus rounded up Christians and threw them in jail or had them stoned and it goes on.

I like the fact that none of these heroes were larger than life on their own. It gives us hope, because most of us were anything but a success before we met the Lord. If anything, God specialises in taking people who are self-willed, arrogant, or just plain ordinary and making a success of them. By successful, I don't mean rich and famous, but humble, loving, and generous and becoming the best they can be in Christ.

What seems to be our tragedy becomes our triumph. We learn how to turn the "messes" of our lives into "messages" and how to change the "tests" into "testimonies," and as my wife often says, "turn our cares into prayers; our worry into worship and last but not least how to find peace in the pain." Our strength is always in God.

What is our biggest hindrance to success - is it failure? - No! We are our own hindrance! Making mistakes is not a hindrance for victory! We see in scripture when Elijah went straight from a great victory into a great flop! Jonah, everything God told him to do - he did the exact opposite! We have all come to that place where we have found our problems were not really the issue; instead we discovered that our problems were actually God given opportunities!

This transpires simply because problems can help make us people who reach out past and beyond our natural abilities. Whereas a person who reaches out to God without any problems or challenges whatsoever, sees little if any change, growth or increase etc.

Problems represent NEEDS!

In reality who needs to look for problems? Problems exist and God has called every one of us to be problem solvers. **Problems represent NEEDS!** Problems are not wrong. They are not negatives if we look at them positively.

They are needs that God has called us and given us the ability and anointing to meet and solve. For sake of illustration there were two salesmen who came back from Africa, one was down and the other was up - thrilled to bits. One said, *"They don't wear shoes in Africa - it's hopeless."* The other said, *"No one has shoes in Africa, they all need our shoes!"*

God told us that we are to get a harvest, to multiply and reproduce. That means we must see and experience "increase" because **God has said. In other words, blessing is not a feeling but a condition** therefore it is important to consider this vital fact:

God's expression for our lives is an expression of His promises.

Chapter 17

Spiritual Gifts vs. Governing Authority

It is true to say, that being "gifted" does not automatically make you "autonomous" *(independent)*. In other words, none of us are an end in ourselves nor can we have authority in ourselves! None of us can function independently from the rest of the "body" and thrive or survive!

In actual fact our gift only operates and functions in its fullest degree and glory when it is functioning with the rest of the body and submitted-to-the-correct-authorities within the body.

> *Has the Lord indeed spoken only by Moses? Has He not spoken also by us?*
>
> *(Numbers 12:2 AMP)*

There is some confusion at large in the body of Christ today, over this very issue, because immaturity and misunderstanding say that because a person operates in a "gifting" *(albeit genuine)* this automatically gives him or her governing-authority. Absolutely Not!

Spiritual Gifting vs. Governing Office

Let's look at it like this: it is a grave mistake to confuse mere spiritual gifting with governing-office. All of us as believers have a measure of authority but this amounts to the general believer's authority and does not include governing-authority or being in an office of authority within the body of Christ.

Therefore having a gift does not give anyone of us an automatic position-of-authority, just a general authority, which is the right of "every" believer. In fact we all have been given significant-authority in order to lay hands on the sick and to raise the dead!

Along with general authority as a believer we have general gifts that have been distributed amongst us - but none of this gives us an automatic "office-of-authority." To help explain this further, scripture tells us clearly that it is the Holy Spirit who is the giver of the gifts but that Jesus Himself is the One who places certain individuals into positions of governing-authority *(called offices)*.

An ordinary believer's authority is something we can gain overnight! But to have a governing-authority in the body of Christ is something else altogether. Irreparable damage has been done because of the lack of adequate understanding in this very area *(see 1 Corinthians 12:4-31; Ephesians 4:11-12)*.

If a person begins to operate in a legitimate gift but after some time refuses to yield themselves over to an established authority structure, then that gifting will become distorted and perverted; warped and void of purity because of its false agenda. **It's far too easy for a person to become disillusioned when they have no real accountability.** Distortion develops with misuse and lack of submission to God's governing authorities.

Now but Not Automatic

The same person, who is gifted now, is not automatically ready to have governing-authority NOW! Mere gifting never gave any man governing-authority, **this only comes via divine appointment and preparation**; being made ready through testing and faithful serving!

For illustration purposes let us refer to Miriam and Aaron who spoke against Moses in the bible *(Numbers 12:1-2)*. Whether they did this openly or privately is not made clear but nonetheless God heard their conversation and was not too happy about it.

We must consider that although both Aaron and Miriam were genuinely gifted and already had some position-of-authority, it was Moses nonetheless who was God's "governing-authority" at that time. Their supernatural gifting *(whether legitimate or not)* afforded neither of them any room whatsoever to usurp Moses governmental-office.

This was a direct insult to God. So serious in fact was this offence before God that Miriam became leprous because of it *(Number 12:10).* However both were forgiven and restored, nevertheless it reveals the dangers of *usurping* God-given and appointed authority. It illustrates perfectly the difference between mere *spiritual gifting* and *governing-authority.*

It might be true to say that not all false prophets *set out* to be false, rather they *become* that way. Just like Miriam and Aaron would have become false, if they had continued using their "gifting" to try and *out-rank* their brother *(Moses).*

It must be understood therefore that no man or woman can assume the kind of authority that Moses had been given by God - certainly not on the grounds of spiritual-gifting! God alone appoints individuals to such positions and we can see just how vehemently God defends it!

We must never forget that none of us can successfully operate outside of God's authority-structure, as our human ability to remain authentic, trustworthy, faithful, reliable, genuine, dependable or accurate - outside of His boundaries of authority - is zero! In fact to remain true rather than false within our gift capacity, we must remain continuously submitted to God given, ordained and appointed authority. No human reasoning or logic can add anything to or take away from this concept.

Conclusion:

In short, we must learn *not* to hold our own opinions too highly or be threatened by the credentials of others. We must work hard to show ourselves approved and be diligent to get genuine instruction and guidance from the Holy Spirit; who will never lead us to usurp authority.

For our gifts to flourish and to live peaceful lives we must not violate the boundaries of God's authoritative structure and governing authority.

We can only enjoy the true benefits of authority, whilst we cooperate with it!

CHAPTER 18

Authority - Who has it?

We all know that we have been given authority through Jesus Christ, to overcome in this life, to lay hands on the sick and to cast out demons etc. Spiritually speaking this means we reign in life and have dominion.

Nevertheless we are all part of the body of Christ, which has a specific structure with leadership - called Church. Whether we perceive we are individually gifted or not - this gives no automatic-right for any of us to become a leader within the local church. *(Qualification for leadership - authoritative office if God appoints - takes a number of years).*

Given to me was all authority in heaven and on earth.
(Matthew 28:18 YLT)

However within this chapter I would like to begin by speaking about the apostolic, the apostles in general. Which means this chapter is not a written spotlight based upon the believer's authority but more specifically in regard to the five-fold-governmental-authority.

(Note: successive chapters will touch on elders and deacons including whether the title "bishop" is just another word for "elder" currently mistaken as the "supreme-title" of the church, replacing that of the apostle!)

Who has Authority?

First and foremost, authority begins and ends with Christ but the question is; who else has authority?

To help answer this we are going to look at the five fold ministry gifts, ordained by none other than Christ Himself and known as the **"resurrection apostles."** The one that we will focus on the most in this chapter is the apostle but before we continue let me make this statement,

"Authority and responsibility can only be given by those who have it."

Our opening scripture above (Matthew 28:18) reveals very clearly that ALL authority - both in heaven and on the earth belongs to Christ. That is a lot of authority! And it's not a power sharing scheme either... all means all. Jesus will never **SHARE** authority power with anyone, but He does **GIVE** it to those He delegates *(chief components in this of course are the ascension or five fold ministry gifts).*

Let's see this again briefly in the following verses: "All authority in heaven and on earth has been given to me" *(Matthew 28:18)*. "It was **he who gave some to be apostles, some to be prophets, some to be evangelists, and some to be pastors and teachers**, to prepare God's people for works of service, so that the body of Christ may be built up" *(Ephesians 4:11-12)*.

"Ministry Gifts" then, exist primarily for the building up and preparing of God's people for works of service. It could be said like this: principally they have earthly authority and receive their ordination directly from the Lord Himself, without human involvement. Such was the case with the original disciples who lived with Jesus during His earthly ministry.

Equally so, however, was the case with Paul who was "...one born out of due time..." *(1 Corinthians 15:8 KJV)* "The things that mark an apostle - signs, wonders and miracles - were done among you with great perseverance" *(2 Corinthians 12:12)*.

Ultimate Authority

Therefore it is true to say that the original New Testament apostles literally had "ultimate authority" on this earth, which was no small thing! For instance if there was a dispute regarding doctrine, then the apostles were the final adjudicators; they had the last say.

Some of the apostles by their very nature also fulfilled the **offices of elder** *(bishop)* **and overseer.** The reverse however does not necessarily apply. A person recognised as an elder is not automatically an apostle or other ministry gift to the church. The apostle is perhaps the most difficult of the five ministry gifts to explain.

Known to us then in more familiar terms as the "five fold ministries" these are perhaps better called the "five ascension gifts" as we already saw revealed in Ephesians 4:11 above: **"apostle, prophet, evangelist, pastor and teacher."**

Let me point out however, these are not just gifts of the Holy Spirit per se, they are "office and gifting" combined, an extension of Christ's headship ministry to the church. **Their primary ministry and function is to teach, train, activate and mature the saints for works of service** *(Ephesians 4:12-13)*.

Laying Foundations

As one of the five and concerning the apostle in particular - the apostle is a **"foundation-laying"** ministry *(Ephesians 2:20)* that we see in the New Testament, establishing new churches *(i.e. Paul's missionary journeys)*, correcting error by establishing proper order and structure *(first epistle to the Corinthians)*, and acting as an oversight ministry that fathers other ministries *(see 1 Corinthians 4:15; 2 Corinthians 11:28)*.

The New Testament apostle has a **"revelatory-anointing"** *(Ephesians 3:5)*. Some major characteristics are great patience and manifestations of signs, wonders and miracles. However we will know more and see greater manifestations surrounding the ministry of the "apostle" during the peak of the Apostolic Movement to come.

A keynote to point out here of course is that no person ever went or ever will walk straight into an apostolic ministry! There is always a process just as we saw with Paul: "In the church at Antioch there were prophets and teachers: Barnabas, Simeon called Niger, Lucius of Cyrene, Manaen *(who had been brought up with Herod tetrarch)* and Saul" *(Acts 13:1)*. Evidently Paul was recognised operating in other ministry gifting *(teacher)* before he was commissioned by the Holy Spirit and then "sent-out" as an apostle by *(his)* the leaders.

This is a good point to remember. In other words, no one is born an apostle. It takes serious preparation and maturity to walk in that office plus it is not chosen by the individual - rather it is bestowed upon them, at God's bidding - not their own. Paul was no volunteer! God had to throw him down off his high horse first and that was just to get his attention. Rather Jesus "informed" Paul of his selection; he was not consulted!

It is a sovereign act of God. Entirely for His choosing and while many are called - few are chosen; few can walk in such an office. Therefore self-assigned or self-appointed apostles are real glutens for punishment, as scripture clearly reveals that it is no walk in the park to be a genuine apostle! It's not a title for glory, it's an office of government; spiritually weighty and generally unpopular!

The Pioneers of the Church

As spearheads and pioneers, they take the brunt of onslaught, while at the same time they faithfully lead others to victory! Not everyone has what it takes! Remembering that part of the calibre and proof of leadership is generally that other people naturally follow! It's self-explanatory, that if no one is *following,* those claiming to be in leadership status are clearly just in wishful thinking! The gift will speak for itself.

Generally if an apostle walks in a room, his presence fills the room and is felt by everyone! They possess such weight in the spirit that rarely goes unnoticed. They become recognised quickly as well as targeted and spoken about quickly! *(A lot!)* These are the true joys of apostle-hood *(with its inherent and unrelenting passion).* No one in their right mind would sign up for a role like this; rather the Lord Himself confers it on man simply because there are no volunteers!

However to continue, the apostle will usually have one or more of the other five fold ministry gifts - as his major gifting as well; this is called his "gift-mixture." For example apostle Paul was a *teacher.* Apostle Peter was a *pastor.* Apostle Barnabas was a *prophet.* We need to look at scripture to see what kind of men these were and what they did to discover their ministries as true apostles of Christ.

The most prominent is shown in the listing found here:

Now you are the body of Christ, and each one of you is a part of it. And in the church God has appointed first of all apostles, second prophets, third teachers, then workers of miracles, also those having gifts of healing, those able to help others, those with gifts of administration, and those speaking in different kinds of tongues.
(1 Corinthians 12:27-28)

So does this apostolic ministry merely exist to bless or to build? To bless is one thing, to build is quite another. We could say it like this: to bless and just excite people all the time, requires humanism, stamina and lots of charisma! This usually results in human appreciation, generally large love-gifts and popular return bookings *(invited back!)*

Yet for God this will *never* be enough! A true apostle cannot be bought or sold. He is not a crowd pleaser. Even if he does please the crowd, that's not his primary intention.

Why? Because Jesus is not interested in *exciting crowds* but in building His church. However building with the **"Master Builder"** *(Jesus)* is genuinely **hard work!** It takes dedication on an unprecedented scale and life-long commitment *(the apostolic ministry is not for the faint hearted!)*

We can say it like this: all apostles are in it for the long haul. They don't need convincing. They don't even sprint! Rather they plod, even when everyone else is having a spiritual sugar rush; running here and there on nervous human energy! In fact by the time others collapse from weariness, the apostle just keeps on keeping on, steady and undeterred. Mature with lengthy staying power - because he has had to learn to suffer-LONG!

No Time to Waste

Apostles generally show no interest for time wasting activities and are notoriously stable. They bring order and Godly discipline wherever they go and exude an admirable stature. People are drawn to them, for all sorts of reasons, both good and bad. In other words they can attract trouble like bees to honey, or moth to a flame simply because they have been dispatched as **God's voice in the earth**; anything and everything wants to shut them up!

In order to build a master plan is required and the master designer is not haphazard. The builders need insight into God's plan and strategy for the church. The apostle in close collaboration with his prophetic teammates **seeks always to build according to the patterns shown on the "mountain" of revelation.**

> *They serve at a sanctuary that is a copy and shadow of what is in heaven. This is why Moses was warned when he was about to build the tabernacle: "See to it that you make everything according to the pattern shown you on the mountain."*
>
> *(Hebrews 8:5)*

Accumulated Rubbish

As it was in Nehemiah's day, there must be a clearing-away of accumulated *rubbish!* Today there exists, to a very large extent, wrong thinking in regards to the actual role of the local church. Many see it as a place to attend only when needing a *blessing*. A cavalier easy-come-easy-go attitude prevails.

In addition there are such individuals who perceive that they can justifiably manipulate the church in order to serve their own ends *(personal gain - financial, sexual or otherwise)* or simply fill a vast ego! Either way Christ is not usually front-and-centre in those types of churches!

Then there are those churches who try to embody new ideas and structures within their services and mingle it in with the old-way. Generally this effects no real or worthwhile change, but instead **introduces competition into their churches - where the old now has to compete with the new!**

We see this featured in Mark 2:21-22, "No one sews a patch of un-shrunk cloth on an old garment. If he does, the new piece will pull away from the old, making the tear worse. And no one pours new wine into old wineskins. If he does, the wine will burst the skins, and both the wine and the wineskins will be ruined. No, he pours new wine into new wineskins" *(Mark 2:21-22)*.

With all intents and purposes an apostle is a prolific builder and will always have that desire to BUILD. He will establish new churches and or re-establish existing ones, but his ministry will always be the same. In fact restoration and pioneering go hand in hand for the apostle - "building" or "re-building" are the same to him - it's all building and precisely what he will be found doing. It is his calling card. To bring into order **"...to build and to establish"** *(see Jeremiah 1:10; 18:9; 31:28; 33:2)*.

Unity Expressed in Diversity

Philip Mohabir in his book, **"Hands of Jesus"** says that, "Paul sets forth in Ephesians 4 the core values and essential virtues that form the kernel from which local church life and practice flow. They are unity expressed in diversity, maturity, stability and corporeity. The ascended Lord gave apostles, prophets, evangelists, pastors and teachers to the church to build these characteristics in the very fiber of local church life.

He has given five gifts for this purpose. We cannot do it with three or even four. In His infinite wisdom, He knew we need five. God is generous but not superfluous. Any other structure, system, strategy, or man-made method will fail to produce the kind of church that Jesus wants and for which He died.

But now is the time when the Lord is restoring the apostolic and apostles to the church. Now is the time for the whole body of Christ to experience the authority and anointing of apostles just as it was in the book of Acts. To see the church rise to its full potential and built according to New Testament pattern, we must rise in vision and faith. To see the church become all that the Lamb died to make it, **we need another apostolic reformation.**

In these days the Lord is preparing the church, His Bride, for glory, equipping her to reap a final gigantic harvest and at the same time preparing the world for judgment.

Worldwide Penetration

As Dr. Sam Matthews said, let us allow the Holy Spirit to orchestrate us into a worldwide penetration of the gospel. **It is time to become part of the second apostolic reformation.** As mentioned before 'the vision is rushing to completion.'

The five ascension gifts are not optional extras, but essential imperatives, ordained by God for the church. Their importance and role to the body are a divine arrangement by Father, Son and Holy Spirit. We cannot fulfil the apostolic mission of the church without their active presence. If the church 2000 years ago needed them, how much more do we need them today when the days are so much more evil? Oh, how we need them!"[5]

Chapter 19

Who Ordains Who?

Ordination is a biblical principle and directive that is found throughout both the Old and New Testaments. It can be seen in operation first of all in the Garden of Eden and then repeatedly during every spiritual awakening right through to the Acts of the Apostles and the early church. There is however, reference to ordination before this time by the prophet Ezekiel, where he says of Lucifer:

You were anointed as a guardian cherub, for so I ordained you. You were on the holy mount of God; you walked among the fiery stones.

(Ezekiel 28:14)

He prophesies concerning Satan that, prior to his rebellion and fall, he was ordained *(or set in place)* by God as an anointed cherub on the holy mount of God.

This pre-time prophetic revelation serves to show the importance of ordination within the kingdom and body of the Lord Jesus Christ. His rejection due to pride, led to rebellion, violence and disorder.

> *...God is not a God of disorder...*
> *(1 Corinthians 14:33)*

Ordaining is God's Nature

The importance and reason for *ordaining ministers is fundamental* to the nature and character of God. He loves order - He created it and used it to bring to birth the world and everything in it - including mankind. He ordained light and darkness. He ordained earth and sky, land and sea and in so doing provided a structured environment for mankind.

> *Now the Lord God had planted a garden in the East, in Eden; and there he put the man he had formed.*
> *(Genesis 2:8)*

When God put Adam in the Garden of Eden, the **wording used implies appointment or ordination.** Adam was firstly appointed to a position provided and prepared for him, later on in verse 15. God completes the call by defining his responsibility i.e. to *"work it" (the garden)* and take care of it.

The principle itself is that of one who has authority, *delegating to another a commission of responsibility and therefore a realm of spiritual authority.* It is the highest form of *"service"* within the body of Christ. Jesus said, *"He who would be chief among you, would be the servant of all!"*

Who Ordains Who?

There are different degrees of ordination as there are different measures of service.

Ordination therefore can be defined thus:

- The appointment of an individual to a place or position of authority
- The delegation to an individual of an area of responsibility. Moses ordained elders to assist in the management of the mighty nation of Israel *(Exodus 18:25)*
- He also ordained the priesthood, with Aaron as high priest *(Exodus 28:1)*
- Towards the end of his life and ministry he ordained Joshua - his disciple - to be his successor

Moses did as the Lord commanded him. He took Joshua and made him stand before Eleazar the priest and the whole assembly. Then he laid his hands on him and commissioned him, as the Lord instructed through Moses *(Numbers 27:18-23)*.

The Pattern Continues

Samuel and David, Elijah and Elisha and many others, each exemplifying ordination as God's purpose for their day. Then Jesus speaking to His disciple's states quite clearly that He chose and ordained them to go and bear fruit *(John 15:16)*.

When speaking to Peter after His resurrection, He commissions Peter to feed and take care of his sheep. In every instance mentioned, each individual had laid aside their own will and desire to take up and submit to, the will and desire of God. In so doing, they fulfilled their destiny and call, to powerful effect!

Who Ordains Who?

Over the years, many have come to me and asked that I would ordain them. Usually I have mixed emotions regarding their request, as not all are genuine in their quest to be ordained. Motives are very important. Before I give any answer, whether it being "Yes or No," **I first ask a number of questions.**

The following are an example:

Am I their apostle? Who have these individuals submitted to so far? And have they already an apostle whom they are in relationship with? *(As you do not want to usurp another's authority and build on another's foundation...)*

Have they split from somebody else, therefore creating a church split? If so, that would have to be dealt with as this will cause them problems later on and reflect on the Lord!

Are they looking to be in association or affiliation? *(There is a big difference between the two.)* The first is that they may take the relationship lightly. In the second case, you are their apostle i.e. Father in the faith... All this has to be qualified for future relationship development; remembering that every relationship must have a foundation of understanding which gives clear boundaries to both parties; stopping any confusion or misgivings.

You have to truly find out what each individual means when they say they want to submit to you! Many of course want to be ordained but don't want to submit to anyone... It's the apostles and the apostolic teams that connect the local churches which in effect stops any isolation of any individual group... i.e. we are one universal body...

Am I ordaining a ministry gift or an elder of the local church? Eldership is governmental, an office of responsibility with authority to rule. Each elder, as we have already seen, is a shepherd *(which does not mean that they are automatically a pastor)* and perhaps, will operate to some degree in their gifting. On the other hand we also then need to recognize that not every elder is a five fold ministry gift.

Submitting one to Another

Remembering, an apostolic ministry does have governmental authority. He can be responsible for a region, territory, nation, etc. Although the other five fold ministry gifts should submit to an apostle that they are in relationship with. They may have some governmental authority but it's meant to operate in submission to the apostolic structure.

As ministry gifts are not necessarily governmental positions, unless they are apostolic, but even then the apostle submits to the authority of the local church... We as apostles only have authority over any individual group as a result of submission through relationship. It is fundamental that the apostolic anointing that we are discussing here is *recognized*.

I only ordain leaders because I know them personally or leadership that is in relationship with me knows the person in question personally. The reason for this is that elders or ministry gifts for that matter *(when I mean ministry gifts, I mean itinerant ministries)* have to be qualified as seen in the New Testament. You cannot personally qualify an individual if you don't know them.

Therefore in the New Testament when elders were being put into a position of leadership, this was done by an apostle and presbytery of apostolic leaders. You will also find in the New Testament that there was an emphasis on elders being recognized by the people, the local body as good and honourable individuals. But once eldership has been appointed they then have the right to ordain anyone who God raises up to a position of elder or ministry gift in the local church *(as the local elders are the authority for their given territory)*. This can be approved by the apostle.

Ordination Service

Once all the above is clarified you then can set a date for the ordination service. This can be done in any given setting. I usually ordain ministers in front of their congregation because the congregation also needs to see that their pastor is submitting to an apostle. This would be a normal Sunday morning, perhaps one would teach on church structure or some other leadership message, referring to ordination. The body of Christ needs to understand what is going on...

Then at the right time, laying hands on the individual to recognize their position and praying for an impartation. This needs to be done with a presbytery of other leaders including other visiting pastors... Words of knowledge and encouragement are also important.

Expect the supernatural, change and increase not only for the minister in question but also for the church as the anointing should then increase. Again you can look at Acts 14:23, Titus 1:5. Even the apostle Paul told Timothy to fight the good fight using the word of prophecy given to him when hands were laid on him: 1 Timothy 1:18.

Regarding ongoing relationships, this is down to the type of relationship that you have agreed upon. Our role as apostles is to help father ministry gifts or elders to become the best that they can be. Watching as a father over their child who is trying to walk for the first time... applauding their victories... loving them enough to overlook their failures... Seeing their future success.

The Instruction of the Holy Spirit

There are many other issues that need to be observed but all that I know I have learned from the Holy Spirit. I have learned that many want to use the gift, which is fine, but I am not so quick to ordain people these days.

The given individual to be ordained has to pay for the traveling expenses, paper work that is incurred, honorarium on the day, and renew their membership fee every January. Why? This keeps them accountable... If however a Senior Pastor says he wants to be in affiliation then they have to tithe the tithe to me as their apostle.

Hope all this is helpful... Remember we don't wear nametags! People are trying to find out how to be an apostle... That is the wrong perspective on it... Whatever is in the bottle will be tasted when the bottle is poured out... You don't learn to be an apostle, you allow the apostle in you to be revealed!

Validating the Selection

As we know it was the apostles who validated the selections made by the people. Remarkably, these men were being given responsibility for what might be considered as a menial task, yet they were required to be full of the Holy Spirit and wisdom. One of the men, Stephen, described as being full of faith, grace and power *(verses 5 and 8)*, displayed signs and wonders befitting any apostle. So much so, that he incurred the wrath of the religious rulers who promptly persecuted him and contrived his death.

The fact that the first man ordained by the apostles should also be the first Christian martyr would indicate the spiritual importance of ordination. Were it to be of little spiritual value, it would not have drawn so much opposition. The pressure on the apostles to refrain from further ordination would have been considerable, *(i.e., "If this is what is going to happen when we ordain people, it doesn't seem like too good an idea!")*

Similarly, the pressure on individuals to hold back from being ordained to ministry would have been great. But then - those full of the Holy Spirit, faith, grace and power are not easily intimidated!

Ordination therefore is carried out by those appointed by God, whose authority is evidenced by the position of responsibility they hold within the body of Christ and by the demonstration of the Holy Spirit's power on their lives. *Such men (apostles) have something of value to impart.*

The Appointment and Ordination of Elders

In the early church, the appointment of elders was very important. In fact, the apostle Paul saw the church as *"unfinished"* until this happened *(Titus 1:5)*. The scriptures suggest that the elders were not selected by apostles or other trans-local ministries *(Acts 14:23; Titus 1:5)*, but were ordained, appointed or installed. It seems they ratified or confirmed the validity of the church's selection of men for the task and then *"officially"* appointed them.

In the new churches, which only had immature believers as members, the apostles *(or church planters)* had to help the church to recognise elders *(as the apostle Paul did when he described the qualifications for eldership)*. Note though that there is no place from scripture for the appointment of elders by democratic vote. It is God who calls, equips and enables elders, not the church members. The church has simply to recognise them, perhaps with apostolic help.

At first, the apostles *(and other trans-local ministries)* exercised authority in the church, *and* then later it was exercised by those they appointed as elders. The trans-local ministries never appointed men immediately a church was established, but appointed some members of the community to this position on subsequent *"missionary"* visits. This allowed time for some members of the new Christian community to mature sufficiently spiritually for others in the group to recognise this and their calling in God to be elders.

After all, there was no point appointing a person, as an elder if the majority of a congregation did not recognise them as such. Members of the congregation would also be able to test the people over time to see if they met the qualifications for eldership stressed by the apostle Paul. Note that elders in the early church were always drawn from the local community.

This meant that elders had to be members of the community, therefore enabling them to know the local situation and people intimately, and be able to make their judgements in the light of this as they carried out their oversight of the church.

Recognised as they Emerge

Men should never be appointed to eldership just because the church does not have elders or to make up the number of elders. Elders should only be recognised as they emerge. In some newly formed churches, it may be necessary to have a leadership, but not a properly constituted eldership. Elders will emerge later in God's time. This process must never be rushed. To end up with people appointed to eldership who are not called by God to the task can be devastating to a local church. Remember that a man is an elder before he is ever recognised as one, because it is a calling of God.

The requirements or qualifications for eldership will simply be met in Him and the church members must recognise this. This is the only way the man will be entrusted and therefore enable him to function as an elder. Note though that not all members of a church will be drawn to the same man for help and counsel etc. *(that is why God's best is plurality of eldership)*, but most members of the flock need at least to be able to look up to and respect those chosen for eldership.

The number of elders recognised will usually be related to church size. God will not raise up ten elders in a church of twenty members. He will also not want one elder in a church of considerable size, as the job will be too great for one man alone. If, in a small church, only one man is recognisable as an elder, it would be wise for him to seek fellowship with other elders in his geographical area, where possible.

This will give him the opportunity to share his burdens and concerns with others and also be helped in his work. It is possible that the early church worked on this principle, as elders could have been appointed to geographical areas with each one overseeing one house-church.

Men should NOT be appointed as elders simply because:

- They are old. Remember though that spiritual maturity and wisdom do not develop overnight, so age is not entirely irrelevant
- They have served the church faithfully for many years
- They have successfully served in another area of church leadership for a number of years and they are due for a promotion
- They have influence, power, money, popularity, are successful, or professionally capable
- They are outgoing, outspoken, eloquent or good communicators
- There is no one else

CHAPTER 20

The Office of an Elder

So let's get back to the teaching on the apostle in regard to those who are promoting the hierarchy of bishops as the top structure of the church. In order to refresh, the word bishop simply means "elder."

> ...I saw four and twenty elders sitting, clothed in white raiment; and they had on their heads crowns of gold.
> (Revelation 4:4 KJV)

The word episkopos occurs five times in the NT: once of Christ *(1 Peter 2:25)* and in four places of "bishops" or "overseers" in local churches *(Acts 20:28; Philippians 1:1; 1 Timothy 3:2, Titus 1:7)*. The verb episkopeo occurs in Hebrews 12:15 *("watching")* and *(in some NT MSS)* 1 Peter 5:2 *("exercising the oversight")*.

A bishop then has "oversight of," he is an "overseer." 1 Peter 5:2 says, "Feed the flock of God which is among you, taking the oversight thereof" *(KJV)*. The Greek word for "oversight" is episkopeo - to oversee, to beware, to look diligently, take the oversight. Extra words given: direction *(about the times)*, have charge of, take aim at *(spy)*, regard, consider, take heed, look at *(on)*, mark.[6]

Elders in the Old Testament

So to continue let's take a look at eldership now in both the New and Old Testaments.

The Hebrew word for elders: *zaqen*, *(OT)* does not necessarily mean an old man, but does imply one of maturity and experience *(Numbers 11:16)*. They were recognised as the highest authoritative body over the people. They acted as the religious representatives of the nation *(Jeremiah 19:1; Joel 1:14; 2:16)*.

As well as handling many political matters and settling inter tribal disputes *(Joshua 22:13-33)*, the town elders were a sort of municipal council, whose duties included acting as judges in apprehending murderers *(Deuteronomy 19:12)*, conducting inquests *(Deuteronomy 21:2)* and settling matrimonial disputes *(Deuteronomy 22:15; 25:7)*.

The **"elders of Israel,"** first heard of in Exodus 3:16-18, were assembled by Moses to receive God's announcement of the liberation of Egypt. The covenant was ratified at Mount Sinai in the presence of 70 elders of Israel *(Exodus 24:1,9,14 cf. 19:7)*, the **"nobles"** *(KJV)* or chief men of the nation *(24:11)*.

Later 70 elders were specially anointed with the Spirit to aid Moses in governing the nation *(Numbers 11:16-25)*. In cases when the whole community sinned, the elders of the congregation or community were to represent it in making atonement *(Leviticus 4:13-15)*.

The authority of the elders was in principle greater than that of the King *(cf, 2 Kings 23:1)*. It was this group, which demanded that Samuel appoint a king *(1 Samuel 8:4-6)*, and they were parties to the royal covenant, which established David as king *(2 Samuel 5:3)*.

In Babylon the elders were the focal point of the Jewish community in exile *(Jeremiah 29:1; Ezra 8:1; 14:1; 20:1-5)*, and after the return to Jerusalem they continued active *(Ezra 5:5, 9; 6:7-8, 14; 10:8, 14)*. While their authority was originally civil, **by New Testament times** the "elders of the people" *(presbyeroi tou laou)* shared with the chief priests the power of determining religious affairs and if necessary of expulsion from the synagogue.

Elders in the New Testament

An elder in the NT is really a bishop. In his vision of heaven, John saw 24 elders seated upon thrones surrounding the throne of God, clothed in white garments and wearing golden crowns *(Revelation 4:4)*. They fall down in worship and cast their crowns before God's throne *(4:10; cf. 11:16; 19:4)*, and with their harps and bowls of incense, symbolising the prayers of the saints, they sing a new song to the Lamb *(5:8-10)*.

As elders they represent God's people; their thrones and crowns symbolise a kingly role, while their acts of worship and the bowls of incense suggest a priestly function. Thus they seem to be the chief representatives of the redeemed as a kingdom of priestly function *(Revelation 1:6; cf. 20:6; 1 Peter 2:5, 9; Exodus 19:6).*

They used the same word for *elder* in the OT and the NT, but the content of the Christian elder's ministry has changed, for it now includes visitation of the sick *(James 5:14).*

Elders are vital components within the structure of the church, including the restoration of the apostolic.

Elders and the apostles must work together. NOT in a power struggle but in complete unison, consulting with one another - bringing stability and strength to the local church.

However it is true to say that as we begin to see the apostles and elders working together again like in the time of the early church, we are going to begin to see an **unleashing of God's** power - restored to the church - a power that this world will NOT be able to resist or refute!

Authority and Power go Hand in Hand

When perfect order is restored *(concerning authority in the local church)* **there will no longer be any shortage of power - in the church of the living God.**

Looking at the early church, where elders seemed to have been **responsible** for groups of house-churches, *(at that* *time there were no church buildings!)* elders were appointed to make sure these groups stayed on the right track spiritually. They exercised the greatest authority of all the members and brought a sense of the fatherhood of God to the local church, such as: faith, security, confidence and spiritual covering.

Elders were also meant to establish and maintain a family atmosphere, which enabled the flow of love between members. This enabled the Holy Spirit to move in power and enabled new converts to be *kept secure* after any evangelistic effort. This meant they had to speak with people personally and not rule by notes in the church newsletter.

Elders were overseers who had spiritual responsibility for local church members. It has already been stated: it was the elders and NOT the apostles - that ruled the local churches in New Testament times. Trans-local ministries such as apostles and prophets did at times bring some correction or exhortation, but the elders carried out their task of overseeing and shepherding the local church unhindered.

Leader of Leaders

From within a group of elders, God typically raises up a "set-elder" - a leader of leaders. This man is often the pastor, vicar, or full-time leader within a church. The elders may be of equal standing, but it would be very unusual for them all to be equal in leadership experience, gift and ability. The man who is called to lead the elders should enable eldership meetings by **"chairing"** them - in other words **"managing"** them and keeping them on the right track.

He is often also the spokesman for the eldership as well as being the main church teacher. Remember, every church member, including the elders, needs to submit to God and to any other person God raises up into a position of authority, i.e. an apostle bringing correction from God or a prophet bringing the "Word" of God. This submission to God and each other enables any church to be coordinated by God and fruitful as it seeks to carry out His will.

The scriptures do not reveal a clear job description for elders, but they do show us something of the way eldership functioned within the early church. Studying this can assist elders today in better understanding their significant role and what it is that God desires of them.

The qualifications we see in scripture concerning those serving in eldership - reveal the sheer **calibre and quality** of such men - chosen and expected to be fit for their task! These men had to serve the church to which they were called in a Christ-like way and other members of the church needed to recognize some measure of spiritual gifting and spiritual maturity in them.

For example those recognized, as elders should: direct the affairs of the church they were entrusted with by God, i.e. they were God's stewards *(Titus 1:1f; 1 Timothy 5:17)*. The Greek word for **"overseer"** is *episkopos* and was used in the secular writings of the time to refer to a person with **administrative and judicial functions.**

Therefore eldership is a governmental function, which has authority, and whose goal in the local church is to increase and maintain the rule of God; this affects each individual member, including their respective families, the church itself and the wider community.

Remember God never instituted "DEMOCRACY" as a means of governing His people. Rather He established "THEOCRACY" which means - government by God Himself. He enables His rule by raising up leadership - through whom He can rule *(principally eldership in a local church setting)*. These men therefore, must walk closely with God and wait on Him, so that they can hear His Word for the church for which they are responsible and obey His directives and take care of God's church.

They should also have a good reputation with those outside the church so that the church will be seen as a place of integrity, where non-Christians can come for help *(1 Timothy 3:5, 7)*. They also need to work hard, help the weak and remember that it is more blessed to give than receive *(Acts 20:35)*.

They must be able to Teach

The Greek word used here is ***didaktikos*** - better translated as "apt or skilled to teach" *(1 Timothy 3:2)*. However, 1 Timothy 5:17 suggests that only *some* had the labour *(or toil)* of preaching and teaching in the local church. This probably referred to those elders whose main function was preaching and teaching and perhaps even their full-time employment; hence the following verse about the worker deserving his wages *(1 Timothy 5:18)*.

All elders need to be able to teach and disciple *(even if it is just in a one-to-one counselling situation)*, however only some are called to preach and teach in a corporate sense.

Elders, when they are asked, anoint with oil in the name of the Lord those who are sick. The prayer offered in faith will make the sick person well, because the Lord will raise them up... *(James 5:14-15)* They also need to be on guard and watch over themselves and the flock of which the Holy Spirit has made them overseers/elders, because savage wolves will attempt to come in and will not spare the flock *(Acts 20:28-31)*.

In closing, elders are willing shepherds of the flock, that God has placed under their care - serving as **overseers** and **examples of Christ-likeness** to their flock *(Acts 20:28; 1 Peter 5:2-3)*. Their example should be Jesus Christ who is the **shepherd and overseer** of our souls *(1 Peter 2:25; 1 John 2:6)*.

Laying hands on and praying for those in their congregation, thus imparting spiritual gifts and prophecy *(1 Timothy 4:14)*. Encourage *(or exhort)* those they oversee by sound doctrine and by holding firmly to the trustworthy message as it has been taught, and refute *(or convict)* those who oppose it *(Titus 1:9)*.

Finally elders are to discern the truth of God in a given situation and guide the church for which they are responsible in the light of that truth.

The elders in Jerusalem did this with the apostles and therefore kept the church on the right path *(Acts 15:1-31; Acts 16:4)*.

CHAPTER 21

Church Government

We were discussing the significance and the role of "elders" in both the Old and New Testaments. Specifically in the New Testament we saw that there was an addition to their function which was that of "visiting the sick" *(as seen in James 5:14)*. We also saw confirmed through scripture that elders appear to be the "chief representatives of the redeemed of the local church" and have a "...priestly function."

> ...*They continued steadfastly in the apostles' doctrine and fellowship, and in breaking of bread, and in prayers.*
> *(Acts 2:42 KJV)*

However as we continue in light of the apostle, it was more in a *"corporate capacity"* by which he provided leadership for the primitive church; and that leadership was effective both in **mercy** *(Acts 2:42)* and in **judgment** *(Acts 5:1-11).*

They exercised a general authority over every congregation, sending two of their number to supervise new developments in Samaria *(Acts 8:14)* and deciding with the elders on a common policy for the admission of Gentiles *(Acts 15).* So in this context, we can see clearly, the apostles and elders working together for the benefit of the whole.

Pressure of Work

In Acts when the pressure of work increased, they appointed seven assistants *(Acts 6:1-6),* elected by the people and ordained by the apostles. They were to administer to the churches charity. These seven have been regarded as deacons from the time of Irenaeus onwards, but Philip, the only one whose later history is clearly known to us, became an evangelist *(Acts 21:8)* with an unrestricted mission to preach the gospel. Church officers with a distinctive name are first found in the elders of Jerusalem, who received gifts *(Acts 11:30)* and took part in Council *(Acts 15:6).*

This office was probably copied from the eldership of the Jewish synagogue. The church itself is called a synagogue in James 2:2 and Jewish elders, who seem to have been ordained by imposition of hands, were responsible for maintaining discipline, with power to excommunicate breakers of the law.

But Christian eldership, as a gospel ministry acquired added pastoral *(James 5:14; 1 Peter 5:1-3)* and preaching *(1 Timothy 1:5);* and although the disturbances at Corinth may suggest that a more complete democracy prevailed in that congregation *(cf. 1 Corinthians 14:26)*, the general pattern of church government in the apostolic age would seem to be a board of elders or pastors. Possibly augmented by prophets and teachers, ruling each of the local congregations, with deacons to help in administration and with a general superintendence of the entire church **provided by apostles (not bishops!)**

Two Distinct Biblical Qualifications

The late Dr. Bob Gordon once wrote, "There are two biblical qualifications for eldership; these are distinct from others… **elders must not be novices and that they must be able to teach.** The other qualifications are a check to make sure that those proposed for eldership are living an exemplary Christian life. Those who are to oversee the church need to be good ambassadors for it, for Christ *(i.e. be models of Christlikeness)*, and for the truths they were teaching and not merely professional leaders.

Elders therefore need to be: men of prayer, true worshippers of God, men of the Word of God, men of true spiritual authority and maturity and men of mature spiritual experience and understanding. Men who are spiritually ahead of those in the church, men of vision *(which is sourced in God)*, who receive God's guidance and revelation and who are sensitive to the moving of the Holy Spirit; and men of faith, because without faith it is impossible to please God.

Elders are recognised by who they are and not what they do, and not by age or official title. They need to be men who have largely got their spiritual priorities right and their life in spiritual order.

The qualifications in the New Testament for an elder (*overseer*) are many:

- Shepherds of God's flock that is under their care, serving as overseers - not because they must, but because they are willing, as God wants them to be *(1 Peter 5:2)*
- Not greedy for money nor a lover of money *(1 Peter 5:2; 1 Timothy 3:3)*
- Eager to serve, of ready mind or willingly *(1 Peter 5:2)*
- Examples to their flock, not lording it over those entrusted to them *(1 Peter 5:3)*
- The husband of but one wife *(1 Timothy 3:2; Titus 1:6). (Note: divorce is allowable in scripture in certain circumstances; therefore, this phrase refers to bigamy or polygamy, not divorce)*
- A man whose children are faithful and not accused of riot or unruly *(Titus 1:6)*
- Blameless *(Titus 1:6-7)*
- Not overbearing *(not self-willed) (Titus 1:7)*
- Not quick tempered *(not soon angry) (Titus 1:7)*
- Not given to much wine *(1 Timothy 3:3: Titus 1:7)*
- Not violent *(no striker or brawler) (1 Timothy 3:3; Titus 1:7)*
- Not pursuing dishonest gain *(Titus 1:7)*

- Hospitable *(a lover of and given to hospitality) (Titus 1:8; 1 Timothy 3:2)*
- One who loves what is good *(Titus 1:8)*
- Self-controlled *(sober) (1 Timothy 3:2)*
- Upright *(just) (Titus 1:8)*
- Holy *(Titus 1:8)*
- Disciplined *(temperate) (Titus 1:8)*
- Able to hold firmly to the trustworthy message as it has been taught, so that they can encourage others by sound doctrine and refute those who oppose it *(Titus 1:9)*
- Above reproach *(1 Timothy 3:2)*
- Temperate *(vigilant) (1 Timothy 3:2)*
- Respectable *(of good behaviour) (1 Timothy 3:2)*
- Able *(apt or skilled)* to teach *(1 Timothy 3:2)*
- Not quarrelsome *(contentious or given to fighting) (1 Timothy 3:3)*
- Gentle *(patient) (1 Timothy 3:3)*
- Not covetous *(1 Timothy 3:3 AV)*
- Able to manage their own family well and see that their children obey them with proper respect... If anyone does not know how to manage *(rule)* their own family *(house)*, how can they take care of God's church *(1 Timothy 3:4-5)*
- Not a recent convert *(a novice)*, or they may become conceited *(puffed up with pride)* and fall under the same judgement as the devil *(1 Timothy 3:6)*

- Of good reputation with outsiders *(have a good testimony among those who are outside)*, so that they will not fall into disgrace and into the devil's trap *(lest they fall into reproach and the snare of the devil)* (1 Timothy 3:7)
- Able to work with other men in mutual submission, because they are called to work as an eldership team and not as individuals *(elders of a congregation are always mentioned in the plural)*

Important note: a true elder will tend the sheep whether recognised or not and will not want position or self-aggrandisement, but rather will simply want to serve the flock to which God has called him.

A man who starts to do this, but gives up because he was not recognised or officially appointed, proves that he is selfishly motivated. Such a man is not serving because 'he is called to the task by God' but is serving for his own gain rather than for the good of the church.'"[7]

CHAPTER 22

Elders are Territorial

As we continue with this concept of the apostle, we have taken the last chapters along with this one to talk about the role of elders in the body of Christ, in yester-world and in today's-world. All authority has "influence" - and all influence has a "realm of influence" over which it operates.

> *Remember your leaders who have spoken God's Word to you. Think about how their lives turned out, and imitate their faith.*
>
> *(Hebrews 13:7 GW)*

Now we are going to look at this in terms of the world territory. So let's begin by looking at what this word **"territory"** actually means. Its literal meaning is as follows: **"an area regarded as owned by the state, social group, individual or animal."**

In addition to this, another significant word that describes territory is "province," which in times-past was the basic **"unit of administration"** within the Roman Empire. Its earliest usage was a general term that referred to the **"magistrate's sphere of administrative action."** This term signified both the **"rule"** of the governor and the **"region"** that was entrusted to his care *(the geographical sense was dominant)*; and included the **"administration of justice."**

Therefore when a province was given to a governor, this was for him to: control, supervise, protect and oversee. It literally became his territory - to rule and to govern - for a specific period of time.

Elders are Territorial

Now when it comes to the spiritual aspect of this matter - there are such things as **"territorial spirits"** *(which are active within the heavenly realms)* but this is another teaching altogether! However as believers it is our right to exercise our authority within any given territory and we too are meant to be territorial!

We are not merely undercover agents that live invisible to the world, with alter egos that no one knows about! We are not a secret society! Rather we ought to govern those areas or regions that God has entrusted to us as scripture speaks about - holding-claim to every place we put our feet! *(see "Territorial Spirits" by C. Peter Wagner)*

This is too general in thought, even though all believers possess authority to a degree - not all believers are called to governmental offices - such as elders and apostles for example. So we must not over generalise this issue. Now let's go beyond this and look more closely at our opening chapter title **"Elders are Territorial."**

This statement refers to the fact that God placed elders within the church to oversee it. Their influence was not merely for the church only, but regionally and spiritually *(in the spirit realm)*. Their influence is far reaching both practically and spiritually. For instance if we go to the Old Testament, we can see that elders often acted as "magistrates" and "judges," who represented the people. Therefore it was their job to "administrate justice" within the areas allocated to them.

Even today this whole structure has NOT changed - because of time! Rather it still continues today; the only thing that has changed is that elders today have the added responsibility of visiting and praying for the sick. They do so in the power of the name of Jesus and His blood!

Elders also represent "pillars" within the church: of maturity, wholeness, purity, integrity, righteousness, doctrine and all that is true.

Every church needs Good Elders!

How then should the church respond to such elders? Well firstly there are three major things that need to be noted from scripture.

Firstly: elders are worthy of double honour, especially those whose work is preaching and teaching *(1 Timothy 5:17)*.

Church members need to respect, uphold and admonish them *(1 Thessalonians 5:12-13)*.

The job of an elder is not easy and the church needs to encourage those who are overseeing them and not pull them down or make their job more difficult than it needs to be. In fact, church members should obey their elders and submit to their authority, because they are men who keep watch over the church and who are accountable before God for it *(Hebrews 13:17)*. Also, if an elder is serving the church on a full-time basis, then the scriptures tell us that the worker deserves his wages *(1 Timothy 5:18)*.

Secondly: church members should not entertain an accusation against an elder unless it is brought by two or three witnesses.

Elders do not need to be the subject of gossip, which only serves to undermine their credibility and authority. Members of the church should stop people who do this and stop something getting out of hand or being blown out of proportion to the truth. However, if an elder is found to be in sin, they are to be rebuked publicly, so that others may take warning *(1 Timothy 5:19-20)*.

Thirdly: the church members should follow the godly example set by the elders *(Hebrews 13:7)*.

We all know that scripture tells us to "seek first the kingdom of God." The word kingdom also represents the **"rule and reign"** of God in scripture. But now we look at the role of elders as they use their God given positions to reign, to rule and to exercise Godly authority wherever they are placed. They actually represent the government of God within the church and must act accordingly.

All of this ties in with the role of the apostle and the apostolic age. The elders do not function under their own authority nor do the apostles. All authority given by God must work together in unity not in contest or rivalry with each other. A house divided falls. It cannot stand and until the elders can work together with the apostles in the local church as they were ordained and equipped to do so, there will always be a certain lack of authority and power.

So bring it on! Bring on the order of God. The church is in need of her power. She needs to be stifled no longer. Let truth be taught and revelation restored to the body of Christ. As all man-made-efforts to rule and to govern, have left her barren and lacking powerful influence within society. But if she regains her position and spiritual possession - with all her dignity in tact - the world will learn once again, what it is to FEAR the authority of the living God - that exists within the local church!

Awesome Authority has Responsibility

Finally, in closing this chapter - my son who is now 21 years, got talking to his mother about the story in the bible of Ananias and Sapphire. They were discussing the awesome authority that the apostles exercised in the early church. However over lunch our son came up with this honest and simple question *(and I quote him word for word simply because I think others would ask the same question!)*: **"If the apostle is being 'restored' where did he go? What happened to him?"**

This legitimate question was deserving of a simple reply! "The fact of the matter is..." I told him, "The apostle never went anywhere! He is not the one being restored, rather the truth about his *role* is being restored to the body of Christ." "Why?" "Because over time, truth was replaced by deception and distortion."

When TRUTH is fully restored to the church *(before Christ returns)* via the revealed Word of God *(the teaching of "revelation")* the apostle will be able to take his rightful place, along with the elders. No longer stuffy relics of an age-old institute or relegated to stain-glass-windows of rotting church buildings. No! They will not remain this ineffective but will take their rightful places in their intended role as POWERFUL EXECUTORS OF GOD'S AUTHORITY & JUSTICE.

The government of God within the local church is vital. The apostle has a huge part to play in this, along with the elders.

May this RESTORATION OF TRUTH advance with speed! How the church needs her divine order - just as God planned it and not as man distorted it - by humanistic ideals and religious **replacement theology!**

❖

CHAPTER 23

Women in Ministry

The apostle Paul clearly states that in God's eyes there is no distinction between male and female.

You are all sons of God through faith in Christ Jesus, for all of you who were baptised into Christ have clothed yourself with Christ. There is neither Jew nor Greek, slave nor free, male nor female, for you are all in Christ Jesus.

(Galatians 3:26-28)

The same man instructed Timothy *(1 Timothy 2:11-14)* that the order of headship between man and woman, irrespective of spiritual equality in God's eyes, must be upheld *(Galatians 3:28)*. He did not permit a woman to teach or have authority over a man.

The statement does not prohibit a woman from teaching in general terms but rather, taking the headship belonging to the man.

They are Significant

Throughout scripture there are accounts of women who have played significant roles within God's order and plan. ***Miriam** (Exodus 15:20),* ***Deborah** (Judges 4:14),* ***Huldah** (2 Kings 22:14),* ***Noadiah** (Nehemiah 6:14).* ***Esther*** was ordained by God to be given within a foreign reign and used greatly to bring in reformation at that time.

There were many women who surrounded Jesus and who were significantly involved with His life in one way or another:

Anna, the prophetess spoke of Him, those who travelled with Him, those who ministered to Him, the last ones at the cross, and the first at the tomb, the first to announce the resurrection (Luke 2:36-38; Matthew 27:55-56; Luke 8:1-3; Mark 14:3; Luke 7:37-37; Mark 15:47; John 20:1; Matthew 28:8).

Jesus never expressed discouragement concerning women and ministry, far from it! The woman Jesus spoke to at the well *(John 4:1-26)* was used by the Holy Spirit to evangelise her hometown.

The evangelist Philip is recorded to have had daughters who prophesied *(Acts 21:9)*. For this information to be included in the Word of God it must have significance beyond that of what Paul spoke in *1 Corinthians 12:7-11.*

God is Not Averse to Promoting Women

History gives record also to the fact that God is not averse to *"promoting"* women to high places of ministry within the body of Christ. Kathryn Kuhlman was a woman mightily anointed by God and her ministry outshines that of many men. She is reported as saying that the reason God used her was because a number of men refused to take the mantle of anointing, so because she was willing God used her. This statement may have considerable credibility but the fact remains – God used her.

She appears to reflect Deborah the prophetess in many ways. Deborah tried to encourage Barak to take the initiative in dealing with their enemy. Because he wouldn't, Deborah prophesied that the glory or credit would go to a woman. This was exactly what happened, *(Judges 4-5)* and it wasn't even Deborah!

Governmental Authority

There is no doubt that God's plan is for the men to carry that responsibility. Adam was created first therefore he had the responsibility and initial relationship with God. Aside from this the physical and emotional differences between man and woman confirm the wisdom of God's order. He created hormones and therefore knew exactly how they would affect the emotional balance of an individual.

God said that the woman's desire would be for her husband and that he would rule over her *(Genesis 3:16)*. Peter talks about women being submissive to their husbands

(1 Peter 3:1-6). It is quite clear therefore that should a woman be looking for position above her husband or striving for equality *(in the wrong sense)*, then this is not of God.

This however does not prevent women from having prominent ministries that flow out from a marriage relationship. The key is found in the heart attitude and submission, primarily to the Lord and then to the husband.

Can a woman be a five fold ministry gift? Can she be a pastor? Can she be an evangelist? Can she be a prophetess? Can she be an apostle, a pioneer or leader?

The answer to each of these questions would have to be, **YES.**

Can a woman be a man? **NO.**

Chapter 24

Mandate for Fellowship with God's Spirit

It is so important in this last chapter to strongly encourage you to **cultivate a deep and *daily* fellowship with the Holy Spirit.** Knowing that when it comes to fellowship with Him, it is vitally important to have a firm understanding of just whom we are relating to. He is not a mystical being for instance, but a distinct person, namely the third person of the trinity.

> *...when the **Friend** comes, the Spirit of the Truth, **he** will take you by the hand and guide you into all the truth there is. **He** won't draw attention to **himself**, but will make sense out of what is about to happen and, indeed, out of all that I have done and said. **He** will honor me; **he** will take from me and deliver it to you...*
>
> (John 16:13 MSG)

As we develop an apostolic lifestyle let's look at what the Spirit does - this will aid us in our grasp of who He really is and how we can relate to Him in our walk and ministries. I have continual mentioned, *"LifeStyle"* or *"daily"* throughout these pages, simply because our fellowship with the Holy Spirit is something that we should pursue daily.

Actually there is much about the Lord in scripture that is "daily" such as: "daily bread" *(Matthew 6:11)*, "fresh manna every morning" *(Exodus 16:21)*, "mercy is new every day" *(Lamentations 3:22-23)*, "take up our cross daily" *(Luke 9:23)* and so forth. Why? Because when something is "living" it is always a "daily experience."

Keeping it daily helps keeping it Fresh!

Bread is predominantly associated with scripture and is something, which for the most part, goes particularly stale after just one day! Same too concerning our relationship with the Holy Spirit, we must keep it fresh. In fact everything about our relationship with God must be kept fresh - not stale, stuffy or religious! We achieve this by approaching Him and welcoming Him afresh - every single day.

This daily pursuit is a journey of discovery that changes our personality in the process. So why don't more people in general try it, what is their cramp? One obvious hurdle that folks have grappled with is the fact that unlike Jesus *(who we saw dwelt amongst us)*, people can't see the Spirit of God with "flesh and bones" *(John 1:14; Luke 24:39)*. This single difficulty throughout church history has led some to either ignore the Spirit completely in their day-to-day Christian lives or keep Him as some kind of spiritual spare tire for emergencies only.

However it is only a sheer lack of understanding that can be the culprit here, for such neglect of this significant member of the Trinity. For example scripture certifies that we are born of the Spirit *(John 3:6)* and that our bodies are the temple of the Holy Spirit - who indwells us, *(Romans 8:9, 11, 14-16)* and that His witness gives us assurance that we are children of God. Also we are baptized by one Spirit into the body of Christ and we have access to God by the same Spirit *(1 Corinthians 12:13; Ephesians 2:14).*

With all this in mind - who would willingly dare to be so casual or caviler in their attitude towards the Holy Spirit? Ignorance can be the only cause; including deception and false teaching that has always dogged and hindered believers in their perception of Him. Our adversary works overtime to ensure this dull perception, knowing better than we just how potent we would be if fully surrendered to the Holy Spirit.

There is a huge difference throughout church history between Christians who walked with the Holy Spirit and those who didn't - quite simply they lacked essential power! Still today we have a choice whether to be "thrilled, filled, or spilled." In other words, mere excitement *(being thrilled)* counts for nothing compared to being fully surrendered *(filled)* and used *(spilled)* by Him!

Nevertheless those who struggle to know the Holy Spirit personally are chiefly those who struggle to see Him as a personality. It is usually the religious folks who have the most difficulty with this!

Nevertheless a definition of personality *(on a human level at least)* refers in general to a complexity of attributes such as; behavioural, temperamental, emotional and mental - that help characterize the uniqueness of an individual. Whereas a more simple definition of personality refers to "person-like-qualities," such as: the ability to talk and to listen *(a.k.a. "the ability to communicate")* to think and to reason; to feel and to have emotions; decision-making and free will.

Personality unmistakably Verified

When broken down like this - especially in reference to the Holy Spirit - it becomes abundantly clear that He does indeed have a person-ality - that of which is unmistakably verified throughout scripture.

For example: Jesus and Paul both continually referred to the Holy Spirit as "He," not "It" *(John 14:16, 17, 26; 15:26; 16:7, 8, 13, 14).* Then our opening scripture refers continually to His "personage" John 16:13; "Howbeit when **He**, the Spirit of truth, is come, **He** will guide you into all truth: for **He** shall not speak of **Himself**; but whatsoever **He** shall hear, that shall **He** speak: and **He** will show you things to come. **He** shall glorify Me..."

Luke 2:26 sees Him "speaking" to man, "...it was revealed unto him by the Holy Ghost" and in various scriptures from both Old and New Testaments, specific qualities of His character are well pointed out: **Goodness** (Nehemiah 9:20; Galatians 5:22, 23); **Holiness** (Romans 1:4); **Truth** (John 14:17; 15:26; 16:13); **Grace** (Hebrews 10:29; Zechariah 12:10); **Comfort** (John 14:26; 15:26); **Patience, Love, Gentleness**, etc. (Galatians 5:22, 23).

Most significantly the Holy Spirit is "one with God" *(Isaiah 48:16; Matthew 28:19; Acts 5:3, 4; 1 Corinthians 3:16; 6:19; 12:4-6; 2 Corinthians 13:14; 1 John 5:7).* Therefore He has all the attributes of God - He is eternal *(Hebrews 9:14).* He was present with God in the creation of the world *(Genesis 1:2, 3; Job 26:13; 33:4; Psalms 104:30).* He is "omnipresent" *(Psalms 139:7-10).* He is "omniscient" *(Isaiah 40:13; 1 Corinthians 2:10, 11).* He is "omnipotent" *(Psalms 104:30).*

Yet He is a distinct personality apart from both the Father and the Son. Besides that, scripture uses many types of symbols to describe His many functions and responsibilities including many Old Testament scriptures that identify Him *(Isaiah 11:2; 42:1; 48:16; 61:1; 63:9; Ezekiel 36:26, 27).* So as far as scripture is concerned the Holy Spirit is undeniably a "personality" and a very powerful one at that!

The Crux of Problem

Consequently those who lack revelation of God's Word will be the ones who struggle to relate to Him. They will posses limited perception of who the Spirit of God is; for example an impersonal "power" or "force" such as electricity!

This impersonal view of Him is the crux of their problem. And while there are "mystical" and "ancient philosophies" that present a plethora of "counterfeit-personalities" for folks to "relate to" - they are no more than cleverly designed plans that appeal to the "spiritual curiosity" of millions who are completely distracted and beguiled from the real McCoy.

Every believer however must eliminate any obstacle that hinders their fellowship with the Holy Spirit and not be duped by religious doctrines or the infiltration of worldly philosophies - which are equally misleading!

For instance it could be said that mainline evangelical Christianity has no problem with the doctrine of the Trinity but their challenge comes with this issue of relating to the Holy Spirit on a personal level. Until this is resolved, fellowship with Him will always be disputed; meaning that many will fail to give Him the place that He truly deserves. The Word and the Holy Spirit must be working in conjunction in our lives, without which we have no revelation and our endeavours will be Godless!

To continue, both Old and New Testaments report the work of the Spirit extensively. "This is the word of the LORD to Zerubbabel: 'Not by might nor by power, but by My Spirit,' says the LORD of hosts" *(Zechariah 4:6 NKJV)*.

> *I will pour out My Spirit on all flesh; your sons and your daughters shall prophesy, your old men shall dream dreams, your young men shall see visions. And also on my menservants and on My maidservants I will pour out My Spirit in those days.*
>
> *(Joel 2:28-29 NKJV)*

Jesus was anointed with the Holy Spirit *(Acts 10:38)* and led by the Spirit to be tempted by Satan and returned in the power of the Spirit *(Luke 4:1-2, 14)*. Jesus cast out evil spirits by the Holy Spirit *(Matthew 12:28)*.

In fact, it would not be incorrect to suggest that the entire ministry of our Lord, was influenced by and "one" with the anointing of the Holy Spirit. Jesus Himself qualified this by saying,

Mandate for Fellowship with God's Spirit

> *The Spirit of the Lord is upon me, because he hath anointed me to preach the gospel to the poor; he hath sent me to heal the broken hearted, to preach deliverance to the captives, and recovering of sight to the blind, to set at liberty them that are bruised, To preach the acceptable year of the Lord.*
> *(Luke 4:18-19 KJV)*

Once we master this continual fellowship with the Holy Spirit, as believers we will also enjoy the intimate bond of fellowship, which binds us together in Christ. There is also fellowship with the Father and the Son as seen here in 1 John 1:3 AMP,

> *What we have seen and [ourselves] heard, we are also telling you, so that you too may realize and enjoy fellowship as partners and partakers with us. And [this] fellowship that we have [which is a distinguishing mark of Christians] is with the Father and with His Son Jesus Christ (the Messiah).*

Then also in 1 Corinthians 1:9 it speaks of specific fellowship with the Son; "God is faithful *(reliable, trustworthy, and therefore ever true to His promise, and He can be depended on);* by Him you were called into companionship and participation with His Son, Jesus Christ our Lord."

One yet Three

However as ONE yet THREE - Father, Son and Spirit - remain very distinct personalities. Even though our fellowship is with all of them our emphasis remains the Holy Spirit and the following list of sins that are directly hostile to the person and ministry of the Holy Spirit, must be avoided by anyone seeking to cultivate a genuine fellowship with Him.

- **Grieving Him:** (Ephesians 4:30) by adopting behaviour contrary to the fruits; bitterness, unforgiveness, etc.
- **Quenching Him:** (1 Thessalonians 5:19) by disallowing the gifts and anointing to work through our lives
- **Insulting Him:** (Hebrews 10:29) through deliberate sin even after receiving knowledge of truth
- **Resisting Him:** (Acts 7:51) going in the opposite direction to the definite guidance of the Spirit
- **Vexing Him:** (Isaiah 63:10) through intentional rebellion against His leadership
- **Lying to Him:** (Acts 5:3) by speaking untruths to His anointed men and women in order to deceive
- **Testing Him:** (Acts 5:9) by provoking Him into action - not out of faith but out of fear
- **Blaspheming Him:** (Matthew 12:31, 32) by attributing the things of Him to demons
- **Striving with Him:** (Genesis 6:3) by walking in the flesh continually against His promptings
- **Rebelling against Him:** (Psalms 106:33) by refusing His instructions

As believers our lives are supernatural. Our fallen natures continue to rage against us *(Galatians 5:16; Romans 7:14-22)* and therefore we continually need to be empowered from within and above in order to live and walk worthy of our calling.

Our Lord explained that the Spirit will guide us into all truth and give us ability to cope with life and its stresses.

Mandate for Fellowship with God's Spirit

With a cultivated lifestyle that is one with Him, we can avoid doctrinal pitfalls and the trickery of our adversary by trusting our "Paraclete" to outwit him *(1 Peter 5:8; John 16:12-13).*

Sensitivity comes via spending time in His presence and is the only way that we can gain firsthand knowledge and gain the skills of detection that we need concerning what grieves and pleases Him moment by moment. Gradually we experience growth in all these areas, the awkwardness flees and a fluent relationship emerges with maturity.

Finally possibly most importantly, as we have an "abandoned devotion" towards God's Word - devouring scripture and making it the final word on every issue - also means that we will always respect the authority of the Spirit who never speaks or gives instruction contrary to the Word.

All in all we eventually find ourselves enjoying His company above all else which finally determines that we have cultivated such a passion for Him, that counts the passions of this world as dung! *(Philippians 3:8)*

Notes

1. Ekman, Ulf. The Prophetic Ministry. Copyright © 1990. Published by Word of Life Publications. Printed in Sweden. p.35

2. Hamon, Bill. Apostles, Prophets and the Coming Moves of God. Copyright © 1997. Published by Destiny Image Publishers, Inc. Printed in USA. p.53

3. Bevere, John. Thus Saith the Lord? Copyright © 1999. Published by Creation House, A Division of Strang Communications Company. Printed in USA. p.120

4. Strong, James. S.T.D., L.L.D. 1890. Strong's Exhaustive Concordance; Dictionaries of the Hebrew and Greek Words. e-Sword ® version 7.6.1 Copyright © 2000-2005. All Rights Reserved. Registered trade mark of Rick Meyers. Equipping Ministries Foundation. USA www.e-sword.net. #G2206

5. Mohabir, Philip. Hands of Jesus. Copyright © 2003. Published by Powerhouse Publishing. Printed in Denmark. p.24, 28-29

6. Strong's Exhaustive Concordance. #G1983

7. Gordon, Bob, and David Fardouly. Master Builders. Copyright © 1990. Published by Sovereign World. Printed in England. p.155-156

Bible Translations:

- Unless otherwise indicated, all scriptural quotations are from the HOLY BIBLE, NEW INTERNATIONAL VERSION ®. NIV ®. Copyright © 1973, 1978, 1984 by the International Bible Society. Used by permission of Zondervan Publishing House. All rights reserved.

- Scripture references marked AMP are taken from The Amplified Bible. Old Testament copyright © 1965, 1987 by Zondervan Corporation, Grand Rapids, Michigan. New Testament copyright © 1958, 1987 by The Lockman Foundation, La Habra, California. All rights reserved.

- Scripture quotations marked AV are taken from the American King James Version.

- Scripture references marked GW are taken from GOD'S WORD®, © 1995 God's Word to the Nations. Used by permission of Baker Publishing Group.

- Scripture references marked KJV are taken from the King James Version of the bible.

- Scripture references marked MSG are taken from The Message. Copyright © 1993, 1994, 1995, 1996, 2000, 2001, 2002. Used by permission of NavPress Publishing Group.

- Scripture references marked NKJV are taken from the New King James Version. Copyright © 1982 by Thomas Nelson, 1982 by Thomas Nelson, Inc. Used by permission. All rights reserved.

- Scripture references marked YLT are taken from the Young's Literal Translation of the bible.

Part Three

PREPARATIONS FOR MINISTRY

CHAPTER 25

Apostolic Pitfalls

Many abort their destiny by catching a glimpse of their future by running off in pursuit in the wrong season of development. They often quote God as being their strength, source and provision but they soon come to realise that something seriously is not working out. One becomes isolated, then discouragement hits.

Remember for these individuals, they have forsaken everything including the God given relationships that God intended to use to increase them. Of course they end up in the recycle tray waiting for God then to reconnect them so that they can get back on the road to what they regard as their destiny.

Fatherlessness vs. Fulfilment

Do we want to "father" when we have never been sons?
(John 8:38; Galatians 4:1-7)

> *Children, obey your parents IN the Lord, for this is right. "Honour your father and mother" – which is the first commandment with a promise – "that it may go well with you and that you may enjoy long life on the earth."*
>
> *(Ephesians 6:1-3)*

As I was thinking about the above scripture, it became obvious to me that for us who are in the ministry – *that there are many trying to be successful* - and yet not fulfilling the vision that is in their hearts. **I call this the pigpen mentality.** For many have wandered from their spiritual fathers, and decided to leave their spiritual homes *(churches)* and look to spend their spiritual inheritance *(anointing)* without a father's care.

This has resulted in frustration and discouragement. The *pigpen* is a place of shame and self-condemnation where no one is able to meet your need for love and intimacy. Who can fulfil that deep desire to be fulfilled with the intimacy that only can come from God? But this comes through spiritual fathers and mothers not even your natural spouse can fulfil that need.

> *Now when he had spent everything, a severe famine occurred in that country, and he began to be in need. And he went and attached himself to one of the citizens of that country, and he sent him into the fields to feed swine. And*

he was longing to fill his stomach with the pods that the swine were eating, and no one was giving anything to him.
(Luke 15:14-16 NASB)

It was not long after the son began to **_devalue_** the relationship that he had with his father that he left his father's house and began to seek wrong answers for right needs for love and intimacy.

In a 1998 interview with Rick Knoth, managing editor of the Assemblies of God Enrichment Journal, Promise Keepers Founder and President Bill McCartney stated that they had researched and found that 62 per cent of Christian men admitted to struggles with sexual sin – pornography, adultery and sensuality. When Christians value the Father more for what He can do for them than for intimacy and love, they eventually begin to seek to fulfil their own selfish desires rather than walk in intimacy with God.

In order to fill the void that has been created, they may begin to pursue one or more counterfeit affections – passions of the flesh, power, possessions or position.

The question must be asked:

- Who is your spiritual father?
- Openness, transparency, and honesty: can you share these qualities with someone you consider your spiritual leader?
- Can you accept admonition and correction from them?
- Do you have a healthy relationship with a local church and its leadership?

- Who is your spiritual parent?
- Can you call yourself a daughter or a son?
- Whose child are you?

Without the spirit of sonship your inheritance is made very difficult. There's no comfort for the fatherless, only isolation and abandonment.

What is an Orphan Spirit?

Are you trying to earn acceptance, or can you rest in your sonship? Are you a servant who earns or the son who rests? Locate yourself, because servants lead like masters! Sons emulate their father's love. Intimate relationship is not necessary to those who seek only the *"position"* of leadership. Without this intimacy in relationship – abuse can occur.

Leadership operating in organizational authority void of relationship – leaves people feeling used, frustrated and induces rebellion.

Leading from the father/son perspective gives first place to relationship above protocol. "My son, I live for our relationship – where I can meet your needs, watching your growth and development. <u>Go beyond my highest achievements and do more than I ever did.</u>" – A son watches his father and reproduces after the same kind. Careful not to grieve his father, the son will prepare himself with fidelity of heart, securing his inheritance.

From the son's perspective, he must be willing to lay down his dreams for the dreams of the father – trusting God for his inheritance.

Delinquent Fathers vs. Responsible Fathers

FATHER... Noun, *patër (πατήρ, 3962), from a root signifying* **"a nourisher, protector, upholder"** *(Lat, pater, Eng., "father," are akin).* Is used:

(a) of the nearest ancestor, e.g., Matthew 2:22;

(b) of a more remote ancestor, the progenitor of the people, a *"forefather,"* e.g., Matthew 3:9; 23:30; 1 Corinthians 10:1; the patriarchs, 2 Peter 3:4;

(c) one advanced in the knowledge of Christ, 1 John 2:13;

(d) metaphorically, of the originator of a family or company of persons animated by the same spirit as himself, as of Abraham, Romans 4:11, 12, 16, 17, 18, or of Satan, John 8:38, 41, 44;

(e) of one who, as a preacher of the gospel and a teacher, stands in a *"father's"* place, caring for his spiritual children.

The Function of "Nourisher, Protector, Upholder"

Moses summoned all the elders of Israel and said to them, "Go at once and select the animals for your families and slaughter the Passover lamb. Take a bunch of hyssop, dip it into the blood in the basin and put some of the blood on the top and on both sides of the doorframe. Not one of you shall go out of the door of his house until morning. When the Lord goes through the land to strike down the Egyptians, he will see the blood on the top and sides of the doorframe and will pass over that doorway, and he will

not permit the destroyer to enter your houses and strike you down.
(Exodus 12:21-23)

This illustrates **the tremendous responsibility of being a father** because the *only* persons in Israel, who could obtain safety and salvation for their people, were *the Fathers of Israel.*

Derek Prince says, **"If the Fathers of Israel had been delinquent, Israel would not have been protected by the Passover."** And goes on to state, "the greatest single social problem that faces us, is delinquent fathers *[slack, neglectful and failing in duty]*… there are no delinquent children; there are only delinquent parents…

All the problems that we are concerned about, abortion drugs the break up of the family, many, many other social evils. I believe if you trace them to their source, their source is *delinquent fathers."*

I have pointed this out to you in this context, because if the fathers had failed; Israel would never have been redeemed. *God's plan depended on the fathers.*

Develop the Spirit of a True Spiritual Parent

True spiritual parents seek to raise up, promote, and send forth sons and daughters who will represent their heart to the nations *(1 Corinthians 4:14-16; 1 Thessalonians 2:7-12).*

True spiritual fathers prioritize relationship over performance, rules, and structure, although there is protocol.

Godly character manifests through a lifestyle of humility and love proved in relationship. Servant-leaders make decisions based upon the benefits and needs of others, not for themselves.

They launch forward into the nations spiritual sons and daughters *(remember discipleships, mentorship is not necessarily sonship)* by helping them to locate, develop and liberate their spiritual gifts and callings. Purity and holiness is the lifestyle outlived before all, having overcome worldly lusts, past hurts, disappointments and obstructions.

True spiritual fathers will provide:

- Security
- Unconditional love and acceptance
- Affirmation
- A sense of purpose and destiny
- Protection
- Role modelling
- Mentoring and equipping
- Responsibility and accountability
- Admonition and correction
- Inheritance – empowerment to go forth to the nations

The Hour is Desperate!

Scott Volk from Fire School of Ministry says, "I hear the younger generation crying out for 'spiritual fathers,' yet, when they're lovingly corrected and biblically rebuked by those very fathers, they write them off as being old-fashioned, traditional, and out of touch with what the Lord is doing in 'their generation.'

Maybe instead of fathers, they really want grandfathers who will simply pat them on the back, offering only grandpa-like encouragement and positive reinforcement.

I hear older men saying that they desire to be 'spiritual fathers,' yet, they're seemingly unwilling to get down in the relational trenches with the very ones that need to be fathered because their ministry schedules are too busy and they have more important things to do. Maybe instead of being spiritual fathers, they really want to be spiritual grandfathers who merely give a thumbs-up when ministry outwardly seems to be going well even though inwardly their grandchild may be withering inside.

Candy Grows on the Carpet

Why is it that children enjoy being around their grandparents? Could it be that at grandpa's house, where candy grows on the carpet and dessert is eaten instead of dinner, life is simply easier? Could it be because at grandpa's house, we can do almost whatever we please since grandpa is really not responsible for disciplining us; he merely desires to keep us happy until we return home?

I want to humbly confront both the generation that is crying out for fathers as well as the generation that says they desire to be fathers, with this simple challenge: it's time to step up to the plate. It's time that our words become something more than spiritual rhetoric. It's time for spiritual wayward sons to honour their fathers and it's time for spiritual deadbeat fathers to change their ways and assume the role that God intended them to have in their spiritual households.

We're living in a generation that is desperate to see the fulfilment of the Malachi 4 scripture that proclaims,

> *He will turn the hearts of the fathers to their children, and the hearts of the children to their fathers; or else I will come and strike the land with a curse.*

It requires a turning on both parties – fathers *turning* to their children and children turning to their fathers. Now more than ever, when biblical standards are being compromised in the name of successful ministries, we need the fathers to lovingly put their arms around their children and guide them into all truth.

Now more than ever, as young people are being commissioned by the word of the Lord, we need to turn to the fathers, lest our youthful zeal and heavenly calling lead us into dangerous areas of pride and arrogance, eventuating in colossal failure and shame.

I believe we're at a desperate hour and that the Lord desires to seize it for His glory. Fathers, let's commit ourselves, by God's grace, to allowing our hearts to be turned to our children; children, let's commit ourselves, by God's grace, to allowing our hearts to be turned to our fathers.

Then and only then will the curse of Malachi 4:6 be avoided" (http://www.fire-school.org).

CHAPTER 26

Promoting the Lord or Self?

There are certain individuals today who assume that they are in leadership when in actual fact they have never legitimately qualified for such position; rather born from ego and hidden agenda than the high calling of God!

> *People should think of us as servants of Christ and managers who are entrusted with God's mysteries. Managers are required to be trustworthy.*
> (1 Corinthians 4:1-2 GW)

So how do we recognise such individuals without starting a witch-hunt! Well they are really quite easy to spot but having said that, what is obvious to the trained eye is not necessarily obvious to the untrained and therefore spiritually vulnerable.

To begin with they are made up of the type of individuals who have for one reason or another been around the church world for many years and have a good grip on Christian "jargon" and "philosophy" yet more out of "head knowledge" and "learnt-behaviour" than from a genuine "living connection" with God! They come to believe that they have in some way been automatically chosen to be a *voice* to the church!

Qualifications and Insights

They even suppose that they have some sort of special "supernatural qualifications" and are convinced that they have some "special insights" that we all need - along with "special authority" to bring "correction" wherever they feel necessary - even to the entire body at large. So we must not fail to ask them, "Who are you and who has qualified you to be in such position?" Once they open their mouths they usually reveal themselves!

To keep things positive let's look at what qualifies a leader rather than what doesn't. According to scripture, there are two major qualifications for leadership.

- **First** of all there must be fruit; fruit of lifestyle and then fruit of ministry.
- **Secondly** there must be recognition and appointment *(see Acts 5:1-11; 6:1-7; Ephesians 4:11)*. But first we must look for the fruits; it's okay having a big mouth, but where is the fruit? Here are some scriptures concerning the "fruit of lifestyle" *(Galatians 5:22; Romans 12:3; 1 Timothy 3:1-f; Titus 1:5-16)*.

Consider our example in this matter; Paul the apostle, who went through years of "testing" once he submitted himself to the leaders at Antioch. *"They must first be tested; and then... let them serve..."* (1 Timothy 3:10) According to this particular scripture, once the "testing" part stops, the "serving" part begins! As Paul found out, this took considerable time.

It remains a fact today that in God's kingdom the way up is always down and the greatest amongst us is the servant of all. It is only the world that glories in arrogance and "ostentatious crowd-pulling" *(entertaining never qualified anyone for leadership!)*

Flamboyant or Humble

Someone with a servant's heart is not *showy or flamboyant* but humble. This is a good sign of leadership quality. In fact, for anyone who has genuinely been called to a leadership position within the body of Christ, one of **the first things that the Holy Spirit is going to deal with is ...*ego!***

Yet as first mentioned above, certain individuals have the ability to "learn behaviour" that seems to be humble when in actual fact it is known as "false-humility." Perhaps we have become so familiar with the false that we no longer recognise the true. True humility is *often* misinterpreted.

Therefore we MUST be led by the Spirit, without Him we are spiritually dull and cannot see. We have eyes to see and yet cannot see; ears to hear but cannot hear. Only the Holy Spirit can REVEAL all truth to us and keep us spiritually alert *(John 16:13)*.

He is the Father's complete provision for us - so that we cannot be so easily misled. But if we choose to walk without Him, to be vulnerable and spiritually ignorant, then no one can be blamed but ourselves! Yet we are meant to be "Over-Comers" in Christ, not gullible or easily led astray, but spiritual laziness is often the cause of dullness *(see apostasy)*.

Now let us emphasise once again the fact that all potential leaders are "separated" or "set apart" by God *(it is never a **natural** selection; as seen in 1 Samuel 16:7)* and this "separation" actually means *"chosen."* Jesus Himself said, *"Many are called, but few are chosen..." (Matthew 22:14 KJV)*, meaning that not many make it through the *"testing"* part! Yet the few who do are successfully "separated" unto the Lord *(so not everyone who claims to be a leader, is one!)*

While many want the name-tag of "leadership" not many want the "costs" or "associated risks!" And while the "separating process" was never intended to be easy, according to scripture, anyone caught "shortcutting" is not legitimate! *(John 10:7; Matthew 7:13)*

Offices and Positions of Service

There are "offices" and "positions of service" mentioned in the bible, *(1 Corinthians 12:28)*. *"And God has appointed these in the church: first apostles, second prophets, third teachers, after that ... helps..." (NKJV)* Once again notice that during those first years in Antioch Paul did *not* occupy a "fivefold-office" *(see Ephesians 4:11)* but instead served in the ministry of helps, only then did he progress to the office of "teacher" *(see 2 Timothy 1:11; Acts 13:1)*.

Promoting the Lord or Self?

In Acts 13:1-2 we can see how Paul was listed along with other teachers in Antioch and how the Holy Spirit wanted them to be specifically "separated" unto Him. The appointed time had finally come, the one who had been called to be an apostle all those years earlier on the road to Damascus in Acts 9:15 had finally, after possibly 14 years of testing and loyal service, been successfully "separated" unto God to be an apostle.

First he was **"called"** then served in **"helps,"** then he progressed to the office of a **"teacher"** and finally the office of an **"apostle."** Why? The reason: Paul was faithful to promote the Lord and not himself *(see 1 Corinthians 4:2).*

Chapter 27

Your Destiny is Developed in Adullam

God has prepared a company of people with an anointing, to see breakthroughs in their own lives as well as in cities and nations. Many of these people are the most unlikely in the natural to be chosen by the Lord. How He loves to take the least likely and demonstrate His ability through them!

David was one of those "unlikely" people that God used to accomplish colossal breakthroughs. Just as the church is stepping into a new season, David came forth at a time when the Lord was transitioning His people from an old religious order *(Eli)* to a fresh new move of His Spirit *(David)*. Whenever God brings His people to a major juncture in history, He always raises up prophets to declare it.

The prophet Samuel stood at a major juncture in history and poured the anointing oil on young David. He declared a new authority was arising to defeat the powers of the enemy and release the will of God in the earth. "Then Samuel took the horn of oil and anointed him in the midst of his brothers; and the Spirit of the Lord came mightily upon David from that day forward..." *(1 Samuel 16:13 NASB)*

And such as do wickedly against the covenant shall he corrupt by flatteries: but the people that do know their God shall be strong, and do exploits.
(Daniel 11:32 KJV)

David's first Anointing

David received his **"first anointing"** in the midst of his own brothers. In an *obscure* place God chose an unlikely individual to accomplish great kingdom exploits *(Daniel 11:32)*. Unfortunately those close to David didn't embrace such an anointing on his life!

As with David, there are people who have known you in the old season of your life. Some of them will try to hold you to an old place, familiar to them. They want you to do the same things you did in the old season. They might enjoy your company but **don't want to go where you are going.**

After David received this "first anointing," he came face to face with the giant Goliath. **The enemy loves to challenge the new anointing in your life.** He doesn't want you to move forward. However, war was not new to David. He had defeated the lion and the bear during the old season. Now he faced the enemy that was resisting David's destiny. An incredible courage rose up in David as he asked the question, "Is there not a cause?" *(1 Samuel 17:29 KJV)*

David was not in the battle for his own benefit. He realized there was a cause at stake, the advancement of God's kingdom in the earth. Those who will be part of the Davidic Company that God is raising up in this hour must be free from fears and selfish interests. It is a time when fears must be replaced with great courage! During this time, we must deal with insecurities, intimidation, limitations, and jealous spirits. All of these are designed to keep this Davidic Company from God's destiny.

After David's "first anointing," he ended up in a dark place. "So David departed from there and escaped to the cave of Adullam; and when his brothers and all his father's household heard of it, they went down there to him" *(1 Samuel 22:1 NASB)*.

Darkness, Obscurity and Confusion

Adullam was a place of darkness, obscurity and confusion. God's future generals often find themselves in obscure places. However, in the dark place of Adullam, David found a place of prayer. **As the seed of destiny dies, we learn that God is our only hope.** In the times of weakness, the Lord becomes our strength *(2 Corinthians 12:9)*.

During David's hour of unpopularity, he discovered whom the people were that would stand with him. Real friends are committed to you in the good and the hard times. Only those who have true heart connections will stand with you in difficult days. The body of Christ is in a time when we will know those whose hearts are knitted to our hearts.

God gathered around David those who were discontented, and those in debt *(1 Samuel 22:2)*. From a small number of unlikely people, God brought forth from the cave a powerful army of 340,000 recruits! The hidden place became a place of multiplication.

Second Anointing and Praise

Today, God is assembling His army. God's Army is made up of those generals who have been in a hidden place in the last season. Their hearts have been knitted together to see King Jesus exalted in the earth. They have come forth with the anointing at Judah. David received his **"second anointing"** at Judah. Judah means praise. **Praise will be a key to victory.**

The seed of destiny in these lives that seemed dead is coming forth now in resurrection life and power! David received his **"third anointing"** at Hebron. Hebron was a place of alliance. It was the place of making commitments, entering relationships and cutting covenants. As a result of these alliances, David and his army was able to take back ground the enemy had stolen.

They were able to declare that God is the God of the Breakthrough. "So David came to Baal-parazim and defeated them there; and he said, *'The Lord has broken through my enemies before me like the breakthrough of waters.'* Therefore he named that place Baal-perazim" *(2 Samuel 5:20 NASB)*.

God is gathering a powerful group of people in these days. Lives are joining together in covenant relationships. Ministries are aligned to see the kingdom of God advance through the earth. Many of the ministries have been in Adullam in the past season. However, they are being properly aligned so the seed of destiny in them is released to accomplish great kingdom exploits.

Destiny has a time for fulfilment. **Great courage will be needed as we embrace our destiny.** These are days when we will see new enemies. Old war strategies and independent spirits will not be able to stand against these enemies.

A synergistic alliance of powerful visionary ministries is emerging as a Davidic Army for the new season. They are anointed for powerful breakthrough in cities, territories and nations. Their testimony proclaims, *"Jesus is God of the Breakthrough!"*

CHAPTER 28

The Strength of the Anointing

T he Bride of Christ, can she handle the strength of her own anointing? Are we fighting the Holy Spirit and not even aware of it...? "Against You, You only, have I sinned" *(Psalm 51:4)*.

Can we contain and understand the season that we are in? Some time ago, I was watching **Billy Brim** on TV in the UK, who was being interviewed in front of a live audience. They were discussing the anointing of the last days to be poured out upon the body of Christ before Jesus returns.

Mention was made to the effect that if the Lord had poured out the kind of anointing upon the church that He plans to before Christ is able to return, then it would most certainly have wiped many people out because the church is still not yet adequately prepared.

People have to be brought to that place where they can handle the anointing and it not kill them, as in the case of Ananias and Sapphira *(Acts 5:5)*.

People aren't going to get away with some of the things they may have got away with up to now in the church. **The apostolic anointing is currently being restored to the church with the strength of the anointing that existed on the apostles in the early church.** If people come against that anointing they will find themselves fighting the Holy Spirit.

I believe this apostolic move of the end times will restore the true FEAR OF GOD back into the church. To be found fighting, resisting or even lying to almighty God is never good! And when we do find ourselves in that position, we usually cause ourselves much unnecessary harm!

Sin directed against the Holy Spirit

David possessed such revelation, as seen in Psalm 51:4 where he is quoted as saying to the Lord, **"Against thee, thee only, have I sinned"** *(KJV)*. This helps to reveal that when Ananias and his wife *lied*, such sin was not directed against the apostles but against the very person of the Holy Spirit. Just think how many people sin against the Holy Spirit and don't even recognize it!

However in their particular case, I do personally believe that the purity of the Holy Spirit and the wickedness of their own hearts caused such a conflict inside of them that it killed them. They could not stand in the presence of a Holy God and we must understand that this sort of thing may begin happening again, as part of the restoration of the apostolic.

The Strength of the Anointing

*O worship the LORD in the beauty of holiness: **fear** before him, all the earth.*

(Psalm 96:9 KJV)

There must be **holiness** in the body of Christ. Jesus is coming back for a bride without spot or wrinkle and without adultery in her heart for the world and her beauty will be as the scripture says, "**...the beauty of Holiness.**" While there are *many* unclean spirits in this world, there is only one **HOLY** Spirit!

The nations once again will posses a fear for the children of God, for the **true unadulterated power in the church of the end times.** Just as in the days of the early church, God will display His power through the apostolic ministry. Even though many will be unprepared and not able to handle such an anointing, it MUST be intensified *(the anointing that is)* before Jesus returns.

Billy Brim continued, "**...as much as the anointing is powerful to create, it is as powerfully destructive of evil.**" Holiness will show up wickedness in the hearts of men.

Think of it like this, when Jesus turned the water into wine at the wedding feast, what kind of powerful reaction went on inside of those jars *(atomic)* and yet it didn't shatter them! **We as the church have got to be able to contain the anointing without it shattering us!**

Resisting the Anointing

To grieve the Holy Spirit is a serious offense and not something to be taken lightly. Apostles are human vessels chosen by God - capable of making mistakes - but the anointing they carry is sacred. God carefully prepares them and we can see this if we carefully study the lives of Paul and the other apostles.

Many end time apostles are walking the earth again, so dead to self, so yielded to obeying Jesus and so perfected in the love walk that the authority they have is unparalleled. Nations are listening to them because God has granted them a genuine "VOICE" that can be heard.

Apostles are greatly opposed but they have the anointing and the help of the Holy Spirit to handle it. *The world is not worthy of them!* The world reacts to them in every way. They live in a perpetual position of vulnerability and yet of great influence! As we saw with Paul, he was never free of temptation or trials but was a powerfully anointed vessel that carried holy *revelations* directly from almighty God.

Don't Kill the Apostle

In the end times, people will carry such anointing, as we have never seen before. **Many will fail to understand and even become "offended."** The reality is that most people don't know how to recognize true anointing; therefore many will find themselves resisting God in these days!

People found themselves wanting to kill Paul without any concept of who or what he really was. They often rose up in violent opposition against him, but were completely ignorant of the true presence and force of God within him. Everywhere he went somebody or something wanted to kill him! So we must not be surprised at the violent reactions that some people will experience - especially when they come up against this apostolic anointing in the wrong way.

> *Saying, Touch not mine anointed, and do my prophets no harm.*
> *(1 Chronicles 16:22; Psalm 105:15 KJV)*

David had a revelation about not touching God's anointed. Even when tempted to *retaliate*, he always resisted. When Saul's behaviour was at its worst, David still recognized the anointing that was upon his king and would not touch Saul. *(This is a healthy **none-negotiable** for us all!)*

During the famous encounter in the cave that Saul visited in order to *relieve* himself, David had the perfect opportunity to kill or capture Saul. He could have said, **"Oh Lord... thank you for finally delivering this wretched man into my hands!"** Instead David did *not* judge the situation by the standards of his flesh but by the revelation of God in his heart, concerning the anointing. Oh how we need this revelation in the church today.

Be Found Walking

It's no small thing to be found resisting or grieving the Holy Spirit. Even though we are heirs of salvation and have the revelation of Jesus Christ, we must still be found walking with the Holy Spirit and by His holiness, especially in these last days!

The world needs to see the church living and walking in the miraculous supernatural power of the resurrection.

THE AGE OF APOSTOLIC APOSTLESHIP

But I say, walk and live [habitually] in the [Holy] Spirit [responsive to and controlled and guided by the Spirit]; then you will certainly not gratify the cravings and desires of the flesh [of human nature without God].
(Galatians 5:16 AMP)

Chapter 29

Humanism vs. The Spirit of God

I warn everyone who hears the words of the prophecy in this book: If anyone adds anything to this, God will strike him... If anyone takes away any words from this book of prophecy, God will take away his portion of the tree of life... *(Revelation 22:18-19 GW)*

Admittedly this focus on "leadership seduction" may seem slightly negative, but a subject that must be addressed nonetheless and always better tackled than left. After all, a lot of us have encountered these types of people who either don't want to change or are completely ignorant that anything is wrong.

Nevertheless we still have the option of heaping up many teachers to tickle our ears as scripture puts it, with tastefully designed and politically correct teachings that only address what we want to hear. Yet avoiding all things negative is not wise and keeps us shallow and uninformed. Awareness *(not conspiracy theory)* prevents spiritual threats, which arrive on the doorstep of *every* church group or ministry. No one is immune; *ask me how I know!*

So to continue, yes - bogus leaders without qualification or recognition hate to be challenged; yet challenge is precisely what reveals their false anointing. They are easily threatened. True anointing attracts trouble, it comes with the territory. But these individuals have a hatred for all things *"challenge"* or *"change"* because they reveal insecurity and weakness like nothing else.

I believe that the Holy Spirit uses change in order to teach us, and sometimes it may even seem that the only "constant" in life is change! It keeps us fresh and unstuck. Change is not synonymous with crisis as some folks treat it. And it helps to keep in mind that our behaviour in the first moments of a crisis reveals who and what we truly believe.

Character Assassination is another Trait

Many of us have had our integrity questioned and it's never pleasant. Generally it doesn't stop with us either but also affects our families, our marriages and every area possible... *(Especially if we are leaders)*. However it is the accuser of the brethren who does this. But there is balance to everything and leaders must not use this as a clock to cover everything by saying, *"...don't question me about anything..."* No! We must remain accountable to our flock, to each other and to the word.

Bogus leaders never enhance unity and leave a trail of separation and disunity in their wake, of marriages, associates, and friends; even longstanding relationships, all left in tatters (see Proverbs 16:28). They don't co-habit and when they have the opportunity they specialize in rescuing and then despising!

Falsehood, *(2 Corinthians 11:4, 26)*. The bible speaks of many falsehoods such as false brethren, false apostles, false spirits, false doctrines and false prophets, to name a few. The point is this, **there is a counterfeit to anything that has an original!** For example we never get to see counterfeit $30 dollar bills or £9 pound notes, simply because there was never an original!

Uncanny ability to Misread

False brethren for instance are those who consistently find something to make an accusation about. They are not unlike false witnesses except they shout about stuff they do witness but don't like! And there's nothing much they do like! The humanism that steers them is not of the Spirit of God; they have the uncanny ability to totally misread everything!

They easily make a controversy over anything and seek to correct their leaders by saying, *"We don't want to undermine you, BUT..."* Usually these same people have such delicate consciences (no faith) that they use this to manipulate their leaders to pass everything by them first; to the effect that nothing happens without their approval!

What all these people struggle with - is *humanism* - more often than not they exalt psychology, science of the mind rather than the very word of God. In fact false leaders love to quote more from their psychology books than from scripture; yet quote just enough scripture to keep it convincing! They offer a complete mix. Mixing the word with anything is dangerous, because it must be kept pure, unadulterated and defined as the true word of God.

Even though psychology has its place, though limited, it certainly must not be mixed with the word of God; especially where people don't know the difference! To qualify this let me say the following: If people insist on using psychology, they must define it as such and not mix it with - add it to - or - mistake it for - the word of God, because pretty soon people in general won't be able to recognise the difference.

The Mind in its Fallen-State

Besides - psychology only applies to the "fallen mind" not to the "renewed mind." Those born of the Spirit know their mind is being renewed by the word of God daily. Psychology only studies the mind in its fallen-state but it cannot renew anything! Humanistic reasoning's must not be added to God's word (see Revelation 22:18).

Clearly not everyone who claims to be genuine and led by the Spirit is what they say they are. However scripture gives us one main source of evidence to prove or disprove the genuine from the bogus - "FRUIT." Its presence or absence speaks volumes. If any of us truly walk by His Spirit, there will always be evidence to prove it! There is always evidence to the life of the Spirit. Tongues for example is evidence of the baptism, fruit is the evidence of the Spirit led life. Whether it is fruit of character or of ministry, there is *always* fruit where the Holy Spirit resides.

Finally, even though we have looked into the behaviour of the false and bogus - none of this is personal or aimed at flesh and blood, rather spiritual forces that are opposed, hostile or anti-Christ (anti-anointing, anti-truth, anti-righteousness!) The anointing breaks every yoke of bondage, which takes genuine authority!

Remember that where the counterfeit can only question Christ, the true anointing reveals Him.

CHAPTER 30

Divination and the Python Spirit

Felt under spiritual attack lately? Well here's a passage that helps describe the kind of spiritual attack we've all been experiencing.

As we were on our way to the place of prayer (church), we were met by a slave girl who was possessed by a spirit of divination (python - see KJV) [claiming to foretell future events and to discover hidden knowledge], and she brought her owners much gain by her fortunetelling. She kept following Paul and [the rest of] us, shouting loudly, These men are the servants of the Most High God! They announce to you the way of salvation! And she did this for many days. Then Paul, being sorely annoyed and worn out, turned and said to the spirit within her, I charge you

in the name of Jesus Christ to come out of her! And it came out that very moment.
(Acts 16:16-18 AMP)

Firstly notice that this was not a spirit of stealth and seduction but of harassment and pestering torment. Divination or python, exposes, provokes, discredits, humiliates and even bankrupts. Notice how it did not just target Paul but his entire apostolic company, "...she kept following Paul **and [the rest of] us,** shouting loudly."

Unpleasant Mental State

Folks, as part of Christ's apostolic company (see Hebrews 3:1 KJV) we too are the targets for such harassment, designed to sorely annoy and wear us out. We know this because it goes on to say, "She did this for **many days.** Then Paul, **sorely annoyed and worn out** turned and said..." According to the dictionary the word "annoyance" refers to an unpleasant mental state that is characterized by such effects as irritation and distraction... and can lead to emotions such as frustration and anger. It refers to the act of making unwelcome intrusions upon another.

The Greek for "grieved" as used in the King James Version (instead of annoyed) means: "to manage with pains, accomplish with great labour; to be troubled, displeased, **offended**, pained and **to be worked up.**"[1]

Perhaps Paul was not on best form after "many days" of such annoying harassment. Plus the original language confirms that it was just "a young female slave" who got under his skin *(annoyed him so much!)* Her masters weren't interested in harassing Paul - there was no money in it for them - she even lost them money. Instead she locked target with Paul *(and the others)* and wouldn't let go - until Paul put an end to it.

Never Take Spiritual Warfare Personally

What's puzzling is, why did Paul take so long to respond? I would suggest to you, that the devil wants us to react to everything and to take *everything* personally. Paul on the other hand knew that she was just a "servant girl." I want to remind you, that it's never a good time to take things personally; especially in spiritual warfare, we are all prone to this! It's hard sometimes because the devil uses people.

Still this spiritual-struggle that we are in, is never against *people*. "Our struggle is **not against flesh and blood,** but against the rulers, against the authorities, against the powers of this dark world and against the spiritual forces of evil in the heavenly realms" (Ephesians 6:12 NIV; John 17:14-16 KJV).

Once we start taking things personally, we have lost the plot completely. Self-preservation makes us lose our focus and our purpose (Christ's agenda was never self preservation). Self-preservation - always motivates us - out of the will of God. We become defensive and our sensitivity to God becomes seriously impaired. All spiritual warfare is targeted at Christ (hence anti-Christ) and is therefore never personal. (Remembering this fact can really help prevent the roots of bitterness - see Hebrews 12:15).

However we know that Paul was capable of being led of the Holy Spirit, because of preceding events mentioned earlier in the same chapter. At each major juncture of their travels, we see an interaction between Paul and his apostolic company and the Holy Spirit.

For example it says in the passage below that, "...**they were forbidden by the Holy Spirit** to preach the word in Asia" (right place - wrong time). We also know that Paul was quick to respond to the Holy Spirit's guidance because it says also, "Now after he [Paul] had seen the vision, *immediately* **we** sought to go to Macedonia, **concluding that the Lord had called us to preach the gospel to them."**

> *Now when they had gone through Phrygia and the region of Galatia, they were <u>**forbidden** by the Holy Spirit</u> to preach the word in Asia. After they had come to Mysia, they tried to go into Bithynia, <u>but the Spirit **did not permit** them</u>. So passing by Mysia, they came down to Troas. And <u>a vision appeared to Paul</u> in the night. A man of Macedonia stood and pleaded with him, saying, "Come over to Macedonia and help us." Now <u>after he had seen the vision, **immediately** we sought to go</u> to Macedonia, concluding that the Lord had called us to preach the gospel to them.*
>
> (Acts 16:6-11 NKJV)

So this apostolic company, who were "forbidden" by the Spirit, also knew to "conclude" when they were permitted to preach the gospel in Macedonia. They knew how to be led by the Holy Spirit. With this in mind, are we to believe they missed it, when it came to a mere "servant girl"?

Did Paul (who responded immediately) suddenly become delinquent? Either Paul concluded deliberately to ignore her for many days, then out of mere exhaustion succumb to the frustration of relentless spiritual harassment (Moses also struck the rock twice out of frustration with the people and suffered the consequences). Paul - waiting on the unction of the Holy Spirit (to minister deliverance) only delayed his response - out of a knowledge of the spiritual climate and what sort of trouble it would stir.

When we read accounts like this in the bible, there was so much going on. Our lives are much the same. It takes great discernment to distinguish what's really happening. On a human level, we've all been annoyed and worn out (especially in the ministry!) So whether Paul acted out of frustration and spiritual exhaustion or not, the servant girl was still delivered and Paul's jailer (and household) were saved!

More than Conquerors

Many other miracles occurred also, and I would suggest, that it was because Paul faced and did not run from spiritual warfare. (He knew about Daniel 7:25 and how it was the enemies ploy to wear him out).

The consequences might have seemed heavy, but what were the alternatives, to do nothing or pursue and recover all without fail like David did in 1 Samuel 30: 1-19? If we just lick our wounds we'll lose everything.

However we are more than conquerors, we triumph through Christ, who is greater in us, than he that's in the world! (Romans 8:37; 2 Corinthians 2:14; 1 John 4:4 KJV paraphrased).

Chapter 31

A Work of Sovereign Grace

We are going to be looking at the "grace" needed for our "appointment." Chiefly looking at the life of Paul the apostle, we see that he too needed grace to do what he was appointed to do.

Having gifts (faculties, talents, qualities) that differ according to the grace given us, let us use them.
(Romans 12:6-8 AMP)

So to begin with, the most important fact to remember is that the call-of-God is actually a working of His sovereign-grace, sovereign – because it is His choice to make and His alone! In other words, God does not always call the most likely or the most naturally talented! In fact His choosing is rarely ever popular and all mystery concerning His "calling" or "election," can only be answered within the very heart of God (1 Corinthians 1:27-29).

However as our opening scripture states and as the NIV continues it says, **"We have different gifts, according to the grace given us.** If a man's gift is prophesying, let him use it in proportion to his faith. If it is serving, let him serve; if it is teaching, let him teach; if it is encouraging, let him encourage; if it is contributing to the needs of others, let him give generously; if it is leadership, let him govern diligently; if it is showing mercy, let him do it cheerfully" (Romans 12:6-8).

Gift Discernment

A major weakness concerning our "gift-discernment" tends to have been our lack of understanding concerning the "responsibility" that is involved in our election. In this respect then, natural talents don't add up too much when answering the specific call of God!

This is where stewardship comes into it, as we see Paul mentioning here in 1 Peter 4:10 (AMP) "As each of you has received a gift (a particular spiritual talent, a gracious divine endowment), employ it for one another as [befits] **good trustees** of God's many-sided grace [**faithful stewards** of the extremely diverse powers and gifts granted to Christians by unmerited favour]."

Granted this is a bit of a mouthful in the Amplified and is perhaps better when more simply put, as here in the Authorised Version, "as every man hath received the gift, even so minister the same one to another, **as good stewards of the manifold grace of God**" (KJV).

Nevertheless we see in both these respected versions of the bible the use of the word "steward." God has simply called us to be good-stewards of His grace (authority and ability). Notice we are not stewards of just anything - but specifically of His grace.

To help us define this word steward a little better, let me say the following, **the biblical doctrine of stewardship defines a man's relationship to God. It identifies God as owner and man as manager.** God makes man His "co-worker" in "administering" all aspects of our life. The apostle Paul explains it best by saying, "For we are God's fellow workers; you are God's field, God's building" (1 Corinthians 3:9 NASB). This helps us to better evaluate our position in this life.

Stewardship Defines our Purpose

In essence then, stewardship defines our purpose in this world - as assigned to us by God Himself. It is our divinely given opportunity to join with God in His worldwide and eternal redemptive movement (Matthew 28:19-20). In truth, stewardship is not God "taking" something from us, rather it is His method of bestowing His richest gifts upon His people.

I suggest that the following words best describe this concept of "stewardship" as seen in scripture: manager, foreman, guardian, governor, procurator and administrator (see Galatians 4:1-2 AMP). In fact we see this more contemporary word of "manager" specifically in the "God's Word Translation" of the bible where it says, **"Each of you as a good manager must use the gift that God has given you to serve others"** (1 Peter 4:10 GW).

Clearly then, our faithfulness in managing God's affairs exceeds the traditional boundaries of just managing finances correctly or faithfully paying our tithes and offerings! Paul likens his own calling to that of an "administrator" or "steward" of God's grace. He viewed God like the master of a great household who wisely administrated His affairs through Paul - an obedient servant of Jesus Christ (see Ephesians 3:2 and 1 Corinthians 9:17).

To continue with our focus on **"grace,"** however it is important to notice how often this word "grace" is actually used by Paul in the scriptures: "The **grace God gave me** to be a minister of Christ Jesus" (Romans 15:15-16); "They recognise **the grace given to me**" (Galatians 2:9); "I became a servant of this gospel by the **gift of God's grace** given me" (Ephesians 3:7); "Assuming that you have heard of the **stewardship of God's grace** (His unmerited favour) that was entrusted to me [to dispense to you] for your benefit" (Ephesians 3:2 AMP).

The Grace Given

I believe that Paul constantly referred to "the-grace-given-to-me," simply because he was overcome by the fact that God had not only put **"grace"** into his life, but more specifically **"a-grace"** into his life. There is a difference! The specific "grace" that God had given to Paul literally controlled and directed his entire life. We see this clearly in Romans 12:3 where he says, "For **by the grace given me** I say to every one of you."

Incidentally - speaking by the grace God had given to him – did not refer to a special eloquence of speech. No! But something far more potent – which was the very "authority" of God! Gracious speech had nothing to do with it; but the "authority-by-which-he-spoke" was the key.

The grace of God refers also to the gift of God, which was given to Paul for his life and ministry – that also warranted him the authority he needed to administrate on God's behalf. Therefore grace can quite simply be seen as the "authority" and the "ability" of God in our lives. Given to us to benefit others and to "manage" God's affairs on His behalf.

Finally, this was Paul's motivation. He knew what the grace was. He identified the grace within his own life. He understood that he was both called "by-grace" and called "into-grace." The authority and the ability of God were with him, to achieve God's purpose through him. And it is with this in mind that we must also refer this to our own lives.

The grace of God and the gift of God go hand in hand. His authority and His ability work together. Continually through scripture we witness this as the words **"gift"** and **"grace"** are always closely linked throughout the New Testament, as seen in the following scriptures:

- "Each one should use whatever **gift** he has received to serve others, faithfully administering **God's grace** in its various forms" (1 Peter 4:10)
- "To each of us **grace** has been given as Christ apportioned it" (Ephesians 4:7)
- "And **gifts** of the Holy Spirit distributed according to His will" (Hebrews 2:4)

- "Now to each one the manifestation of the Spirit is given for the common good" (1 Corinthians 12:7)
- "There are different kinds of **gifts**, but the same Spirit" (1 Corinthians 12:4)

In closing, most of the spiritual "gifts" are for the body and why they can be referred to as the body gifts. Examples of these are listed in 1 Corinthians 12:7-11. However while there are general gifts for the body, there are also specifically gifted individuals to the body (see 1 Corinthians 12: 27-31, or Ephesians 4:7-13).

In other words there are callings and gifting and then there are specific "offices" that hold a specific governing authority and ability. All as God wills it according to His master plan and His glory!

Chapter 32

Staying Accountable

Then, having fasted and prayed, and laid hands on them, THEY SENT THEM away. So, being sent out by the Holy Spirit, they went... (Acts 13:3-4 NKJV)

Now the emphasis here is twofold; "They sent them..." and "...sent out by the Holy Spirit." This means that to have "official" leadership you need the authentic commissioning of the Holy Spirit alongside "recognition" that is necessary from other leaders. In order to promote Paul the apostle, God used the established leadership with whom Paul had already faithfully served, during his years of testing and ministry of helps.

Some misguided folks think that they can go around saying, "I am anointed - I don't need anybody else and I don't care what they think!" This sounds impressive to some perhaps, but really it's nothing short of "stupid!" Without recognition from other leaders our own position can never be legitimized, only jeopardized.

It's vital to work together with others. Having said this, it is also normal to lose any reputation before you gain one! Losing your life, before you save it! Dying to self so that the "person" can be built before the "ministry" and the ego dissolved! Jesus had the wilderness for this process, we have a lifetime!

Nevertheless when we humble ourselves God promises to raise us up. Therefore to go any distance in leadership and gain that recognition from other leaders, this involves humility on our part. However this doesn't mean that everybody who is in leadership becomes our apostle or mentor!

No Lone Ranger

God never called anyone to be a lone ranger. We must never work alone. There may be seasons where God strips us back, to deal with our heart motives but even in the Adullam cave, David had a small crowd going on! (1 Samuel 22:1) Paul did travel alone at times but not all the time. More importantly he did not operate alone or solely under his own authority. He worked in collaboration with other recognised leaders; especially from Antioch and Jerusalem from where he was sent out.

From inception then, it's crucial to remember that it is before God AND men that we must serve. Recognition comes from God first and then from men, but not just anyone. That's why it's important that other recognised leaders recognise us before God.

Sensationalism Evaporates

Not all will of course; but there certainly should be some! Especially those who God has brought you into divine connection with. Without this, there is no lasting influence or authority. Sensationalism evaporates; yet true anointing and genuine recognition can last a lifetime.

Certainly to begin with and on a continual basis, there must be humility and submission towards others in leadership. God did not use anyone Paul was not in submission to; instead He used an established authority that had already been set up in Antioch. God will never undermine the leadership of the body of Christ just in order to raise up someone else into a position of leadership! With recognition comes appointment (ordination) by other leaders, in other words confirmation of certain leadership qualities (Acts 5:1-11; 6:1-7; Ephesians 4:11).

However, on the other side of the spectrum there are those who want to lead without first being led. Those who have no intention of ever operating in or out from a place of submission and yet expect submission wherever they go! These types of people have to assume leadership, because they have not gone the proper way. Usually in fact they have no recognition except for their own imagination! Their assumptive leadership behaviour operates something like this:

They like to have influence (where possible) straight at the top. They like to steer where they have no authority to steer. They start by infiltrating a church or group where they have had little if any input, nor developed any real relationship or invested any quality time and yet insist on airing unqualified opinions.

Even their silence suggests something! They leave people hanging, waiting, and wondering, so that even when they are absent, everyone is still thinking about them, almost possessed in their thoughts, something that ends up completely controlling. A false dependency upon their opinions develops and this is dangerous.

Intelligence Collecting

Having successfully infiltrated and gained trust they begin to draw back causing a little confusion and hurt; making others push in even harder to them. However a big characteristic, of these unauthorised leaders is that they remain very guarded and safe about their own personal lives. They only share so much as to get you interested or impressed and then they stop. They withhold information to make people feel that they have to earn their acceptance!

All the while these bogus leaders are gaining intelligence on everything and everyone else, because knowledge is power to them. Their self-preservation goes undetected at first but then it's realised that they never give anything away about themselves. They never indulge information about their own lives yet they manage to extract information from others, about *everything,* what they are doing, how and why,

Staying Accountable

only to use that information to pass judgment! They use all information they can get as strategic ammunition for such times they feel threatened!

Eventually those around them feel more and more raped of information each time they enter conversation with them. They try to resist the urge to gush but always give in to the seduction, which induces the feeling of depression, like they are literally giving their lives away.

The seduction works so well because they give off the sense that they are really interested and want to know, but less is always more with these people. The less that is shared with them the better! Their genuine concern is appealing however and they usually succeed in seducing their victim.

The depth of their concern is revealed in time, especially when they use that information just to prove their theories and issue an, "I told you so..." They estimate themselves so highly and regard their opinions as law that they act out of extreme self-righteousness and pride. But they fear exposure! So they cover their tracks so carefully so that no one tells on them!

Seduction is not always Sexual

Ever met anyone like this? I am sure that you have. We all have. Seduction is not always sexual. It can be intellectual, informational; anything that makes us feel that we must have what they have. But it's very safe for them to stay aloof, watching and judging everything from the side-lines.

Endlessly analysing, assessing, criticising but never doing anything, they are too afraid to really commit to anything - that might affect their safety zone or expose them in any way. They don't ever reveal their own weaknesses - but they want to reveal everyone else's! They feel they must rescue everybody by correcting and coaching them in the things of God! When really the greatest need is theirs! They prey on the vulnerable and it's only a matter of time before the vulnerable eventually wise up!

Most importantly they cannot prove anything; they only have words! And yet they indulge in making everyone else feel like they have achieved nothing. Nothing worthy in their sight that is! Regardless of all the proof and genuine achievements!

When they do come across genuine success it challenges their theology - and they look for ways to disprove its legitimacy and prove it wrong. They bide there time, watching, analysing and waiting for leaked bits of information that they can use. After all, anyone who is not just like them must be wrong...!

Risk of Criticizing

This is absurd. Anyone can assume the role of judge; watching everything yet remaining unaffected by anything. Anyone can do this. People who do this don't want to pay their own price - they'd rather reap the benefits of the risks that others are willing to take. After all, the bible does say - watch and pray - not watch and judge. In fact if you hear someone constantly criticizing others, just ask them when they last prayed for those same people. Their reaction should say it all.

Finally all of us should be accountable to leadership - in one-way or another. This stops us getting carried away and helps make us more careful. We cannot be established alone. Submission is not harmful for us - long term it's more than healthy. Covering - keeps us from being vulnerable and open to attack from the bogus and false.

Ultimately, anyone who persistently says "No" to the Holy Spirit - is a dangerous character. Remember, the misguided always want to steer others! And fruitless people always have big opinions that only measure up to their own dreams but not to reality.

Chapter 33

Honouring your Apostle

One of the questions that I had for many years regarding finance was in relation to *"Does a leader need to tithe the tithe?"* The answer to this is found right here in Numbers 18:26-29 where the Levite priests were commanded to pay a tithe from the tithe that they received from the people and give it to Aaron. We can call this, **"The Aaron's Tithe."**

Leaders themselves must be responsible to tithe the tithe. "Give these instructions to the Levites: When you receive from the people of Israel the tithes I have assigned as your allotment, give a tenth of the tithes you receive to the LORD...

You must present one-tenth of the tithe received from the Israelites as a sacred offering to the LORD. This is the

Lord's sacred portion, and you must present it to Aaron the priest. **Be sure to give to the LORD the best portions of the gifts given to you"** *(Numbers 18:26-29 NLT).*

Out of interest the same scripture in the Message Bible reads: "When you get the tithe from the people... you must tithe that tithe and present it as an offering to GOD. Your offerings will be treated the same as other people's gifts... This is your procedure for making offerings to GOD from all the tithes you get from the People... give God's portion from these tithes to Aaron the priest. Make sure that God's portion is the best... and holiest of everything you get" *(Numbers 18:26-29 MSG).*

The Best of the Best

And we see very clearly that the priests lived off of the tithe, something that we must be clear about in our teaching when we teach on the subject of *God's ways of Financial Increase.* Then in regard to church leadership, pastors and directors of Christian organizations or apostolic networks, the principle remains the same, that if we teach one thing and then excuse ourselves because of our preference of position - this is completely hypocritical.

Many pastors of churches give offerings *(but they don't necessarily tithe)* - for example towards the random itinerant ministry gifts that come through and minister in their churches, including towards their own structural developments and outreach projects.

Now of course these things are wonderful but it is not what God was instructing in Numbers 18:26-29; and such *gifts* are geared to sure up one's own agenda rather than giving the best and holiest to God, which is what tithing for leaders on this level is all about.

Now developing the vision that God has given us is not wrong in itself, nor is it wrong encouraging our members to give into certain projects that in turn will enhance them. And yes teaching our people to tithe and give offerings into the storehouse so that there is meat in God's house and an open heaven where they can prosper is all good. On the other hand however when you step back and look at this theory, superficially it all looks wonderful when actually it is also teetering over the trap of deception.

Church Extension needs Financing

For instance I believe that in these end times not only will there be a greater development of networking, where ministries are concerned, but also the network of spiritual fathering via the apostolic ministry. It's important to remain connected, committed and under the right structural covering. Every leader or pastor needs to be in a relationship that is accountable in an apostolic way.

Even as an apostolic itinerant ministry myself, I can say that my wife and I are committed to other leaders that God has directed us to be accountable to, including our own pastor who is our apostolic covering.

This carries the point over that not only are our individual members called to be responsible through their connection with their local church and with their leadership, but we as ministers also must experience connectedness with the wider body and specifically apostolically, because essentially the life flow of God's anointing and blessing comes so richly and through these avenues of: connectedness, apostolic relationship and unity *(Psalm 133:1, 3).*

And while it's important to teach our people all about tithing we also, as organizational leaders, ministries ought to be tithing faithfully to God through "tithing the tithe" to those whom God has specifically connected us to apostolically speaking.

As leaders we are not "exempt" from tithing, rather we should be "exemplary" in it by giving tithe to the "Aaron" that God has specifically placed in our lives.

So... this is where we place the tithe of the tithe - not to random itinerant ministries or events *(that flow in and out of our lives without accountability).* When we tithe in a correct manner, we are tithing the best of the best "unto the Lord." And to this you might say, "well I'm connected and in relationship with so many!" While this might be correct, ask yourself, of all those you are "connected" to **who is your apostle?**

The Best and Holiest

Who has been assigned to be an Aaron in your life? This is something that has to be settled between you and God and not something you can change or rearrange, *(like the goal posts)* when it suits you! Again the question has to be asked, "Whom do you ultimately submit to besides the Lord? And who represents God in your life? Who can speak for Him when you are not seeing straight?"

We are discussing a certain figure in your life who goes beyond mere acquaintance or friendship; someone who has a "voice" into your life, a voice that holds considerable weight when it really matters. Whoever that person is, this then is where you should be tithing your tithe *(the best and holiest part of everything given to you...v29)* to honour the Lord. And I don't mean your wage; I mean 10% of the income of the WHOLE of your ministry or church. Re-read Numbers where it says "the best of everything."

I stress, this is not an idea of mine that I have stumbled across, nor is it an effort to conjure up finances for my own ministry. As much as I relish the support that we so need, I am rather forced to correct an "incorrectness" that exists in the body by addressing this subject and using very clear scriptural instruction to do so, that is very often swept under a religious and proverbial carpet.

Don't sidestep your Responsibility

We often conveniently sidestep such issues especially those that threaten our personal economy and create a levy upon our finances!

But if we will obey scripture on this point, then this will not only release an open heaven over our personal lives as ministers but will flow down through every branch of our vision *(it is our tithe that opens up the floodgate)*. And then of course our offerings that go to those random itinerant ministries on occasion, can still bring a harvest of supply to our ministries and churches that will positively affect all of our people and only then will we be living what we teach.

Let me say, that during my travels over many years, I discovered that many pastors possess the attitude, that their own ministries are the only ones within the church that should receive a *wage* or the tithe of the tithe. However let me ask, *"IS THIS GOD'S WAY?"* I don't believe it is.

Simply because now we have various *gifts* starting churches - just to *finance* their ministries! They play the role of a pastor, with the notion that this is the only way to fund their true ministry identity. People have hidden behind the safe title of "pastor" for generations, because it is unassuming and less offensive. Nevertheless it is unscriptural for *everyone* to relinquish their true identities and callings within the body, in order to become pastors.

Restoration and Revelation

It's ludicrous and only with a restoration of all-things-apostolic can these haphazard notions be lifted. It has caused internal restrictions within the body of Christ, not allowing gifts to function as they truly should and as God designed to best benefit the whole church.

Clearly then what is really needed is a return towards the apostolic and apostolic teams working together within the body, where all gifts are recognized and can enhance one another to create a balanced fivefold ministry for its people. With a financial structure capable of supporting them with regular income and causing each *gift* to thrive and not just *survive* in the wrong position.

God has made every provision for us to be successful and to remain so. My ministry motto has always been; **"His voice is all the provision you need."** Because every instruction we need is right within His word. If we fall short, it is only when we negate on that word or fail to obey it!

CHAPTER 34

God in Three-Perfect Deity

For all those who are preparing for ministry and ordination it's important to have a clear understanding of the God we serve.

But first of all let me say that all Christians can enjoy the presence of the Holy Spirit in their lives from the moment they accept Jesus Christ as Saviour. Remembering that our new birth experience *(salvation)* brings about a remedy for the condition of man.

For God so loved the world that he gave his one and only Son, Jesus.

(John 3:16)

For His purpose is that all of mankind may have eternal life, a relationship with the living God whose desire it is that we may have the fullness of the Spirit. To bring this about

Jesus tells us that no one can see the kingdom of God unless he is born-again *(John 3:3-7)*. He goes on to explain this experience by stating that flesh gives birth to flesh, but the spirit gives birth to spirit. This happens when we hear the word of truth, the gospel of our salvation:

> *You however, are controlled not by the sinful nature but by the Spirit, if the Spirit of God lives in you. And if anyone does not have the Spirit of Christ, he does not belong to Christ.*
>
> *...But if by the Spirit you put to death the misdeeds of the body, you will live, because those who are led by the Spirit of God, are sons of God.*
>
> *The Spirit himself testifies with our spirits that we are God's children.*
>
> *(Romans 8:9, 13-14, 16)*

From this, we see that the Holy Spirit indwells the human spirit at the time of salvation. We can categorise this by saying or stating this to be the **"Baptism into the Body"** i.e., **"The Body of Christ"** or the **"First Baptism."**

The Second Baptism is of course **"Water Baptism"** an outward confession of what has happened within, a symbol that we are cleansed or washed clean by the blood of the Lamb, Jesus, and His word, *(Acts 22:16; Revelation 1:5; John 15:3)*.

But then we see quite clearly that the rest of our body has to be brought into obedience. This is a lifetime event, for we are to put off the old self and put on the new *(Colossians 3:5-17)*.

Jesus taught that salvation could not be achieved by a person's own effort, self-improvement or religious celebrations. Rather it takes place when God brings about rebirth at the centre of a person's being; something new must happen.

Paul Yonggi Cho says "Think of it this way: However well a monkey imitates man, it cannot become a human being because monkeys are fundamentally different from humans in the level of their existence."[2]

John 1:13 declares that to become children of God we must be born of God: *"Which were born, not of blood, nor of the will of the flesh, nor of the will of man, but of God."*

An Outward Confession

What then does it mean that God enables sinners to be born again by water and the Holy Spirit? It is said that some people think that being born of water means physical baptism of water. But as we have already discovered that water baptism is an outward confession of what has happened within, simply a sign, a command, and a symbol.

Jesus clarifies this to Nicodemus in John 3:5,

> *Jesus answered, "I tell you the truth, no one can enter the kingdom of God unless he is born of <u>water</u> and the Spirit. Flesh gives birth to flesh, but the Spirit gives birth to the Spirit. You should not be surprised at my saying, 'You must be born again.' The wind blows wherever it pleases. You hear its sound, but you cannot tell where it comes from or where it is going. So it is with everyone born of the Spirit."*

The word *"water"* here in the scripture, above all means, *"washing."* The teaching of the bible elsewhere says, that we are washed by the word of God. Jesus said to His disciples, *"Now ye are clean through the word which I have spoken unto you"* (John 15:3 KJV). *"Now,"* not *"you are going to be,"* so the cleanliness referred to here was a present experience before the cross and before Pentecost.

Paul wrote,

> *That he might sanctify and cleanse it [the Church] with the washing of water by the word.*
> *(Ephesians 5:26 KJV)*

When Jesus says we must be **"born of water and of the Spirit,"** He is referring to the word of God and the Holy Spirit. Who could be the word of God but Jesus Himself?

> *The Word became flesh and made his dwelling among us. We have seen His glory, the glory of the One and Only, who came from the father, full of grace and truth.*
> *(John 1:14)*

Only the precious blood of Jesus, who is the living word, can make us clean – and that blood is the very word, which cleanses us.

But Jesus said we are born again **"of water"** – or the word – **"and the Spirit."** Then what does the Holy Spirit do? Ezekiel 36:26 describes beautifully how sinners are changed into new creatures by the Spirit of God:

> *A new heart also will I give you, and a new spirit will I put within you: and I will take away the stony heart out of*

your flesh and I will give you an heart of flesh.
(see also Ezekiel 11:19)

Today our Saviour Jesus Christ can neither be understood nor explained except through the Holy Spirit, the author of miracles and of salvation. He is the administrative agent of God's salvation, reproving us of our sin through the word and revealing Christ, who becomes our righteousness and declares the judgement to Satan:

When he comes, he will convict the world of guilt in regard to sin and righteousness and judgement.
(John 16:8 AMP)

In John 16:14, Jesus showed that He revealed Himself only through the vessel of the Holy Spirit: *"He shall glorify me: for he shall receive of mine, and shall show it unto you."*

"The Holy Spirit carries out the new creative work that transforms a person by leading him to receive eternal life and the nature of God. But the Holy Spirit goes a step beyond regeneration, and that's what the baptism of the Holy Spirit is all about."

Regeneration or Baptism

Dr. Cho goes on to say, "Regeneration is not the same experience as the baptism of *(or with)* the Holy Spirit. Of course, both regeneration and the baptism of the Holy Spirit can happen at the same time. But in other cases there is an interval of time between the two experiences."[3]

Before we take a biblical look at the difference between regeneration and the baptism of the Holy Spirit, we need to make it clear for those who may not understand the characteristics of God, that He is not three gods but **ONE GOD** who manifests Himself as **Triune**.

GOD Revealed in JESUS CHRIST

When a scribe asked Jesus to outline the chief commandment in the law, He answered, *"The most important one is this: hear, O Israel, the Lord our God, the Lord is one"* (Mark 12:29), to which the teacher of the law replied: "Well said, teacher, you are right in saying that God is One and there is no other but Him" *(v32)*.

Ulf Ekman the founder of Word of Life Church, in Uppsala, Sweden, says, "We live in days when the Christian message is increasingly diluted and twisted. Ancient Judeo-Christian values are no longer the unquestioned norms of modern secular society, and even queried by some church leaders. Today it is vital to clearly establish, defend and uphold fundamental Christian truth and our genuine spiritual heritage."

On speaking of the triune God, Ulf Ekman says that, "God steps out of glory and manifests His unity, His eternal nature and omnipotence by means of revelation. All His other characteristics stem from these three, so that we can see, understand, love and obey Him. His personality is first outlined in the scriptures and then summarised and made plain in the incarnation of His Son, Jesus Christ."[4]

In Hebrews 1:3, we read that Jesus is the radiance of God's glory and the exact representation of His being. So we see that God steps out of eternity into full view through:

- Representations and outlines of Himself in nature
- Revelation in the scriptures
- His Son, Jesus Christ, the image of the invisible God *(Colossians 1:15)*, in whom all the fullness of the Deity lives in bodily form *(Colossians 2:9)*
- Nowhere can we find a clearer image, a better understanding and a closer communion with God than in Christ Jesus!

A Triune GOD

Now that God appears in all His majesty, He appears as the only God and as the one God, a unity.

Exodus 20:2-3 says:

I am the Lord your God, who brought you out of Egypt, out of the land of slavery. You shall have no other gods before me.

Pastor Ekman goes on to say, **"God is one!** Yet the New Testament refers to Him **as Triune,** which has caused difficulties for many. Some evade the question of the Trinity, others try to explain it away and still others deny it. But none of these responses is necessary. We do not need to grasp everything through our intellect; we need only to accept the plain, unambiguous testimony of scripture that **God is simultaneously ONE and THREE.** He is not three gods but **One God who manifests Himself as triune."**

Jesus emphasises this in the Great Commission:

> ...*baptising them in the name of the Father and of the Son and of the Holy Spirit...*
>
> *(Matthew 28:19)*

"So we see that **GOD IS ONE**, yet reveals Himself in three persons. Each of these three persons is *Individually Eternal and Omnipotent,* while UNITED IN ONE SINGLE DEITY. They share one being, one will and the same characteristics while, within the Deity, they have distinct roles. Man's limited intellect cannot comprehend a God who is simultaneously one indivisible being and yet three persons. This has led to countless doctrinal arguments about the Trinity and various descriptions of the Godhead."[5]

No matter what people think, the bible teaches that God is a triune being. For instance, Paul says in 2 Corinthians 13:14; "May the grace of the Lord Jesus Christ, and the love of God and the fellowship of the Holy Spirit be with you all."

We have another example when Jesus says; *"I and the Father are one...anyone who has seen me has seen the Father"* (John 10:30; 14:9). And in 1 John 2:23 He says, *"No one who denies the Son has the Father; whoever acknowledges the Son has the Father also."*

One FATHER, one SON, one HOLY SPIRIT

Since the time of the early church, the bible's teaching on the Trinity is nowhere better described than in the Athanasian Creed:

...we worship one God in Trinity and the Trinity in Unity; Neither confusing the Persons nor dividing the substance... For like as we are compelled by the Christian verity: to confess each Person by himself to be both God and Lord; so we are forbidden by the Catholic (read, Universal) Religion: to speak of three Gods or three Lords.

The Father is made of none: not created, nor begotten. The Son is of the father alone: not made, nor created, but begotten.

The Holy Ghost is of the Father and the Son: not made, nor created, nor begotten, but proceeding.

There is therefore one Father, not three Fathers; one Son, not three Sons; one Holy Ghost, not three Holy Ghosts.

And in this Trinity there is no before or after: not greater or less.

But all three Persons are co-eternal together: and co-equal. So that in all ways, as is aforesaid: both the Trinity is to be worshipped in Unity and the Unity in Trinity.

Mr. Ekman in his summary says, "The only, invisible, eternal, omnipotent God reveals Himself so that man can understand Him, communicate with Him, receive from Him and follow Him. He does all this through the scriptures and in Christ.

Some feminist-theologians strongly object to God being called the 'Father.' God's being does not comprise both the masculine and the feminine and when God created humankind in His image, He included both man and woman.

Nevertheless, the bible expressly calls God *'Our Father,'* and *'Lord'* and Jesus talked about his ***'Father.'*** To call God, *'Mother'* is not only utter blasphemy and gross misuse of scripture, but tantamount to replacing the God of the bible with a New Age deity."[6]

CHAPTER 35

Baptism of the Holy Spirit

Now we have an understanding of the characteristics of God, we can now move on and look at the difference between regeneration and the baptism of the Holy Spirit. Jesus promised power to all believers through the Holy Spirit after He had ascended:

> *But you will receive power when the Holy Spirit comes on you; and you will be my witnesses in Jerusalem, and in all Judea and Samaria, and to the ends of the earth.*
>
> *(Acts 1:8)*

He did not say "some of you, one or two of you, those who have specialist ministries," He said "All! All!" We exercise this power out of our position being adopted into God's family, with all the right of a child of God.

Dr. Martyn Lloyd-Jones says when writing in the Westminster Record in September 1964:

"There is nothing, I am convinced, that so quenches the Spirit as the teaching which identifies the baptism of the Holy Spirit with regeneration, but it is a very commonly held teaching today, indeed it has been the popular view for many years.

They say that the baptism of the Holy Spirit is *'non-experimental,'* that it happens to everybody at regeneration. So we say 'ah-well, I am already baptised in the Holy Spirit, it happened when I was born again, it happened at my conversion; there is nothing for me to seek, I have got it all.'

Got it all? Well, if you have got it all, I simply ask in the name of God why are you as you are? If you have got it all, why are you so unlike those apostles, why are you unlike New Testament Christians? Got it all! Got it all at your conversion! Well, where is it I ask."

Baptism or Infilling

In the bible there is clear mention of born-again believers who had not received the baptism or infilling with the Holy Spirit. For instance the Old Testament saints had many experiences and blessing, as follows:

They were **filled** *(Exodus 28:3; 31:3; 35:31; Deuteronomy 34:9; Micah 3:8)* and had the Spirit *in* *(Genesis 41:38; Numbers 27:18; Daniel 4:8-9, 18; 5:11-14; 6:3);* ***within*** *(Psalms 51:10-11; Isaiah 63:10-14; Ezekiel 11:19);* ***into*** *(Ezekiel 2:2; 3:24; Acts 3:21);*

Baptism of the Holy Spirit

upon *(Numbers 11:17-29; Judges 3:10; 6:34; 11:29; 14:6, 19; 15:14);* and He ***moved*** many *(Judges 13:25; Acts 3:21; 2 Peter 1:21),* but none were baptised in the Spirit.

John the Baptist and others were filled with the Spirit, but not baptised *(Luke 1:15-17, 41, 67; 2:25-38).* Mary was filled about 35 years before she was baptised with the Holy Spirit at Pentecost and spoke in Tongues *(Luke 1:46-56; Acts 1:13-15, 2:1-4).* Jesus was filled about 30 years before He was baptised with the Spirit *(Isaiah 50:4-5; Luke 2:40-52; Matthew 3:16-17).* The disciples were filled and had the Spirit in them 3 years before they were baptised with the Spirit *(Matthew 10:8, 20; Acts 1:4-8; 2:1-4, 23).*

Before Jesus' death His disciples had already received eternal life, for Jesus called them in person and they obeyed Him, believing that He was the Son of God.

Jesus said, "Verily, verily, I say unto you, He that heareth my word, and believeth on him that sent me, hath everlasting life."

(John 5:24 KJV)

Jesus also testified in John 13:10 that His disciples were all clean except Judas Iscariot. And when the seventy disciples returned from preaching and told Jesus how the devils were subject to them, Jesus admitted that the seventy disciples had already received everlasting life *(see Luke 10:20).* But Jesus did not say that they had received the baptism of the Holy Spirit from the moment they believed, as some theologians today claim.

It's quite clear that they hadn't yet received the fullness of the Spirit. Before He ascended into heaven, Jesus told His disciples that they should not depart from Jerusalem yet:

Wait for the promise of the Father, which ye have heard of me. For John truly baptised with water; but ye shall be baptised with the Holy Ghost not many days hence.
(Acts 1:4, 5 KJV)

Some people agree that the believing disciples needed the baptism of the Holy Spirit, but they say, that was only because they were believers before Pentecost. The argument goes that any believer since Pentecost, when the church was born and the Holy Spirit descended, received the baptism of the Holy Spirit at this time of conversion. But New Testament accounts show such a theory to be wrong.

Distinctions

The distinction between being born again *(conversion)* and the baptism with the Holy Spirit can be seen in the accounts of this manifestation recorded in the book of Acts. On numerous occasions, believers were prayed for to receive the baptism or infilling with the Holy Spirit, after they had been converted.

In Acts 8:4-24 we can see that the gospel was being preached by Philip in Samaria. The people there "with one accord gave heed unto those things which Philip spake, hearing and seeing the miracles which he did" (KJV). As a result, "…unclean spirits, crying with loud voice, came out of many that were possessed with them: and many taken with palsies and that were lame, were healed. And there was great joy in that city" (KJV).

Those who believed what Philip was preaching were baptised in water, a sign of a person's entrance into the body of Christ. Jesus had said, *"He who has believed and has been baptised shall be saved"* (Mark 16:16 NASB). Thus, these Samaritans were saved, members of the body of Christ, and *"there was much rejoicing in that city"* (Acts 8:8 NASB). And yet, they had not yet received the infilling of the Spirit. *"For He (the Spirit) had not yet fallen on any of them"* (Acts 8:16 NASB).

Not one of the Same

We can see from this passage that the new birth and the baptism in the Holy Spirit are not one and the same. The Samaritans were born again *(saved)* when they *"received the word of God"* (Acts 8:14 NASB). But, this did not automatically give them the infilling of the Holy Spirit, that manifestation came when the apostles laid hands on them.

> *Now when the apostles which were at Jerusalem heard that Samaria had received the word of God, they sent unto them Peter and John: Who, when they were come down, prayed for them, that they might receive the Holy Ghost: (For as yet he was fallen upon none of them: only they were baptised in the name of the Lord Jesus.) Then laid they their hands on them, and they received the Holy Ghost.*
>
> *(Acts 8:14-17 KJV)*

Again in Acts 9:1-19 we see another distinction where Paul tells a vivid account of his conversion and experience of being filled with the Holy Spirit, which didn't happen simultaneously.

With a letter of authority from the high priests, Saul and his friends went toward Damascus, the capital of Syria, to persecute those who believed in Jesus and bring them into prison. But when he and his followers came near Damascus, *"suddenly there shined round about him a light from heaven"* which blinded him.

This new birth is evidence by the fact that he addressed the risen Christ as *"Lord" (Acts 9:5)*, and then asked Jesus what He wanted him to do *(Acts 22:10)* and obeyed Him. Saul subsequently called Paul, said later that this was his witness of the resurrection *(1 Corinthians 15:8)*.

The man who was led blind into the city of Damascus was a man who had witnessed and believed in the resurrected Christ and had submitted himself to His Lordship. Saul fasted and prayed for three days. From this we see that he has become a new creature in Christ. Then Ananias put his hands on Saul and prayed that he be filled with the Holy Spirit, which he was.

Struggling is a Sign

"Another example is the church at Ephesus, which had been established through the eloquent preaching of Apollos. But when Paul visited that Church, he found it struggling and weak. The first question Paul asked was this: *'Have ye received the Holy Ghost since ye believe?' (Acts 19:2 KJV)* Paul knew that if they had received the Holy Spirit, they wouldn't have been so powerless and feeble with only twelve or so members.

If Christians always received the Holy Spirit when they believed, why would Paul have deliberately asked the unnecessary question, *'Have ye received the Holy Ghost since ye believed?'* Faith does not mean that one automatically receives the fullness of the Holy Spirit. It is something a believer should pray and ask for.

I'm not saying that one cannot be saved and filled with the Holy Spirit at the same time. Cornelius and his household had the Holy Spirit fall upon them as they were listening to Peter preach. No appeal was made to Cornelius to repent or confess; the Spirit fell upon him as he believed what Peter was saying about the Lord Jesus *(Acts 10:44).*

However, this does not mean that those two works of God are one and the same. If that were the case, the Samaritans *(who had received the word and been baptised in water)* would not have needed to afterward receive the Spirit. If being born again meant the same thing as being filled with the Spirit, the convert Saul would not have needed Ananias to lay his hands on him to be filled with the Holy Spirit.

A Necessary Qualification

In fact, first-century Spirit-filled believers thought that Christians who weren't Spirit-filled lacked a necessary qualification for service. Because of this, new believers as a rule prayed earnestly to receive the Holy Spirit. Before the believers at Ephesus received the Holy Spirit, the church was miserably weak and sick. But after the people received the fullness of the Holy Spirit through Paul's ministry, a wonderful vitality and power of faith exploded in their midst. After a while it became a famous church that filled all of Asia Minor with the word of God.

When we take all these accounts into consideration, we can see that regeneration and the baptism with the Holy Spirit are two distinctly different experiences. Regeneration is the experience of receiving the life of the Lord by being grafted into the body of Christ through the Holy Spirit and the scriptures. The baptism of the Holy Spirit is the experience in which Jesus fills believers with the power of God for ministry, service and victorious living.

Regeneration Grants a Person Everlasting Life

While the baptism of the Holy Spirit grants regenerated believers the power of God to preach Christ. Christians today are not powerless, sick and spiritless because they are not born again, but because they have not received the fullness of the Holy Spirit, the tremendous power of God for service.

Without the baptism of the Holy Spirit the church today can never display God's power as did the early church – a combative, challenging and victorious power to evangelise a generation. For this reason, we should renounce the foolish, weak and lethargic excuse that all believers immediately receive the Holy Spirit when they believe. Rather we should pray to receive the fullness of the Holy Spirit."[7]

Old Testament saints had gifts and fruit of the Spirit *(1 Kings 3:12; 17:1; 2 Kings 13:25; Acts 3:21; Hebrews 11)*; different measures of the Spirit *(Numbers 11:16-25; 2 Kings 2:9; Luke 1:17)* but not the Spirit baptism or the Spirit *"without measure" (John 3:34; 7:37-39)*. The disciples had gifts and great power years before the Spirit baptism *(Matthew 10:1-8, 16-20; Mark 6:7-13; Luke 10)*, but were told to get the Spirit baptism before starting their ministry *(Luke 24:49; John 7:37-39; 14:12; Acts 1:4-8)*.

Saints and disciples of Christ had salvation *(Psalms 51:12);* **redemption** *(Psalms 31:5);* **grace** *(Psalms 84:11);* **bodily healing** *(Exodus 15:26);* **names written in heaven** *(Exodus 32:32-33; Luke 10:20);* **the new birth** *(Galatians 4:28-30);* **conversion** *(Psalms 19:7);* **righteousness** *(Romans 4);* **the gospel** *(Galatians 3:6-14; Hebrews 4:2);* **justification** *(Romans 4);* **holiness** *(Acts 3:21: 2 Peter 1:21);* **pure hearts** *(Psalms 24:4);* **sanctification** *(Exodus 29:42-44; 31:13; Ezekiel 20:12; John 15:3);* **and many other spiritual blessings before Pentecost** *(John 7:37-39; Acts 2:33)*.

Therefore, one should **not take any of these blessings as evidence of a Spirit baptism.** From all this we gather that the Spirit baptism is the fullness of God in the lives of believers, not the Spirit by measure as in OT times *(John 3:34; 7:37-39; Luke 24:49; Acts 10:38; Isaiah 61:1; Romans 15:29; Ephesians 3:19)*.

The late Bob Gordon said, "If the Lord Jesus needed to be filled *(Luke 4:1, 14)*, the apostles needed to be filled *(Acts 2:2-4)*, and Paul needed to be filled *(Acts 9:17)*, we also need to be filled with the Holy Spirit.

Deposit or Baptism

This is not simply becoming a Christian and receiving the Holy Spirit as a deposit guaranteeing our salvation *(Ephesians 1:13-14)*. Jesus was conceived by the Holy Spirit

(Matthew 1:18), and so has the Holy Spirit in Him all His life, but He still needed to be filled or baptised with the Holy Spirit in order to fulfil all that His Father had sent Him to do.

This happened when He was baptised in water at the river Jordan *(Luke 3:21-22).* The disciples received the Holy Spirit when Jesus breathed on them *(John 20:22),* but they were told to wait until they had received the baptism with the Holy Spirit before they began their ministry *(Acts 1:4-5; 2:2-4).*

The bible uses many different ways to describe this filling. These include being filled *(Acts 2:4);* being baptised *(Acts 1:5);* the Holy Spirit coming upon *(Acts1:8);* receiving the Holy Spirit *(Acts 8:17);* pouring out of the Holy Spirit *(Acts 10:45).* It is not the label that matters but what actually happens, that is, we are enabled to do God's will and to be true disciples of our Lord Jesus Christ."[8]

It must be remembered that we are not just to be filled once and leave it at that. **We need to be CONTINUALLY FILLED WITH THE HOLY SPIRIT** *(Ephesians 5:18; Acts 2:1-4; 4:31).*

CHAPTER 36

New Days – New Ways

They dress the wound of my people as though it were not serious. "Peace, peace," they say, when there is no peace (Jeremiah 6:14).

In this final chapter we will cover an interesting topic, especially considering current events, involving such figureheads as the Pope and the Catholic Church. However from the outset let me clarify that currently my wife and I are living in Tuscany, Italy *(even though we have offices in other parts of the world)* and I have preached more than once in Catholic churches here, whom I have always found to be open if not more-open-and-hungry for the things of God than other churches I experience!

For instance, there have been the occasions that I have gone up to preach for Padre Don Stefano, who lived on top of a mountain here in Tuscany - and have enjoyed some spectacular events with him *(a mountain that takes roughly two and a half hours to ascend - even with a car!)*

The precise reason that he was placed there was due to his sincere belief in the things of the Holy Spirit. Something that his peers in the Catholic Church did not collectively appreciate some decades before and decidedly put-him-out-to-graze in order to minimize the influence of his beliefs on others. In other words, his own church effectively ostracized him in an attempt to quench the Holy Spirit's fire.

No one can Stop You

However as it stats in John 12:32, if Jesus is lifted up, all men will be drawn to Him. Therefore we know and have confidence that the Holy Spirit will always find a way to draw people unto Christ. Despite all their efforts, those in the hierarchy in the Catholic Church were unable to hinder the moving of the Holy Spirit for long, as Padre Don Stefano regularly attracts hundreds upon hundreds to his meetings on the mountain top.

Many came via the coach load *(totally disregarding the difficulty of logistics!)* especially for such calendar events as "Pentecost," where typically Don Stefano would invite known "Pentecostals" to come and preach for him on those specific occasions - which is where I came in of course!

So as you can tell, I have always and will always preach where the doors are open and where I feel the leading of God's Spirit, whom over the years I have discovered, will transcend any humanistic boundary and anoint me to preach right across the board; with strong love without ever compromising the scriptures.

So having said all this - by way of small disclaimer - nothing changes the fact that there are obvious discrepancies within the doctrine of the Catholic Church! Yet with nothing posing too great of a challenge or a threat for the Holy Spirit - keeping this in mind - let us read on, from this excerpt taken from my own book material on the End Times - entitled, **"Israel, The Church And The End Times."**

It was interesting that several years ago, Archbishop Runcie who was the head of the Church of England, told *"Time Magazine"* that he had given a ring to Pope John Paul II as *"an engagement ring"* in view of the coming marriage between the Roman Catholic Church and the Church of England.

What Ecumenical Union?

Remember the Church of Rome has not renounced any of the fundamental doctrinal errors that provoked the Protestant Reformation in AD 1520. **The non-Catholic members of the union are making this Ecumenical union on the basis of theological compromise.**

Even Catholic theologians admit that John Paul II was the most traditional Pope of this last century and the strongest advocate of worship of Mary, Queen of Heaven, Mother of God, as the *"co-redenitrix"* along with Jesus Christ. However a process of intense ecumenical dialogue has proceeded quietly during the last twenty years or so! The church leaders are very close to healing the schism between the Greek and Russian Orthodox Churches and the Church of Rome. The Pope has met with Buddhist, Muslim, and Jewish religious leaders from around the world.

For the first time in history the Vatican has sought to establish ties with those other churches. He has engaged in ecumenical religious rituals and services with other religions that would have been unimaginable for any previous Pope.

The danger today is that in opting for a man-made unity based on compromise; and abandoning the Protestant Reformation and the truths of the scriptures that were sealed in the blood of martyrs, we are heading back to whence we came.

Love is not always Truth

Michael de Semlyen says, today in Britain, there is a *"love gospel"* about, which confines itself exclusively to what is called *"the positive."* It is claimed that as long as Jesus Christ is proclaimed as Saviour and Lord, we are all as one in Him. Differences over doctrine must not be allowed to get in the way of this. They say, **"we can affirm truth, but not confront error!"**

Even Evangelical Alliance, UK Director *(at the time)*, Clive Calver said: "More barriers need to come down if a true alliance of evangelicals in the UK is to emerge. There are thousands more with whom we wish to stand shoulder to shoulder." Is this part of the New World Order? It must be said that those who are pointing the finger and accusing many whom are standing for truth, as "SECTS," are very often part of the so-called unity at any cost; which is part of the Babylonian church!

A.W. Tozer said, "Every century needs its prophetic voices. Those men who have been gifted by God with an incisive cutting edge to expose hypocrisy, denounce compromise, and call for holiness."

He also said, "If THE CHURCH in the second half of this century is to recover from the injuries which she suffered in the first half, there must appear a new type of preacher. The proper ruler of the synagogue type will never do. Neither will the priestly type of man who carries out his duties, takes his pay and asks no questions, nor the smooth talking pastoral type who knows how to make the Christian religion acceptable to everyone.

All these have been tried and found wanting. Another kind of religious leader must arise among us. He must be of the old prophet type, a man who has seen visions of God and has heard a voice from the throne.

Peace at any Cost

The Protestant martyrs, godly and loving men, 'could have taken this same position of, peace at any cost, within the wider church of their day. They could have confined themselves to avoiding all controversy and to agreeing with their persecutors about many of the 'positives'. But, the scripture commanded them to 'exhort and convince by sound doctrine' and to 'flee from idolatry.'

They obeyed; they saw the error and the idolatry, and as responsible leaders, as pastors trusted to guide their flocks into green pastures, they exposed and opposed it all roundly. They could so easily have chosen to look the other way and concentrate on the many truths of the Christian faith, which was common ground. They could have elected to please men, rather than please God."

The Reformers saw the whole Catholic system as anti-Christian. Luther and Calvin went so far as to identify the Papacy with the Antichrist and they like Wycliffe, Tyndale, Matthew Henry, Spurgeon, Llyod-Jones and many others saw the Roman Catholic Institution as Mystery Babylon, the Mother of Harlots, vividly described in Revelation 17. The Spirit-filled life is filled with testimony of experience which of course is not wrong in itself, but **"New Days, New Ways"** is a dangerous way of life!

A New Cross

"I well knew how many smooth arguments can be marshalled in support of the new cross," says A.W. Tozer. Does not the new cross win converts and make many followers and so carry the advantage of numerical success? **Should we not adjust ourselves to the changing times?** Have we not heard the slogan, *"New days, New ways?"* And who but someone very old and very conservative would insist upon death as the appointed way to life? And who today is interested in a gloomy mysticism that would sentence its flesh to a cross and recommend self-effacing humility as a virtue actually to be practised by modern Christians?

These are the arguments along with many more flippant still, which are brought forward to give an appearance of wisdom to the hollow and meaningless cross of popular Christianity.

He says (Tozer) "Doubtless there are many whose eyes are open to the tragedy of our times, but why are they so silent when their testimony is so sorely needed. **In the name of Christ men have made void the cross of Christ.**

'The noise of them that sing do I hear.' Men have fashioned a golden cross with a graving tool, and before it they sit down to eat and drink and rise up to play. In their blindness they have substituted the work of their own hands for the working of God's power. Perhaps our greatest present need may be the coming of a prophet to dash the stones at the foot of the mountain and call the Church out to repentance or to judgment.

Please Lord send a Prophet

Before all who wish to follow Christ the way lies clear. It is the way of death unto life. Always life stands just beyond death and beckons the man who is sick of himself to come and know the life more abundant. But to reach the new life he must pass through the valley of the shadow of death, and I know that at the sound of those words many will turn back and follow Christ no more. But to whom shall we go? 'Thou hast the words of eternal life.'"[9]

To close, let us be mindful of all that has been brought out in this part three, **Preparations for Ministry**, and resist becoming part of a false "Doctrine," whether Catholic, Anglican, Protestant or Pentecostal that cries peace when there is no peace! (Jeremiah 6:14) For those of us who entered into the life of Christ, we chose to be identified as such; an identity that we cannot afford to compromise.

In fact we live in a day where the distinctions are becoming more and more acute - in the context that the dark is getting darker and the brightness is getting brighter! In other words the dividing lines, although fudged, for many are still strong. We must make our daily choices wisely and never lean back into deception.

Let us therefore not be fearful of hearing the voice of God's prophets. Satan has undermined the authority of the apostolic and prophet in every generation, including this one - simply because they threaten him the most!

Remember that God Himself singles them out when He declares, "Come not against Mine anointed ones, and against My prophets do not evil" *(1 Chronicles 16:22 YLT)*. They will always be singled-out so we must not be timid about them. Instead let us become a generation that develops ears to hear the voice of His prophets - resisting our human instinct that despises this gift.

They may not be as smooth talking as the other gifts, even much less articulate perhaps especially to the humanistic crowd; but oh how we need this potent gift in the body of Christ today! Amen.

Notes

1. Strong, James. S.T.D., L.L.D. 1890. Strong's Exhaustive Concordance; Dictionaries of the Hebrew and Greek Words. e-Sword ® version 7.6.1 Copyright © 2000-2005. All Rights Reserved. Registered trade mark of Rick Meyers. Equipping Ministries Foundation. USA www.e-sword.net. #G1278

2. Cho, Paul Y. The Holy Spirit My Senior Partner. Copyright © 1989. Published by Charismas Media. Printed in USA. p.98

3. The Holy Spirit My Senior Partner. p.100

4. Ekman, Ulf. Doctrine. Copyright © 1996. Published by Word of Life Publications. Printed in Sweden. p.42

5. Doctrine. p.44

6. Doctrine. p.45

7. The Holy Spirit My Senior Partner. p.103

8. Gordon, Bob, and David Fardouly. The Foundations of Christian Living. Copyright © 1988. Published by Sovereign World. Printed in England. p.47

9. Tozer, A.W. The Divine Conquest. Copyright © 1995. Published by Living Books. Printed in USA.

Bible Translations:

- Unless otherwise indicated, all scriptural quotations are from the HOLY BIBLE, NEW INTERNATIONAL VERSION ®. NIV ®. Copyright © 1973, 1978, 1984 by the International Bible Society. Used by permission of Zondervan Publishing House. All rights reserved.

- Scripture references marked AMP are taken from The Amplified Bible. Old Testament copyright © 1965, 1987 by Zondervan Corporation, Grand Rapids, Michigan. New Testament copyright © 1958, 1987 by The Lockman Foundation, La Habra, California. All rights reserved.

- Scripture references marked GW are taken from GOD'S WORD®, © 1995 God's Word to the Nations. Used by permission of Baker Publishing Group.

- Scripture references marked KJV are taken from the King James Version of the bible.

- Scripture references marked MSG are taken from The Message. Copyright © 1993, 1994, 1995, 1996, 2000, 2001, 2002. Used by permission of NavPress Publishing Group.

- Scripture references marked NASB are taken from New American Standard Bible®, Copyright © 1960, 1962, 1963, 1968, 1971, 1972, 1973, 1975, 1977, 1995 by The Lockman Foundation. Used by permission.

- Scripture references marked NKJV are taken from the New King James Version. Copyright © 1982 by Thomas Nelson, 1982 by Thomas Nelson, Inc. Used by permission. All rights reserved.

- Scripture references marked NLT are taken from the Holy Bible, New Living Translation, copyright © 1996, 2004, 2007 by Tyndale House Foundation. Used by permission of Tyndale House Publishers, Inc., Carol Stream, Illinois 60188. All rights reserved.

- Scripture references marked YLT are taken from the Young's Literal Translation of the bible.

Part Four

DEVELOPMENTS AND PROVISION

CHAPTER 37

Interest and Concerns

It's important to remember that this is part four of *a four book series* of "The Age of the Apostolic Apostleship." The first covers "Laying Foundations," the second "Apostles and the Local Church," the third the "Preparations for Ministry" and the fourth "Developments and Provision," which you are about to read. To understand the context you need to have read books one, two and three.

Our heart and passion behind **"Connecting for Excellence International Apostolic Network"** is for *"A Network of Relationships,"* apostolic companies that the Holy Spirit has and is developing for this **end time move** of God. These relationships look for apostolic support and encouragement. In so doing, our desire is to encourage the men and women of God to move boldly and powerfully in the Holy Spirit. *Being released to fulfil their destinies* for the glory of God.

The Developments and Provision of a Network

This is the linking of people with a common interest or area of concern. As we move on in this New Millennium and apostolic age we will see a new emphasis and the development of denominational and associational networking working together.

Dr. Bill Hamon says, "Networking does not imply that all groups should come under some Pope type figure or apostolic movement. Networking simply implies associations or people with a net such as a fishing net.

Each member of the network is like that of a knot that ties the net together. Those who have vision, grace and wisdom, to network with other networks will become the great fishing net that God will use to draw in the great multitude of souls. This gives the Holy Spirit the opportunity to bring a greater unity and corporate vision within the body of Christ.

This will enable all available resources to be harnessed to work together towards assisting the body of Christ to initiate and sustain an effective thrust towards souls. The common meeting ground is to have the corporate vision of reaping the great end time harvest and proclaiming Jesus Christ as Lord over all the earth."[1]

Effectively, the network depends upon people *(pastors and ministers)* who are totally committed in every aspect of their life to the Lord Jesus Christ, people who are willing to

Interest and Concerns

use their God given talents and abilities without regard to the cost, with great joy.

Remembering that this relationship of association networking is not to threaten or contradict denominational loyalties or cause division but to help bring strength, depth, unity, clarity, and the word of God that can only enhance better skills and insights into sharing the word of God.

Spiritual Hubs of Government

Their aim is to help establish ministry centres of excellence and significance for this present move of God, Spiritual Hubs of Government that **enhance His kingdom** and to provide a platform for ministry gifts to speak into the cities and nations in an effective way.

To develop ministries, enhancing and bringing them into positions of leadership, to influence every area of society. To combine their skills, experience and abilities, to make increasing individual and corporate impact in the regions of their influence for the *kingdom of God* and for the glory of the Lord Jesus Christ.

The awareness of a situation, need or opportunity will need collaboration of many Christians *(the body of Christ)* from across the different denominational lines in related expertise and location that is required to meet the need. Setting initial meetings with individuals known to identify with the need and clarify the need to pray, share and hear what God is saying.

Of this "Core-Group" making its works known to others, local organisations interested in that activity, and visit others working that field. Introduce the "Core Group," to the media, to assist finding wider support and publicise its work. Offering to make a continued contribution and support in every possible way and linking the "Core Group" to businessmen who can help provide funds, services and expertise. Seek to support and help from the rest of the body.

Network Objectives

To find and bring together apostolic leadership *(Connecting for Excellence)* with a heart for God and a call on their lives, who have a common vision, to enable them to work together with initiatives to promote the kingdom of God in their sphere of work or ministry, providing spiritual support, teaching and training, fellowship and encouragement, advisory and other services relevant. Being a vehicle for the setting up and establishing new works, fellowships, bible schools, and businesses in areas of their location.

This vision in every factor of society taking full advantage of opportunities that is open to Christians in position of leadership and influence, to implement and fulfil their visions. ***To advance the Christian faith by the proclamation and furtherance of the gospel of God*** concerning His Son Jesus Christ our Lord and the preaching and teaching of the word of God in one's region, town, city, nation and the world.

With the doctrines and articles of belief conducting with the consent *(where possible)* of the relevant authorities, to conduct open-air crusades, to establish apostolic bible schools for ministry development, setting forth a prescribed curriculum and course of study.

To course to be written and printed, or otherwise reproduced and circulated gratuitously or otherwise periodicals, magazines, books, leaflets or other documents or films recorded tapes or by any other media which is or may be available. Raising finance to permit the ongoing of all the above.

Functional Practice

The leaders or overseer of "Connecting for Excellence International Apostolic Network" do not have the right to interfere in the internal running of its individual members or churches, *(elders and pastors are responsible for the local church)* but has the machinery to act and deal with issues and problems on the invitation of members. The senior overseer and boards of directors *DO NOT* hold authoritative power over members or churches.

But within the power of the association or network, speak, act and work for and on behalf of its partners, churches, and ministries of the Christian faith by virtue of the power vested in the association itself. ***Remember that which you will find in this book is only a guideline for foundational purposes only.***

Every ministry in the local body of the church has the right, if it so desires to appoint internally for its own intern pastoral convenience. To appoint pastors and officers as they see fit, and such officers or elders are expected to fulfil the duties of that office to which he or she has been appointed internally in his or her own congregation.

This however does not mean that such a person has reached the standard of spiritual development required to be selected for ordination, this is where apostolic oversight comes in. Remember ministers should have at least a Bachelor's degree.

Those who are selected or ordained to any position will have ecumenical, national and international recognition by the "Connecting for Excellence International Apostolic Network."

CHAPTER 38

Apostolic Association Network

As an apostolic network we continue to advise that all fellowships, ministries, church organisations, bible schools etc.; to be in a relationship with an apostolic-association or network. Apostolically no individual part of the body functions without the *flow of life* that comes through being directly joint in unity to the whole body of Christ. Isolation brings a stagnancy and eventual deception.

You have to, however be able to accept the basis and commitment of such an organisational structure. The apostolic presbytery of a said network *(one of)* will provide them with authenticity, a platform of recognition for the force of support, the welfare of its people, evangelisation and the spreading of the gospel. We also as a network urge that *(all)* partners fight *(speak out)* against: Anti-Semitism, racism, sexism, classism, abortion, etc.

Specific Responsibilities

To safeguard and maintain the purity of the nature of the association, is related to the understanding of the *"The Apostolic and Prophetic Movement."*

Boldness, strength, fervency, commitment, strong worship, warfare and intercession, above all living a life of righteousness, holiness, compassion and love *(1 Corinthians 13:1-13)*.

To this end he or she must ensure that wherever they have charge, **that they** impart to the people **and encourage people** to be of the same spirit and mind. Also it must be held that any ministerial or other relationships that may develop, do not conflict or offer hindrances to the unity of the association and its out-working, in either the lives of the main body of the churches or its apostolic relationships.

- To safeguard against division at all times, *"Make every effort to keep the unity of the Spirit through the bond of peace" (Ephesians 4:3).*

- Teaching and exemplifying a life of consecration and holiness. Standing against all unrighteousness *(Leviticus 20:7; Hebrews 12:14; 1 Peter 3:18).*

- Teach the principles of tithing and the giving of offerings *(seed)* and the giving of alms as essential to pleasing God and receiving the associated blessings, individually and corporately *(Malachi 3:10; Proverbs 28:27; 2 Corinthians 9:6; Galatians 6:7; Matthew 13:8).*

- Develop relationships with other gifts, pastors etc., enhancing trust, reliability and confidence. Your title is not a job description but a mandate to service.

- Develop true disciples but not at the expense of those who may *not* be ready to respond to the cost of such commitment. Holding fast to the *"no compromise stance,"* yet realising babies don't grow into adults over night.

- Impart the vision for the local community, i.e. evangelism and care etc.

- Help to mobilise the local body **to action** consistent with the vision of God.

- To build whenever possible, relationships with other local leaders, outside of your ministry and association, without loss of the vision and its standards of excellence, not relinquishing spiritual values gained.

- Personal standards and presentation and hygiene must be exemplary. Equally high standards of cleanliness and excellence must be reflected in the homes and all other aspects of the minister's life, i.e. the office, the car etc., **being a standard to others.**

Christian Representation

Note: No church leader or ministry who *invents buys or sells documents* that falsely create the belief that someone is trained or ordained, will not be recognised by this Network Association.

His or her ministry would be seen as undesirable to the Christian faith. Ordained ministers must seek to bring such people to the integrity of the Christian representation.

Restoration is also important, therefore if it is brought to our attention that a pastor or leader is in sin or dealing with feelings of failure or sexual misconduct, marriage difficulties or any other misgivings, and perhaps about to say, "I quit." Then we want to help them.

> *Brethren, if a man is overtaken in any trespass, you who are spiritual restore such a one in a spirit of gentleness, considering yourself lest you also be tempted.*
>
> *(Galatians 6:1 NKJV)*

Sending Progress Report

If any member of the network goes for a period of *"one year"* without sending a progress report, we will see this as *a lack of response or commitment* on their part. We then will send a letter of concern. If this then is ignored we will take it that their desire to be associated with the association has come to a close.

Remember:

"Connecting for Excellence International Apostolic Network of Churches and Ministries in Association" is an "umbrella title" for those in:

- **Association:** i.e. body of persons organised for joint purpose; connection of ideas and fellowship

- **Affiliation:** i.e. "affiliating or being affiliated - order, compelling... help and support." An obligatory relationship between "Connecting for Excellence International Apostolic Network" and "LifeStyle International Christian University," and those affiliated

We have an obligation to help aid and support if one comes under the umbrella of affiliation.

❖

CHAPTER 39

Preventing Ministry Burnout

According to some studies 1,500 pastors per month quit the ministry. You don't have to be the next statistic. **Therefore the question is,** "Are you guarding your ministry from ministry burnout?"

Ministry Today magazine, which serves and empowers church leaders or Spirit-led ministers, by providing practical, relevant tools for growth, asked Larry Huch what he believes pastors can do to prevent burnout. Here's what he had to say:

Keep Your Priorities Straight

- *First* – God; if I don't have a relationship *with* Him, I can't minister *for* Him

- *Second* is my wife; if I lose her, I lose my destiny
- *Third* are my children; why do we work so hard to get other people into heaven and then ignore our own children?
- *Fourth* is our staff
- *Fifth* is our church

Jesus says that His yoke is easy, and His burden is light. This doesn't mean you don't work hard – you just don't work *"worried."* You have to believe you are going to win and keep the victory. One of the ways you do that is through the right fellowship with others.

Don't sacrifice everything for the church. God does not need that. I know of one man who wants nothing to do with Christianity because even though his father was a pastor and everyone thought he was a great man of God, **he had a mistress.** If the mistress needed carpet, furniture or money, it was there, but if the man's wife or family had a need, it wasn't there. ***The "mistress" wasn't a woman – it was the church.***

Don't Let Everyone Dump on You

You cannot let people call you 24 hours a day. My job is to motivate and teach. I have trained my staff to handle various areas of responsibility; they don't come to me with everything. ***You have to guard the anointing.***

Know when it's time to step up to a new level. When you're pioneering a church, you do everything. But as the church grows, you have to train people to do the work of the ministry. As a pastor, you need to stay fresh in your relationship with God so you can bring a fresh word to the people.

Don't put people in a position to win their loyalty. Pastors spend too much time trying to lure people in, or back into the church, when these people aren't going to make it anyway – they just want to manipulate you.

Quit baby-sitting Christians and win souls, and you'll stay fresh. If somebody backslides, I'll go after him or her. But not if somebody leaves because they're mad nobody called them. I'm not here to baby-sit. If you're three weeks old, we'll change your diaper; but if you're 30 years old, we have a problem.

Know your calling. Many people who are pastoring churches are doing something they are not called to do. Maybe they're called to be pastors, but not *senior* pastors. If you are not in the right position on the team, it will wear you out.

Take Joe Montana, one of the greatest quarterbacks of all time. If you give him the same ball, the same place, the same game and the same team, but change his number to a line-backer, not only will he not be the best, *he'll die*. He won't make it because he's in the wrong position. You have to know your calling. And no matter how good you are, you have to build the right team around you.

There must be a Mentoring Process for Ministry

Get good training and mentorship. In addition to biblical knowledge, you also need to have other skills, such as people skills and hands-on ministry experience. I like the pattern of some of the large churches in South America.

- *First,* you have to be saved
- *Then* filled with the Spirit
- *Then* able to win people on the streets
- *Then* able to build a cell group, and out of that birth other cell groups
- *Then* you start a church that becomes self-supporting
- *Then* you are brought home, and leadership lays hands on you
- **<u>And then you are called a pastor</u>**

Finally, embrace God's love. God is a good God. He is more interested in you, the worker, than He is in your work. You are not alone. God will build relationships – we are in this together. You will see visions and dreams that were stolen given back.

This is the greatest era the church has ever seen.

Chapter 40

Team Ministry

Forbes Magazine once said, "Success is 10% ability, 30% credibility and 60% visibility. Ability + credibility = visibility." Help a person develop their ability to meet the needs of others. When people begin to experience healing through another person, this makes that person's ministry credible.

They will then begin to encourage others to get involved in your ministry. Visibility will be a natural by-product and your ministry will be released to the nations.

Recommend a list of helpful books that will benefit your spiritual sons and daughters develop and take on your spirit. Explain why each is important and have all the team reading the same book for a month. So that everyone is being impacted at the same time, then you can have collective and constructive dialogue.

In addition ensure personal contact each month with every individual on the team. This can be achieved over meals, coffee, prayer times, counselling and recreation time or calls. Possibly, your team is too large for this, so then it's necessary to raise up team leaders or a team pastor who possesses your heart to keep the personal touch in the ministry. Training and development – personal time – maturity!

Recognise spiritual sons and Daughters

- Start praying for and recognise spiritual sons and daughters that God wants to add to your ministry (Matthew 4:18-22; 2 Peter 1:3-11)
- Cultivate parameters and credentials for ministry team participation
- Define and list various areas of duty and potential team involvement
- Pray 1 Chronicles 28:21, "…every willing man of any skill will be with you in all the work for all kinds of service" (NASB)
- Increase the training process of your spiritual sons and daughters, concentrating more upon *impartation* than information (John 5:19,20; John 17:4-8)

Single-mindedness is required for impact. All you do is an employment of time, initiative and resources. The most effective use of your time is to centre it up on the right people who can replicate your heart and ministry. The more people involved in meeting the needs of others, the more others will contribute the resources to meet your operating costs.

The ultimate confirmation of true spiritual fathers is the commissioning of spiritual sons to the nations.

- Jesus did the work and others spectated
- Jesus did the work and others aided
- Others did the work and Jesus spectated!
- Others did the work and Jesus departed

Cultivate clear parameters, strategies, boundaries, and targets for your ministry team (Romans 13; Ephesians 4:22-32). People need to know what is expected and where they stand. 80% of the development of future leaders involves giving them reachable goals, occasion for responsibility, problems to solve and the resources to succeed.

Give each team member a variety of opportunities to serve and prove their ability to handle responsibility. Find out which areas draw the best from them and which draw out the worst. What nurtures their gifts and what kills them.

Growth in the team requires the development of team leaders or pastors (Numbers 11:16, 17). Team leaders are influencers, who people naturally like to follow. They recognise what needs doing and get it done. They are fixers, discerning the needs of each member and are always looking to meet them. They are problem solvers.

Catching the Vision

Team leaders are good managers, who take pleasure in catching the vision of the leader and then motivating others.

Others usually follow them because of the influence of the spiritual father. In other words they are better at managing than leading! Functioning best as a number two rather than a number one. In the kind of support role, that listens to the vision of the spiritual father and then helps to execute it to the max.

The team leader influences the spiritual atmosphere of the whole team. He or she is the one with whom people will most likely be vulnerable and discuss their problems with. They are responsible to ensure that each individual team member walks in the central values of the ministry. Bringing correction where it's needed, with humility and encouragement.

Teachers are gifted with the ability to communicate the deeper things of God in a simple and coherent manner, so that each person is able to comprehend. They are not just distributors of digital information, but midwives that help birth revelation through the act of impartation into the lives of others.

Bringing forth a Ministry

In Luke 1:26-38 we can read the account where the angel Gabriel gave Mary a personal prophecy about bringing forth a ministry (Christ) that would bless the world. The natural process that she had to undergo parallels the spiritual process that we must undergo to bring forth a spiritual baby (ordained ministry).

- Isaiah 66:8 – Zion in labour – then she gives birth
- Romans 8:26 – the Spirit helps us

Prior to the birthing process, we must develop an intimate relationship with God who causes His Spirit to plant seeds of faith and vision, which develop and grow like a baby in the womb of our spirit. Patience and flexibility are required for the long process from conception to delivery.

- James 1:15 – sin is also birthed, when full-grown gives birth to death
- James 1:21 – humbly accept the word planted in you, which can save you

Like an expectant Mary whose womb was stretched, we are stretched until we feel we cannot grow anymore. We become awkward and like the pregnant woman after nine months, we feel that we can take no more! Yet things must get worse before they get better, with the hardest labour pains coming at delivery.

The Twelfth Hour Experience

The 12th hour experience can be drawn out and just before our promise comes forth into the light, we experience our darkest hour of labour and intensity. We are visited with doubting thoughts like, "Why did I ask for this, I don't want to go through with it. It's not worth it!"

Instead, as we flow with the labour pains, before we realize it, the fruit of our labour is revealed! Our ministry comes forth for all to see. And like any new baby, a ministry will go through its first vulnerable years of dependency. As we pour out our lives into it, it will eventually self-advocate. All it will require from us is our parental vision, care, counsel and covering.

Any "success" born outside of due process, will not be able to sustain itself or reach fullest potential (Isaiah 66:7-8).

1) Life		a) Parental vision
2) Energy	in time	b) Care
3) Time		c) Counsel
4) Ability		d) Covering

Discouragement diminishes once you realise - God is moving indeed!

CHAPTER 41

Thoughtful Questions

What is required of me to be a part of the "Connecting for Excellence International Apostolic Network of Churches and Ministries in Association?"

A. You must have some type of relational connection with the Board of Directors whether they are Senior Pastors/Apostles and/or the Senior Overseer.

Q. What type of authoritative jurisdiction am I giving to the "Connecting for Excellence International Apostolic Network" in order for me to become a partner?

A. None as such, it is our belief that each pastor or leader is responsible before God for his or her group of people that has been given to them by God. I.e. it is your ordained ministry. Itinerant ministries on the other hand should be submitting to an apostolic pastor, elders or an apostolic team.

We believe entirely on kingdom structure, whereas one has to ask the question, "Are they a local pastor or some other ministry gift?" (Ephesians 4:11-16)

The ministry gifts are mentioned throughout the bible, but the church as a whole seems to be in total confusion about who's who and where they fit in! And yet no area of ministry has been so well documented, so well developed in the New Testament as the ministry of the apostle.

Scripture is Clear

These apostolic ministries have so often been misunderstood, in fact many people refuse to acknowledge such gifts because of misunderstanding. Just because we neglect or choose to ignore that there is a structure of authority, does not mean that it doesn't exist. This causes great damage in the body of Christ, because the scriptures are clear, that it's these apostolic gifts that prepare God's people for works of service.

If the ministry of an apostle does not function properly within and over, then nothing else will. It has to be said that there is a lot of ambition and rebellion amongst those who have so-called ministries.

They have been raised to go their own way and do what they please with an attitude that says, "No one is going to tell me what to do, this is my ministry and I'm submitting it to no man. I'm serving Jesus!"

You cannot serve Jesus in ministry without submitting to His delegated authority. Remember, if you have the above attitude, you will have problems that you don't need to bear.

When the Holy Spirit speaks to the church and reveals things to the body of Christ, He always brings order and discipline to accomplish His work. Everyone loves a good meeting and enjoys revelation and anointing and power, but dislikes order, reproof, discipline. We need to come to that place where we can enjoy every aspect of God's word.

The apostle and prophet's ministry is of course the foundational gifting that we need to build on and to a great extent deal with the disciplining of the saints. The apostle can see how things should be maintained and developed and to bring order where there is confusion. But many are trying to build their house without foundations that will support all that God desires.

Not Imposing but Order

The apostolic brings order and stability; many might think that the apostolic ministry is imposing. For God's work to be truly established it will require God's strength and order. This is why the ministry of the apostle is as essential as are all the other ministry gifts.

The last portion of Ephesians 4:8 says, "He...gave gifts to men." "He" refers to Jesus, who is the one who gives the gifts and places them in the church (1 Corinthians 12:18).

Despite their different functions, the gifts should work together. Ulf Ekman in his book, "The Apostolic Ministry" says on page 10, "That first we need to realise that the ministry gifts are individuals with a task from heaven, they are gifts to the body of Christ and should be accepted as such. Some consider ministry gifts as a threat, while others become confused and uncertain. But if we want to benefit from them, then we must accept them as they are.

We read in the forth chapter of Ephesians that God wants us to come to a point of spiritual maturity. He wants us to attain to the whole measure of the fullness of Christ, no longer driven by every wind of teaching. The Holy Spirit has the same desire you have for people to be saved and edified, and for God's glory and for the works of Jesus to be made manifest.

God's Ordained Order

He longs to affect the world in a way that makes the kingdom of God 'visible.' This is achieved as the body of Christ is built up through the ministry gifts. However, this is often overlooked and becomes one of the major causes for the problems and attacks against the body of Christ among the ministry gifts.

The enemy strikes here more than anywhere else, because if the ministry gifts don't function, as they should, then neither will anything else. They are an inherent part of God's planed and ordained order.

Some people teach that the ministry gifts are unimportant or unnecessary, as long as everything is functioning well. Everyone needs to be involved in the body of Christ, but this can only happen when the ministry gifts function effectively.

'But this has nothing to do with me! I'm just an ordinary Christian. I'm not called to the ministry gifts.' You're wrong! You still need to recognise God's servants, and discern between true and false in this vital area. You are directly affected whether you have a special calling or not. You need to know and accept how God works through His servants."[2]

CHAPTER 42

Financial Economy

What is my financial obligation to the "Connecting for Excellence International Apostolic Network?"

A. We teach from Malachi 3:8-10, which tells us to bring our tithes and offerings into the storehouse. You as a pastor or an itinerant ministry would not exist without this financial, biblical, God given teaching. We also teach that the members of our churches should tithe to the church (storehouse) to which the member belongs. Encouraging them from the biblical concept that ten per cent of their income should be their tithe.

It is our belief that if partners of "Connecting for Excellence International Apostolic Network, Churches and Ministries in Association" are serious about their covenant relationship, they would not hesitate to give tithes and offerings to the said mentioned association.

This is a gift set aside monthly to help the association help others. Remember for our partners we are the storehouse.

God's ways of Order of Finance

As mentioned in chapter thirty-three, "Honouring Your Apostle" that one of the questions that I had for many years regarding finance was in relation to, "Does a leader need to tithe the tithe?" The answer to this is found in Numbers 18:26-29; remember the Levite priests were commanded to pay a tithe from the tithe that they received from the people.

> *Speak to the Levites and say to them: "When you receive from the Israelites the tithe I give you as your inheritance, you must present a tenth of that tithe as the Lord's offering. Your offering will be reckoned to you as grain from the threshing-floor or juice from the winepress. In this way you also will present an offering to the LORD from all the tithes you receive from the Israelites. From these tithes you must give* <u>the LORD's portion to Aaron</u> **(your apostle)** *the priest. You must present as the LORD's portion the best and holiest part of everything given to you."*

As in the reference we see in the Old Testament where the priests lived off of the tithe, we then must be clear in our teaching when we teach on the subject of *God's ways of order of finance*. In regard to church leadership or directors of a Christian organization, regardless of terminology, denominational preference or apostolic network the principle being that we teach one thing and then excuse ourselves because of our preference of position – this is completely hypocritical.

Many churches, pastors give offerings – such as to the itinerant ministry that has been ministering in their church. Or to their structural development or outreach project. Of course these things are wonderful but usually these gifts are given in regard to ones own vision.

This is no different for many in relationship to develop one's own business. This is not wrong in itself, God wants us to develop the vision that He has given to us, one encourages members to give to such things *(this will enhance those members)*. Encourage them to tithe and give offerings into the storehouse so that there will be meat in God's house and an open heaven, then the people thereof can prosper. But when one stands back – this in theory looks wonderful, yet actually is also falling into the trap of deception.

In these endtimes not only will there be a greater development of networking, where ministries are concerned, but also the network of the apostolic ministry. I believe that it's important to remain connected, committed and under the right structural covering. For example every leader or pastor needs to be in relationship and accountable.

Not only are individual members called to be responsible in being connected to the body of Christ, i.e. the local church but also each church, leadership, or pastor needs to be connected to the wider body. The flow of God's anointing and blessing comes through connection, apostolic relationship and unity *(Psalms 133:1, 3)*.

What am I saying then?

It's important to teach on tithing but you as an organization or church should also be tithing to whom God has connected you to. You might say, well I'm in relationship to many. Yes, that may be true and certainly correct, **but who is *your* pastor or apostle? Who is the person that you submit yourself to?** This is where you should tithe, the best and holiest part of everything given to you…v29. And I don't mean your wage I mean 10% of the income of the WHOLE of your ministry or church.

This will not only release an open heaven over your ministry, which will flow down through every branch of your vision *(remembering that your tithe opens up the floodgate)*. And then of course your offering that goes to those itinerant ministries etc. will bring a harvest of supply to you and your ministry, which will affect also your people.

You then will be living what you teach. Let me just mention this, more as a statement; there are many that are in ministry that are not pastors or leaders. They might be an evangelist, prophet etc., but what I find as I travel is that pastors have an attitude that their ministry should be the only ministry in the church to receive a wage. They might pay their secretary or heads of departments etc., but what about the apostolic itinerary ministries?

Because what we have is ministry gifts starting churches because they perceive that the only way to finance their ministry is to pastor. What they really needed was to be part of an apostolic team, where the leader considered it his role

Financial Economy

to make sure that he enhances a balanced ministry. They then can at least have a financial foundation i.e. weekly support – so they can focus on what God has called them to do rather than look to try and survive in the wrong position.

Praise the Lord for true accountability, for honesty, for love, for protection, for wisdom. It all comes from God and we are not to be wading out there all alone without them.

God has made every provision for us to be successful and stay that way and *"not go down in defeat for one split second"* if only we will heed to His voice and obey His wisdom found in His word. All we need is there – that's where our motto originates from – *"His voice is all the provision you need."* Because every guideline – plumb line – guiding fork and instruction manual is right there in the word of God. If we fall short, we fall short of our knowledge of that word or our willingness to obey it!

Q. What if I am already financially supporting other organisations?

A. "Connecting for Excellence International Apostolic Network" is not looking to be the only organisation that you are involved with. As you will discover from part one, two and three of these books, "The Age of Apostolic Apostleship." You can be a partner that is in association, i.e. being part of a body of persons organised for joint purpose, connection or ideas and fellowship.

Q. Where do my monthly contributions *(seed)* to the association network go?

A. Your monthly support is separated into several categories; firstly there is of course the administration of any organisation. The expense of stationery and printing of what you find in your hands. Also travelling expenses for the senior overseer, to those churches and ministries who are diligently looking to be faithful, this has to be shown through their consistency of pushing into the said organisation.

Endtime devastations, flooding, earthquakes, fire etc., or the economy that has escalated or collapsed. We find this problem of collapsed economy in many countries around the would, I know in Uganda for instance, where we help a number of churches, that the tithes and offerings from these village churches hardly produce any currency at all, just enough to feed perhaps a pastor.

In these cases I might add we must do our utmost to help as God directs (Romans 15:23-28).

Chapter 43

Ministry Ordination

Can the "Connecting for Excellence International Apostolic Network" ordain me?

A. Yes. There is a two-level plan *(in theory)*, of and leading up to ordination. Firstly, you have to become a "partner" of "Connecting for Excellence International Apostolic Network," *(there needs to be a relationship first)* and then you can apply for ordination.

Increasing numbers of men and women in full time ministry have been ordained, receiving ordination. I have had the pleasure of ordaining some five hundred people to date of this book as a result of the apostolic ministry – and we are now seeing their ministries and churches multiply, growing in strength and maturity.

For example Pastor Luke of the "Royal Priesthood Mission Centre International," Kenya, wrote and said, "your teachings and general interaction in ministry was fatherly, what we saw was the true mark of an apostle. As a matter of fact we have been praying to God to give us a man with an apostolic calling to oversee our church and many that the Lord will lead us to pioneer. We being an independent ministry need someone we can look to for advise and can speak insight into our lives as the Lord directs him."

The church in Kenya can also enable a National Platform, where other apostolic ministries can gather and be heard. This will enhance leadership. My heart is not to take from but to serve these leaders, providing platforms, with teaching seminars etc., celebration meetings and the development of a world class Christian University, LifeStyle International with extension campuses.

Q. Do I have to do away with or disconnect from my affiliation with other organisations that I am already ordained with in order to join "Connecting for Excellence International Apostolic Network?"

A. No. This is not a denomination although it is a structure, nor is it a dictatorship. What we desire is an affiliation of association in relationship to what the Spirit of God is doing and saying. Our purpose is not to gain control. Apostolic ministries are not meant to have a Pope-like figure at the point of some triangle. This ministry is foundational and will enhance your foundations. It's to focus your attention to ministry growth and development, helping you to become established as a ministry of excellence, to obtain all that God has for you.

When one is ordained the following items shall be provided *(if requested),*

- Letter of recognition
- Certificate
- Ministers identification card; this is to help with hospital visitation i.e.
- Apostle Doctor Alan Pateman's four books on The Age of Apostleship, on behalf of "Connecting for Excellence International Apostolic Network, Churches and Ministries in Association."

Chapter 44

What is Ordination?

Ordination is a biblical principle and directive that is found throughout both the Old and New Testaments. It can be seen in operation first of all in the Garden of Eden and then repeatedly during every spiritual awakening right through to the Acts of the Apostles and the early church. There is however, reference to ordination before this time by the prophet Ezekiel, where he says of Lucifer,

> *You were anointed as a guardian cherub, for so I ordained you. You were on the holy mount of God; you walked among the fiery stones.*
>
> *(Ezekiel 28:14)*

He prophesies concerning Satan that, prior to his rebellion and fall, he was ordained *(or set in place)* by God as an anointed cherub on the holy mount of God.

This pre-time prophetic revelation serves to show the importance of ordination within the kingdom and body of the Lord Jesus Christ. His rejection due to pride, led to rebellion, violence and disorder.

> *...God is not a God of disorder...*
> *(1 Corinthians 14:33)*

The importance and reason for **ordaining ministers is fundamental** to the nature and character of God. He loves order - He created it and used it to bring to birth the world and everything in it - including mankind. He ordained light and darkness. He ordained earth and sky, land and sea and in so doing provided a structured environment for mankind.

> *Now the Lord God had planted a garden in the East, in Eden; and there he put the man he had formed.*
> *(Genesis 2:8)*

When God put Adam in the Garden of Eden, the **wording used implies appointment or ordination.** Adam was firstly appointed to a position provided and prepared for him; later on in verse 15, God completes the call by defining his responsibility i.e. to *"work it"* *(the garden)* and take care of it.

The principle itself is that of one who has authority, *delegating to another a commission of responsibility and therefore a realm of spiritual authority.* It is the highest form of *"service"* within the body of Christ. Jesus said, *"He who would be chief among you, would be the servant of all!"*

There are different degrees of ordination as there are different measures of service. Ordination therefore can be defined thus:

What is Ordination?

- The appointment of an individual to a place or position of authority
- The delegation to an individual of an area of responsibility; Moses ordained elders to assist in the management of the mighty nation of Israel

He chose capable men from all Israel and made them leaders of the people, officials over thousands, hundreds, fifties and tens.

(Exodus 18:25)

He also ordained the priesthood, with Aaron as high priest.

Have Aaron your brother brought to you from the Israelites, with his sons Nadab and Abihu, Eleazar and Ithamar, so that they may serve me as priests.

(Exodus 28:1)

Towards the end of his life and ministry he ordained Joshua - his disciple - to be his successor.

So the Lord said to Moses, "Take Joshua son of Nun, a man in whom is the spirit, and lay your hand on him. Make him stand before Eleazar the priest and the entire assembly and commission him in their presence. Give him some of your authority so that the whole Israelite community will obey him. He is to stand before Eleazar the priest, who will obtain decisions for him by inquiring of the Urim before the Lord. At his command, he and the entire community of the Israelites will go out, and at his command they will come in..."

> *Moses did as the Lord commanded him. He took Joshua and made him stand before Eleazar the priest and the whole assembly. Then he laid his hands on him and commissioned him, as the Lord instructed through Moses.*
> *(Numbers 27:18-23)*

The pattern continues with Samuel and David, Elijah and Elisha and many others, each exemplifying ordination as God's purpose for their day. Then Jesus speaking to His disciples states quite clearly that He chose and ordained them to go and bear fruit.

> *You did not choose me, but I chose you and **appointed** you to go and bear fruit - fruit that will last - then the Father will give you whatever you ask in my name.*
> *(John 15:16)*

When speaking to Peter after His resurrection. He commissions Peter to feed and take care of His sheep. In every instance mentioned, each individual had laid aside their own will and desire to take up and submit to, the will and desire of God. In so doing, they fulfilled their destiny and call, to powerful effect!

Q. If I am ordained as a part of the "Connecting for Excellence International Apostolic Network, Churches and Ministries Association," can I *(my church or ministry)* benefit from the association's non-profit/trust/charitable status?

A. Yes, yet only if you are in one of the nations within which we have an CFE Office. We encourage every member or organisation whether you are a pastor, an itinerant ministry, group, bible school etc., to apply for their-own non-profit or charitable trust status that is legal within one's own country.

Chapter 45

Covenant Partnership

Can I be a partner only of the "Connecting for Excellence International Apostolic Network, Churches and Ministries in Association?"

A. Yes. "Partnership is not a new idea nor is it just a new way to raise money. It is a systematic method, or ordinance, initiated by God, to bring a manifestation of increase into every area of the life of every believer" (Roberts Liardon).

Being a covenant partner has its benefits, like special offers on all book and audio material, reserved seating at CFE conferences, our staff and of course Jenny and I praying for you on a regular basis. We want you to be blessed, healthy, and full of the Holy Spirit and of course strong in faith.

To be a covenant partner you will also receive a Quarterly Newsletter *(Hearing His Voice)* that you will find full of news and encouragement. Just remember that every person who is saved, healed, delivered and touched by the power of God through this ministry has you to thank. Why? Because, when you link up with us at CFE in Covenant Partnership you literally become part of the work that we are doing.

Remember covenant partnership is a relationship where we both work toward the same goal for everyone's good. It is a commitment of both parties standing together in faith, joining their resources to accomplish a common goal or vision.

Perfect Opportunity

Perhaps you have wanted to go to the nations and to somehow be part of what God is doing in the world today and not known how! Well, here is your perfect opportunity! By supporting this ministry both financially and prayerfully, it can be just as rewarding for you as if you had been to the nations personally, (Matthew 10:41-42).

You don't miss out on any of the excitement because all of the testimony and all of the experience, stories and knowledge gained on trips will be brought back and given to you through our newsletter! (Romans 8:37)

Living life at home and yet still being active in the rest of the world at the same time! All it takes is money that's all, and with a little help from our friends we'll go all over the world with God's word, God's power, God's healing and God's love.

Covenant Partnership

We are believing for an army of 10,000 PARTNERS who will faithfully pray and support with their finance this ministry and association on a monthly basis *(50 Euros a month)*. Nothing can stop us if we stand together – there is power in agreement!

Chapter 46

Responsive Thoughts

Will we receive regular updates and addresses of all member churches and ministries for relationship purposes and the invitation of those in the itinerant apostolic ministry team?

A. There should be on a yearly basis an update (report) of the ministry, changes that have been made, new members etc. This is separate from the newsletter called "Truth for the Journey." But you are welcome to write in for any details on any of the above.

Q. Are there any rules that I need to be aware of?

A. Yes as you have already discovered, but in this section let me suggest a number one rule in everything you do; and that is, *"to hear the Voice of the Lord."*

Q. Can we introduce or recommend fellow colleagues to this network?

A. As it has already been stated we believe that all local pastors / ministry gifts should be involved within some kind of structure. Therefore encourage all those isolated and yet gifted men and women to be involved in what we believe a true Network of Association should entail.

Q. Can we write or ring directly to the senior apostle?

A. Yes, of course it is important to be able to speak to the Senior Overseer, but this needs to be directed through one of the directors, two to three days before, so that no inconvenience is caused. Please state general concern or question. Then you will be instructed to "a given time." This is not to delay or put you off, it is out of respect as Apostle Alan is very busy. Writing (or email) usually is a better way of contact; letters can be sent directly to the international address.

Q. Do I need to be at an annual CFE apostolic, national or international conference?

A. Yes please. It is important for all associate ministers to be part of a national conference. For one, we have at these conferences, teaching for pastors and leaders. This is where impartation can be given, yearly updates, apostolic relationships built. Also it is of the utmost importance to encourage as many of your people to attend, as this builds unity and fervour for the upcoming months.

Q. How does one apply?

Responsive Thoughts

A. Your application form is available on our website, www.cfeapostolicnetwork.com, please see instructions in the back of this book. The form needs to be sent to the International Head Offices. We will need three passport photos with your application; one of these is for the minister's identification card, if you desire one.

❖

CHAPTER 47

Theological Education

Can you explain what **"LifeStyle International Christian University"** is all about and do I have to attend?

A. Seasons might be changing but God's word remains the same. My heart is to help train, equip and be a blessing to those men and women who will be willing to fulfil their potential in ministry and be properly equipped for service. We desire for you to walk and live in the authority and power of God's word and His precious Holy Spirit.

Theological education is held for ministers and lay people alike. This is an interdenominational apostolic ministry of the Holy Spirit. Degrees offered at our university range from a "Diploma in Theology" to a "Doctor of Philosophy" for those who decide to go through the full university program. Remember, Christian believers are called by God to mature spiritually and to have an active (LifeStyle) part in Christian service regardless of their status.

It's undeniable that in today's world, recognized education has become indispensable; therefore it is our desire to offer well-balanced and well-structured courses. Those that have been written by gifted and talented ministers of God, who seek to be inspired by God's word and His Holy Spirit.

Excellent Curriculum

Consequently we have put together an **excellent curriculum**, designed both for correspondence students and extension campuses, which is a strategy to reach the distant learner, whether provincial, national or international.

Teaching and equipping people to reach their divine destiny in God is the main focus of "Connecting for Excellence International Apostolic Network." With hundreds of students trained throughout the globe.

So, it's without any fear of contradiction that we say this is a growing platform, where men and women of dignity and passion can grow and be established in their God given endeavours. As God is the healer of the nations, we pray and believe that many of our alumni will go on to **become world changers** in their own right.

And yes you need to consider becoming one of our international students! It would be our privilege to welcome you from around the world to LifeStyle International Christian University.

Theological Education

Your Advantages:

- Internationally recognised credits
- Opportunity to complete your Diploma, Associate, Bachelor, Master and Doctoral degree!
- Affordable student tuition through our one course one payment scheme
- Incentives and free tuition for every one who finds 5 paying students
- Up to 70% scholarships
- Practical tools to release students into their destinies
- Relevant studies
- Helping to equip students for life and ministry
- Teaching syllabuses authored by internationally well-known teachers
- **HONORARY DEGREES available!**
- And Ordination

CHAPTER 48

The Apostolic Doctrines, Articles of Belief

Apostle Doctor Christian Harfouche says, "From the first years of the Church—as the Apostles gave themselves to prayer and the ministry of the Word, as the New Testament Scriptures were inspired, confirmed, written, and distributed, the earliest Church communities in Jerusalem, Antioch, and beyond developed certain scriptural statements of faith, creeds.

Some were very simple, others more complex, however for centuries, all over the world, these words of confirmation and agreement were spoken by the Body of Christ, preserving and transmitting the true Orthodoxy—or right way—of the Apostolic Doctrine, the Faith delivered to us.

In the three-hundreds, the Church consolidated and amplified these creeds into a single, universally-accepted statement of the quintessential Christian Faith. The result was a singular Creed, accepted and promulgated by a worldwide gathering of Christian leaders, representing every Christian community spread across the globe.

This ecumenical, pre-denominational unity and agreement continued to transmit and impart a scriptural record of understanding that confirms unequivocally that our Apostolic Faith stands upon the original First Century Faith of the Church of Jerusalem, the Church of Antioch, and the Christian Faith as it is expressed and believed to date by all genuine Christian families worldwide" (globalrevival.com/about/statement-of-faith).

Statement of Faith

The programme of activities of the ministry of CFE shall be based upon and at all times shall be consistent with the following beliefs and statement of faith:

The Scriptures Inspired:

The scriptures, both the Old and the New Testament, are verbally inspired of God and are the revelation of God to man, the infallible, authoritative rule of faith and conduct *(2 Timothy 3:15-17, 1 Thessalonians 2:13, 2 Peter 1:21).*

The One True God:

The one true God has revealed Himself as the eternally self-existent "I AM" the creator of heaven and earth and the redeemer of mankind. He has further revealed Himself as embodying the principles of relationship and association as Father, Son and Holy Ghost *(Deuteronomy 6:4; Isaiah 43:10-11; Matthew 28:29; Luke 3:22).*

The Deity of the Lord Jesus Christ:

The Lord Jesus Christ is the eternal Son of God. The scriptures declare:

- His virgin birth *(Matthew 1:23; Luke 1:31-35)*
- His sinless life *(Hebrews 7:26; 1 Peter 2:22)*
- His miracles *(Acts 2:22; 10:38)*
- His substitutionary work on the cross *(1 Corinthians 15:3; 2 Corinthians 5:21)*
- His bodily resurrection from the dead *(Matthew 28:6; Luke 24:39; 1 Corinthians 15:4)*
- His exaltation to the right hand of God *(Acts 1:9,11; 2:33; Philippians 2:9-11; Hebrews 1-3)*

The Fall of Man:

Man was created good and upright, for God said, "Let us make man in our image, after our likeness." However, man, by voluntary transgression fell, and thereby incurred not only physical death but also spiritual death, which is separation from God *(Genesis 1:26, 27; 2:17; 3:6; Romans 5:12-19).*

The Salvation of Man:

Man's only hope of redemption is through the shed blood of Jesus Christ the Son of God.

- Conditions of Salvation:
  Salvation is received through repentance toward God and faith toward the Lord Jesus Christ. By the washing of regeneration and renewing of the Holy Ghost, being justified through faith, man becomes an heir of God according to the hope of eternal life *(Luke 24:47; John 3:3; Romans 10:13-15; Ephesians 2:8; Titus 2:11; 3:5-7).*

- The Evidence of Salvation:
  The inward evidence of Salvation is the direct witness of the Spirit *(Romans 8:16).*

  The outward evidence to all men is a life of righteousness and true holiness *(Ephesians 4:24; Titus 2:12).*

The Ordinances of The Church:

- Baptism in Water:
  The ordinance of baptism by immersion is commanded in the scriptures. All who repent and believe of the Christ as Saviour and Lord are to be baptised. Thus they declare to the world that they have died with Christ and that they also have been raised with Him to walk in newness of life *(Matthew 28:19; Mark 16:16; Acts 10:47-48; Romans 6:4).*

- The Holy Communion:
  The Lord's Supper consisting of the elements – bread and the fruit of the vine – is the symbol expressing our sharing the divine nature of our Lord Jesus Christ *(2 Peter 1:4)*, a memorial of His suffering and death *(1 Corinthians 11:26)*, and is enjoined on all believers "...till He come."

The Baptism in the Holy Spirit:

All believers are entitled to and should ardently expect and earnestly seek the promise of the Father, the baptism in the Holy Ghost and fire, according to the command of our Lord Jesus Christ.

This was the normal experience of all in the early Christian Church. With it comes the endowment of power for life and service, the bestowal of the gifts and their uses in the work of the ministry *(Luke 24:49; Acts 1:4,8; 1 Corinthians 12:1-31).*

This experience is distinct from and subsequent to the experience of the new birth *(Acts 8:12-17; 19:44-46; 11:14-16; 15:7-9).* With the baptism in the Holy Ghost comes such experience as an ever-flowing fullness of the Spirit *(John 7:37-39; Acts 4:8)* and a more active love for Christ, for His word and for the lost *(Mark 16:20).*

The Evidence of the Baptism in the Holy Spirit:

The baptism of believers in the Holy Ghost is witnessed by the initial physical sign of speaking with other tongues as the Spirit of God gives them utterance *(Acts 2:4).* The speaking in tongues in this instance, is the same in essence as the gift of tongues *(1 Corinthians 12:4-10, 28),* but different in purpose and use.

Sanctification:

Sanctification is an act of separation from that which is evil and of dedication unto God *(Romans 12:1; 1 Thessalonians 4:23; Hebrews 13:12).* The scriptures teach a life of "holiness without which no man shall see the Lord" *(Hebrews 12:14)*, and by the power of the Holy Spirit we are able to obey the command *"Be ye holy, for I am holy" (1 Peter 1:15, 16)*.

Sanctification is realised in the believer by recognising his identification with Christ in His death and resurrection and by faith reckoning daily upon the fact that union and by offering every faculty continually to the dominion of the Holy Spirit *(Romans 6:1-11,13; 8:1,2,13; Galatians 2:20; Philippians 2:12-13; 1 Peter 1:5)*.

The Church:

The Church is the body of Christ, the habitation of God through the Spirit with divine appointments for the fulfilment of her great commission. Each believer, born of the Spirit, is an integral part of the General Assembly and Church of the first-born, which are written in heaven *(Ephesians 1:22-23; 2:22; Hebrews 12:23)*.

The Ministry:

A divinely called and scripturally ordained ministry has been provided by our Lord for a two-fold purpose:

- The Evangelization of the World
- The edifying of the body of Christ *(Mark 16:15-20; Ephesians 4:11-13)*

Divine Healing:

Divine healing is an integral part of the gospel. Deliverance from sickness is provided for in the atonement and is the privilege of all believers *(Isaiah 53:4-5; Matthew 8:16-17; James 5:14-16).*

The Blessed Hope:

The second coming of Christ includes the rapture of the saints which is one blessed hope, followed by the visible return of Christ with his saints to reign on the earth for one thousand years *(Zechariah 14:5; Matthew 24:27-30; Revelation 1:7; 19:11-14; 20:1-6).*

This millennial reign will bring salvation of national Israel *(Ezekiel 37:21-22; Zephaniah 3:19-20; Romans 11:26-27)* and the establishment of universal peace *(Isaiah 11:6-9; Psalms 72:3-8; Micah 4:3-4).*

The Final Judgement:

There will be a final judgement in which the wicked dead will be raised and judged according to their works. Whosoever is not found written in the Book of Life, together with the devil and his angels, the beast and the false prophet, will be consigned to everlasting punishment in the lake, which burneth with fire and brimstone, which is the second death *(Matthew 9:43-48; Revelation 19:20; 20:11-15; 21:8).*

The Heaven and the New Earth:

We according to his promise, look for new heavens and a new earth, wherein dwelleth righteousness.
(2 Peter 3:13; Revelation 21:22)

Ordinances:

The ordinance of baptism by immersion in water *(Matthew 28:19)* shall be administered to all those who have repented of their sins and who have believed of the Lord Jesus Christ to the saving of their souls, and who give clear evidence of their salvation *(Romans 6:3-5, Colossians 2:12)*.

The ordinance of the Lord's Supper shall be observed regularly as enjoined in the scriptures *(Luke 22:19-20; 1 Corinthians 11:23-26)*.

Notes

1. Hamon, Bill. Apostles, Prophets and the Coming Moves of God. Copyright © 1997. Published by Destiny Image Publishers, Inc. Printed in USA. p.14

2. Ekman, Ulf. The Apostolic Ministry. Copyright © 1995. Published by Word of Life Publications. Printed in Sweden. p.10-11

Bible Translations:

- Unless otherwise indicated, all scriptural quotations are from the HOLY BIBLE, NEW INTERNATIONAL VERSION ®. NIV ®. Copyright © 1973, 1978, 1984 by the International Bible Society. Used by permission of Zondervan Publishing House. All rights reserved.

- Scripture references marked NASB are taken from New American Standard Bible®, Copyright © 1960, 1962, 1963, 1968, 1971, 1972, 1973, 1975, 1977, 1995 by The Lockman Foundation. Used by permission.

- Scripture references marked NKJV are taken from the New King James Version. Copyright © 1982 by Thomas Nelson, 1982 by Thomas Nelson, Inc. Used by permission. All rights reserved.

Your Network

Our heart and passion behind **"Connecting for Excellence International Apostolic Network"** is to reach out to the world with the gospel, making disciples. It is our passion to raise up the leaders of tomorrow, who will have influence in all realms of authority, men and women of strategy, wisdom, and true godliness, who'll stand with stature and maturity in this hour.

A vision to develop networks of relationships *(apostolic companies)*, which the Holy Spirit is developing, these relationships look for apostolic support and encouragement. In so doing our desire is to encourage the body of Christ to move boldly and powerfully in the supernatural, released to fulfil their divine destinies for the glory of God.

Too many talented and sincere people experience misalignments in their lives, which only serve to quash, distract and take away from God's purpose. Misalignments can only ever take away. However divine connections are a lifeline.

Genuine relationships are not easily come by. They are forged out of life through commitment, time and energy. There is a price to such relationships, but the price is greater still if we don't take the time to ever pursue such connections.

Relationship – can be such a loose word but in the context of ministry or even business you cannot survive without the right connections or contacts. With God involved these become divine connections.

The vision provides the opportunity for:

- Apostolic relationships
- Networking
- Mentoring for ministry development
- Prophetic impartation and integration
- Teaching through LICU
- Making disciples and teaching them to walk in the power of the resurrection
- Ministry Ordination

Apply Today

Please go to our Connecting for Excellence International Apostolic Network website at www.cfeapostolicnetwork.com, where you can find the **Application Form** as a PDF file on the "Services" page.

When you click on the link, the PDF document <u>downloads automatically</u> unto your computer or device, from where you can <u>print</u> out the form.

Once you have <u>filled</u> all pages, you may return your form along with **three passport photos** to our Head Office *(please see address details enclosed on the form)*. Alternatively you may scan and submit your form as a PDF file to our email address at info@cfeapostolicnetwork.com.

Please also remember to click on the link for the **Minister Recommendation** letters *(which are found on the same page)*. Please give one of these letters to your Pastor or someone credentialed/ordained in full-time ministry, the other two recommendations also need to be completed by ministers; one of which would be accepted by a friend or someone you have known for at least 3 years.

    Website: www.cfeapostolicnetwork.com
    Email: info@cfeapostolicnetwork.com

Ministry Profile

Doctor Alan Pateman, an apostle, is the President and Founder of **"Alan Pateman Ministries International"** (APMI), which was established in England back in 1987, a Christian-based *(parachurch)* non-profit and non-denominational outreach. This ministry is now focusing in two main areas: First **"Connecting for Excellence"** Apostolic Networking (CFE) and secondly, the teaching arm, **"LifeStyle International Christian University"** (LICU).

CFE is a multi-facetted missions organisation with the purpose of connecting leaders for divine opportunities and building lasting relationships, to touch the lives of leaders literally the world over. Apostle Dr Alan Pateman has to date ordained more than 500 ministers in over 50 NATIONS. In addition there are ministries, churches and schools who are in Association or Affiliation, looking to him for apostolic counsel and oversight.

Secondly LICU, which was founded in 2007, is a study program to help people discover their purpose and destiny. A global network of university campuses and correspondence students, demonstrating the Supernatural Kingdom of God through Doctrinal, Apostolic and Prophetic Teaching. Dr Alan holds the position of President/CEO, Professor of Theology, Biblical Studies and Apostolic Ministry. LICU is exploding throughout Europe, Asia and Africa, enhancing the Body of Christ

Dr Alan has authored more than 40 books including numerous teaching materials and LICU university courses (30) along with hundreds of Truth for the Journey articles on kingdom lifestyle *(that are regularly distributed globally via the internet).*

He is recognised as an Apostle, Bishop, Leadership Mentor, University Educator, Motivational Speaker, Connector and Author, who has also been featured on national and international TV and radio networks throughout the years.

Currently Apostle Alan, his wife Dr Jennifer reside in Lucca *(Tuscany)* Italy and travel out from their Apostolic Company.

- Alan Pateman Ph.D., D.Min., D.D., M.A., B.Th.

Academic Background

Dr. Alan Pateman attended several colleges throughout his training *(including studying Theology at Roffey Place, Horsham, UK and a Member of Kerygma - with Rev. Colin Urquhart and Dr. Bob Gordon - 1985-1987)* before being awarded a Doctorate of Divinity *(2006)* in recognition of his lifetime achievements by the International College of Excellence, now "DanEl Christian College" *(President: Dr. Robb Thompson USA)* also "Life Christian University" *(Dr. Douglas Wingate USA)* where he also earned a Bachelor of Theology B.Th. *(2006),* a Master of Arts in Theology M.A., a Doctor of Ministry in Theology D.Min., *(2007)* and Doctor of Philosophy in Theology Ph.D. *(2013)* from LICU.

To Contact the Author

Please email:

Alan Pateman Ministries International

Email: apostledr@alanpateman.com
Web: www.AlanPatemanMinistries.com

*Please include your prayer requests
and comments when you write.*

Other Books

Winning by Mastering Your Mind

Someone once said, "Happiness begins between your ears and your mind is the drawing room for tomorrow's circumstances..." Remember, what happens in your mind will happen in time, and therefore one of our first priorities must be mind-management.

ISBN: 978-1-909132-40-5, Pages: 136,
Format: Paperback, Published: 2017
Also available in eBook format!

Media, Spiritual Gateway

Let's face it; we live in the era of fake news! It's always existed, but never been quite so prominent. Today it's an all-out-war between fact and political fiction. The media has been sabotaged by political activism. Gone are the days of impartiality and objective unbiased reporting, with many sources saying that true journalism is dead.

ISBN: 978-1-909132-54-2, Pages: 192,
Format: Paperback, Published: 2018
Also available in eBook format!

Truth for the Journey Books

Millennial Myopia, From a Biblical Perspective

The standard for every generation is Jesus. However Millennial Myopia describes the trap of focusing everything on one particular generation or demographic cohort, at the exclusion and expense of all others. The Church cannot afford to make this mistake too. Loaded with research, this book takes readers on a journey of discovery, revealing the true nature of kingdom diversity.

ISBN: 978-1-909132-67-2, Pages: 216,
Format: Paperback, Published: 2017
Also available in eBook format!

Equipped for Spiritual Warfare

This book "Equipped for Spiritual Warfare" helps all believers and disciples of Christ to become warriors for these end times and to know where they belong… " Teaching you how to stand in His authority and dunamis power as an heir in Christ Jesus.

ISBN: 978-1-9091321-3-9, Pages: 148,
Format: Paperback, Published: 2020
Also available in eBook format!

TONGUES, Our Supernatural Prayer Language

In writing to the church at Corinth, Paul encouraged them to continue the practice of speaking with other tongues in their worship of God and in their prayer lives as a means of spiritual edification. "He that speaketh in an unknown tongue edifies, charges, builds himself up like a battery."

ISBN: 978-1-909132-44-3, Pages: 144,
Format: Paperback, Published: 2016
Also available in eBook format!

Dear Friends,

Have you considered becoming one of our international students? We are privileged to welcome you, from around the world, to "LifeStyle International Christian University" *(the teaching arm of Alan Pateman Ministries International)*. **An English speaking university** dedicated to your success; to see you trained and equipped to fully succeed in your God given Destiny.

It is our passion to raise up the leaders of tomorrow, who will have influence in all realms of authority, including the Body of Christ. Men and women of strategy, wisdom and true godliness, who'll stand with stature and maturity in this hour.

It's undeniable that in today's world, recognised education has become indispensable, therefore it is our desire to offer well balanced and well structured courses. Those that have been written by gifted and talented ministers of God, who seek to be inspired by God's Holy Spirit.

Consequently we have put together a **flexible curriculum,** designed both for correspondence students and campuses, which is a strategy to reach the distant learner; whether provincial, national or international. In fact we have many correspondence students from around the world, including a growing number of successful campuses, in various countries.

This is a growing platform, where men and women of dignity and passion, can grow and be established in their God given endeavours. As God is the healer of the nations, we pray and believe that many of our alumni will go on to **become world changers** in their own right.

We are proud of each and every one of our LICU students.
It would be our pleasure if you would join them on this incredible journey!

Doctor Alan Pateman

Alan Pateman Prof. Ph.D., D.Min., D.D., M.A., B.Th.
PRESIDENT AND CEO
www.licuuniversity.com   www.cfeapostolicnetwork.com
Email: info@licuuniversity.com   Mob: +39 366 329 1315

For more information visit our website/facebook or contact our office, using the details below:

Website: www.licuuniversity.com
Facebook: www.facebook.com/LICUMainCampus
Email: info@licuuniversity.com
Telephone: +39 366 329 1315

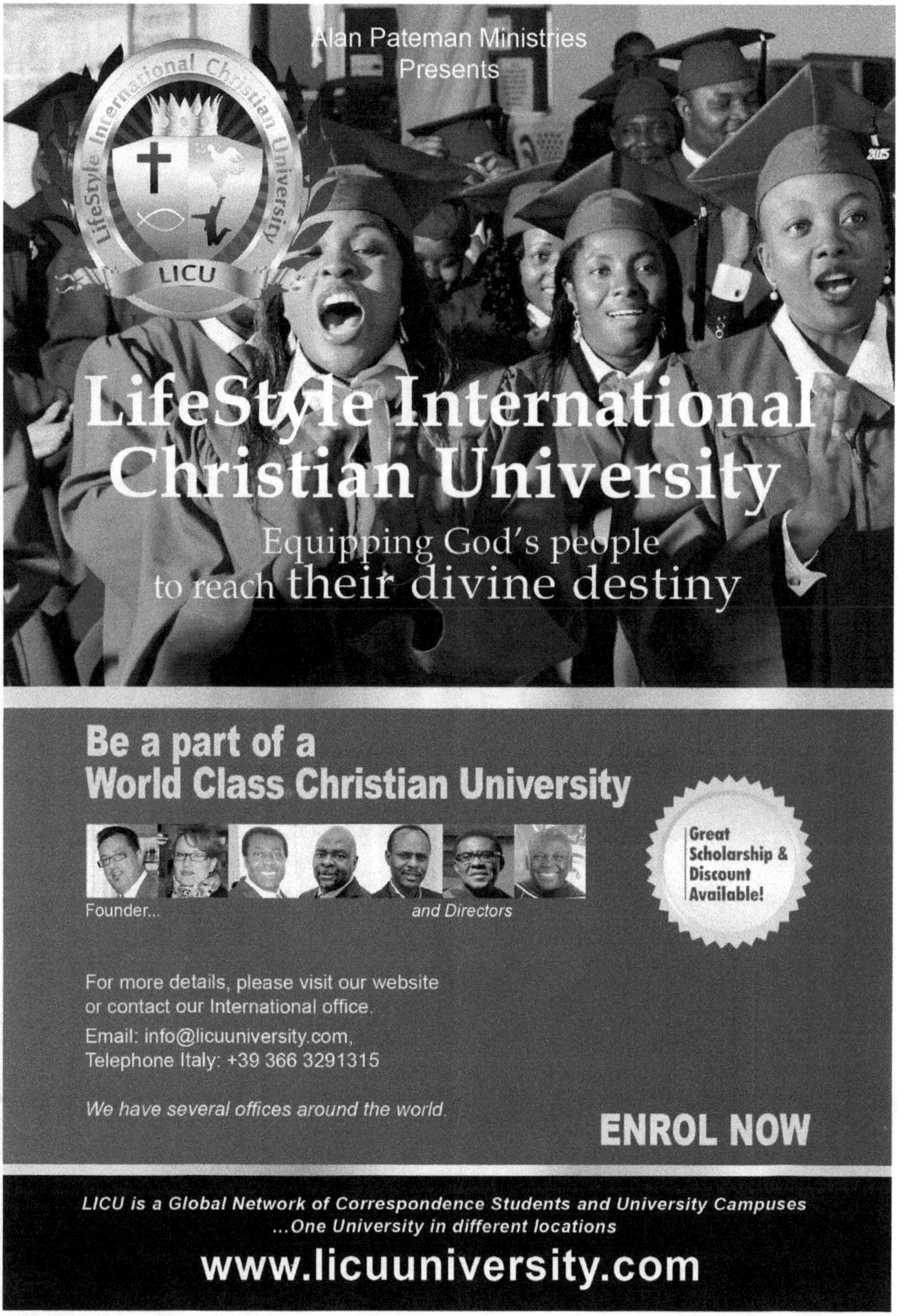

Alan Pateman Ministries
Presents

LifeStyle International Christian University

Equipping God's people to reach their divine destiny

Be a part of a World Class Christian University

Founder...   and Directors

Great Scholarship & Discount Available!

For more details, please visit our website or contact our International office.
Email: info@licuuniversity.com,
Telephone Italy: +39 366 3291315

We have several offices around the world.

ENROL NOW

LICU is a Global Network of Correspondence Students and University Campuses ...One University in different locations

www.licuuniversity.com

We are looking to impact the world with the gospel, together we can do more! Join with us to equip the Body of Christ through our Apostolic Network, LICU university program, campuses, associated schools, missions, conferences, television programs, publication of articles and Truth for the Journey books.

You can become an APMI FOUNDATION PARTNER with a regular contribution of any amount, whether it is once a month or once a year.

- Receive monthly newsletters
- Connect with partners and leaders at our Connecting for Excellence international meetings
- Partners Dinners
- Personal availability for mentoring by Doctor Alan
- Enjoy complimentary books by Doctors Alan and Jennifer
- For those who GIVE EVERY MONTH £10, £15, £20, £30 or more will save money with special discounts on products, hotel rooms, conferences, and more

Partner With Us Today!
Call Italy: +39 366 3291315
Email: partners@alanpatemanministries.com
www.AlanPatemanMinistries.com

All Books Available

at

APMI PUBLICATIONS

Email: publications@alanpateman.com
*Also Available from Amazon.com
and other retail outlets.*

If you purchased this book through Amazon.com or other and enjoyed reading it, or perhaps one of my other books, I would be grateful if you could take a couple of minutes to write a Customer Review, many thanks.

Resources on the Apostolic Prophetic Ministry

- Abboud, Michael, and Brooke Mackie and Victor Korabelnifkoff. Canaan Land Prophetic Journal #94. "Comest Thou in Peace?" Australia: Canaan Land Publications, 1994.

- Arnott, John. The Father's Blessing. Orlando, Florida: Creation House, 1995.

- Basham, Don. True and False Prophets. Grand Rapids, Michigan: Chosen Books, 1986.

- Cannistraci, David. Apostles and the Emerging Apostolic Movement. Ventura, California: Regal Books, 2007.

- Cannistraci, David. The Gift of the Apostle. Ventura, California: Regal Books, 1979.

- Chadwick, Henry. The Early Church. England: Penguin Books, 1967.

- Conner, Kevin J. The Church in the New Testament. Australia: Acacia Press, 1982.

- Crist, Terry. A Time of War. Tulsa, Oklahoma: Terry Crist Ministries, 1986.

- Crist, Terry. Interceding Against the Powers of Darkness. Tulsa, Oklahoma: Terry Crist Ministries, 1991.

- Crist, Terry. Warring According to Prophecy. Tulsa, Oklahoma: Whitaker House, 1989.

- Deere, Jack. Surprised by the Voice of God. Grand Rapids, Michigan: Zondervan Publishing, 1996.

- Eckhardt, John. Moving in the Apostolic. Ventura, California: Regal Books, 1999.

- Eckhardt, John. The Apostolic Church. Chicago, Illinois: Crusader Ministries, 1996.

- Eckhardt, John. The Ministry Anointing of the Apostle. Chicago, Illinois: Crusader Publications, 1993.
- Ekman, Ulf. The Apostolic Ministry – Can the Church Live Without It? Word of Life Publishing Sweden. Kingsway Publications LTD UK, 1996.
- Ekman, Ulf. The Church of the Living God. Uppsala, Sweden: Word of Life Publications, 1994.
- Ekman, Ulf. The Prophetic Ministry. Uppsala, Sweden: Word of Life Publications, 1990.
- Enlow, Johnny. The Seven Mountain Prophecy. Lake Mary, Florida: Creation House, 2008.
- Gay, Robert. Silencing the Gates of the Enemy. Lake Mary, Florida: Creation House, 1993.
- Hamon, Bill. Prophetic Destiny and the Apostolic Reformation. Santa Rosa Beach, Florida: Christian International Publishing, 1997.
- Hamon, Bill. Prophets and Personal Prophecy. Shippensburg, Pennsylvania: Destiny Image, 1990.
- Hamon, Bill. Prophets, Pitfalls and Principles. Shippensburg, Pennsylvania: Destiny Image, 1991.
- Hamon, Bill. Prophets and the Prophetic Movement. Shippensburg, Pennsylvania: Destiny Image, 1987.
- Hamon, Bill. The Eternal Church. Santa Rosa Beach, Florida: Christian International Publishers, 1981.
- Harfouche, Christian. Authority Over the Powers of Darkness. Shalimar, Florida: Christian Publications, 1993.
- Harfouche, Christian. The Miracle Ministry of the Prophet. Shalimar, Florida: Christian Publications, 1993.
- Harrison, Everet F. The Apostolic Church. Grand Rapids, Michigan: Eerdmans, 1985.
- Hawtin, George R. "The Ministry of the Apostle." The Sharon Star (April/May 1951).
- Jacobs, Cindy. The Voice of God. Ventura, California: Regal Books, 1995.

- LaCoss, Lee. I Will Build My Church. Ørum, Denmark: Lychnos Publishing, 2001.
- Lockyer, Herbert. All the Apostles of the Bible. Grand Rapids, Michigan: Zondervan Publishing, 1972.
- Marocco, James. The Invisible War. Kahulu, Hawaii: Bartemaeus Publishing, 1992.
- McBirnie, William Steuart. The Search for the Twelve Apostles. Wheaton, Illinois: Tyndale House, 1978.
- Mohabir, Philip. Hands of Jesus. Denmark: Powerhouse Publishing, 2003.
- Pickett, Fuchsia. For Such a Time as This. Shippensburg, Pennsylvania: Destiny Image, 1992.
- Pickett, Fuchsia. God's Dream. Shippensburg, Pennsylvania: Destiny Image, 1991.
- Pickett, Fuchsia. Presenting the Holy Spirit. Shippensburg, Pennsylvania: Destiny Image, 1994.
- Pickett, Fuchsia. The Next Move of God. Orlando, Florida: Creation House, 1994.
- Sapp, Roger. The Last Apostles on Earth. Shippensburg, Pennsylvania: Companion Press, 1995.
- Schidler, Bill. The New Testament Church and Its Ministries. Portland, Oregon: Bible Temple, 1980.
- Schultz, Steve. Mentoring & Fathering. Santa Rosa Beach, Florida: Companion Press, 1996.
- Schultz, Steve. Radical Warriors Require Radical Training. Santa Rosa Beach, Florida: D. Steven Schultz, 1991.
- Schultz, Steve. Restoration of the Modern-day Prophet. Santa Rosa Beach, Florida: D. Stephen Schultz, 1990.
- Sheets, Dutch. Intercessory Prayer. Centura, California: Regal Books, 1996.
- Stebins, J.E. Moses and the Prophets; Christ and the Apostles; Fathers & Martyrs. Herlbut, Kellogg & Co.,

Hartford, Connecticut: American Subscription Publishing House, 1861.
- Thigpen, Travis. Prophetic Evangelism: A Course on Spirit-Led Witnessing. Richmond, Virginia: Travis Thigpen, 1996.
- Wagner, C. Peter. Apostles and Prophets: The Foundation of the Church. Ventura, California: Regal Books, 2000.
- Wagner, C. Peter. Blazing the Way. Ventura, California: Regal Books, 1995.
- Wagner, C. Peter. Confronting the Powers. Ventura, California: Regal Books, 1979.
- Wagner, C. Peter. Lighting the World. Ventura, California: Regal Books, 1995.
- Wagner, C. Peter. "New Equipment for the Final Thrust," Ministers Today Orlando, Florida: Strang Communications, (January/February 1994).
- Wagner, C. Peter. Spreading the Fire. Ventura, California: Regal Books, 1979.
- Wagner, C. Peter. The New Apostolic Churches. Ventura, California: Regal Books, 1998.
- Wallnau, Lance, and Bill Johnson. Invading Babylon: The 7 Mountain Mandate. Shippensburg, Pennsylvania: Destiny Image, 2013.
- Wyatt, Kenneth. The Apostles. Amarillo, Texas: Y-8 Publishing Company, 1989.

www.ingramcontent.com/pod-product-compliance
Lightning Source LLC
Chambersburg PA
CBHW050417170426
43201CB00008B/445